NEW ZEALAND

TOP SIGHTS, AUTHENTIC EXPERIENCES

...CHED BY

...tt,

Pe... ...ay, Lee Slater

Plan Your Trip
Ultimate New Zealand Itinerary

This is Lonely Planet's ultimate New Zealand itinerary, which ensures you'll see the best of everything the country has to offer.

For other recommended paths to travel, check out our itineraries section (p26). For inspiration on themed travel, see If You Like... (p20).

From left: Hiker on the Routeburn Track (p265); Whale-watching, Kaikoura (p188); Urupukapuka Island, Bay of Islands (p64)

NARUEDOM YAEMPONGSA/SHUTTERSTOCK ©, CHRISADAM/GETTY IMAGES ©, MICAH WRIGHT/DESIGN PICS/GETTY IMAGES ©

Week 1

Christchurch to Te Anau

❶ Explore **Christchurch's** recovery after the 2010 and 2011 earthquakes.
🚗 1½ hours or 🚌 1¾ hours

❷ Take a day trip to **Akaroa**, combining French colonial history with wildlife-watching.
🚗 3½ hours or 🚌 4½ hours

❸ From Christchurch, cross the Southern Alps to **Greymouth** and the nearby **Pancake Rocks**.
🚗 2½ hours or 🚌 4 hours

❹ Continue from Greymouth down the West Coast to stunning **Franz Josef Glacier**.
🚗 4½ hours or 🚌 8 hours

❺ Travel from Franz Josef Glacier to **Queenstown** for adventures and views.
🚗 2 hours or 🚌 3 hours

❻ Head to **Te Anau** to explore spectacular Milford Sound.
🚗 7½ hours or 🚗 2 hours then ✈ 45 minutes

Week 2

Te Anau to Wellington

7 From Te Anau travel back to Queenstown and from there fly or drive back to **Christchurch**.

🚗 2½ hours or 🚌 3 hours

8 From Christchurch head up the east coast for whale-watching in the cool Pacific waters off **Kaikoura**.

🚗 3¾ hours or 🚌 5 hours

9 Head to **Nelson** and the **Marlborough region** for wine touring around Blenheim and kayaking or hiking around **Abel Tasman National Park**.

🚗 1¾ hours then ⛴ 3 hours or ✈ 35 minutes

10 Cross by ferry from **Picton** to the North Island and enjoy excellent museums and a happening craft beer scene in **Wellington**. Flying's faster but much less spectacular.

🚗 5½ hours or 🚌 10 hours

Staying Longer

Wellington to the Bay of Islands

11 Head north to **Taupo,** stopping to hike the one-day **Tongariro Alpine Crossing**.

🚗 45 minutes or 🚌 1 hour

12 From Taupo, continue to **Rotorua** for more geothermal thrills and Māori culture.

🚗 1½ hours or 🚌 2 hours

13 Next stop is riverside **Hamilton**, a convenient base the **Waitomo Caves** and **Hobbiton**.

🚗 2 hours or 🚌 4 hours

14 From Hamilton, continue to **Hahei** and **Cathedral Cove**.

🚗 3 hours or 🚌 4½ hours

15 Time for **Auckland's** cosmopolitan Pacific vibe and **Waiheke Island**.

🚗 3 hours or 🚌 4¼ hours

16 Finish off with history and marine excursions around the **Bay of Islands**.

Contents

Aoraki/Mt Cook (p211)

Plan Your Trip
New Zealand's Top 12

APEXPHOTOS/GETTY IMAGES ©

Queenstown

Adventures, stunning scenery and world-class wine

Queenstown (p232) may be world-renowned as the birthplace of bungy jumping, but there's more to NZ's adventure hub than leaping off a bridge attached to a giant rubber band. Against the jagged indigo profile of the Remarkables mountain range, travellers can spend days skiing, hiking or mountain biking, before dining in cosmopolitan restaurants or partying in some of NZ's best bars. Next-day options include easing into your NZ holiday with sleepier detours to Arrowtown or Glenorchy.

DOUGLAS PEEBLES/GETTY IMAGES ©

MATTEO COLOMBO/GETTY IMAGES ©

Marlborough

Sunshine, water, wine and whales

After a few days sipping fine Marlborough sauvignon blanc or Nelson craft beer made with locally grown hops, nearby Abel Tasman National Park offers tramping, kayaking and swimming amid golden sandy coves and a crystal-clear sea. Kaikoura is the ultimate coastal destination to watch whales, spy NZ fur seals, and be at one with the local bird life.

2

FILIP FUXA/SHUTTERSTOCK ©

Fiordland

Majestic mountains, fiords and lakes

Wish to see Milford Sound on a clear, sunny day, when the world-beating collage of waterfalls, cliffs and peaks, and dark cobalt waters is at its best. More likely, though, is a combination of mist and drizzle, with the iconic profile of Mitre Peak revealed slowly through rain. Approaching via the Milford Track is an iconic NZ adventure, and further south, a kayak is a superb way to explore the serried coastline of remote Doubtful Sound. Milford Sound (p260)

3

Taupo & Around

Outdoor adventures amid mighty volcanic vistas

At the centre of the North Island, Tongariro National Park presents an alien landscape of alpine desert punctuated by three smoking and smouldering volcanoes. The one-day Tongariro Alpine Crossing (p138) hike skirts two of the mountains, providing views of craters, iridescent lakes and the vast Central Plateau. Around the lakeside town of Taupo (p144), echoes of the region's volcanic past linger at geothermal Wairakei. Trout fishing, lake cruising and mountain biking are other essential reasons to experience the North Island's rugged heart.

Meads Wall, Tongariro National Park

Bay of Islands

Sublime coastlines shelter New Zealand's history

Turquoise waters lapping pretty bays, dolphins frolicking at the bows of boats, pods of orcas gliding gracefully by: these are the kinds of experiences that the Bay of Islands (p64) delivers so well. Whether you're a hardened sea dog or a confirmed landlubber, there are myriad options to tempt you out on the water to explore the 150-odd islands dotting this beautiful bay. Between maritime excursions, discover New Zealand's shared colonial and Māori history in Russell and Waitangi, and dive into a world of gourmet treats around Kerikeri. Stone Store (p72) and Mission House (p73), Kerikeri

6

Auckland

A vibrant city, a glittering harbour

Cradled by two harbours, Auckland (p34) isn't your average metropolis. Flanked by wine regions, it's regularly rated one of the world's most liveable cities, and has a thriving dining, drinking and live-music scene. In close proximity, Waiheke Island is many Aucklanders' favourite isle of art, wine and beaches, and on the Auckland region's west coast, the beaches are more wild and forested and surging with surf. Cultural festivals are celebrated with gusto in this ethnically diverse city, which has the distinction of having the world's largest Pacific Islander population.

SCOTT E BARBOUR/GETTY IMAGES ©

CHAMELEONSEYE/SHUTTERSTOCK©

7

Coromandel Peninsula

Brilliant beaches nestled against cobalt sea

A favourite destination of Aucklanders for decades, the Coromandel Peninsula (p80) conceals superb beaches and hidden coves, often enlivened by the summertime scarlet bloom of pohutukawa trees. Head to Hahei to swim beneath the natural arch of Cathedral Cove, dig your own DIY jacuzzi at Hot Water Beach, and learn about the region's gold-mining past amid the heritage ambience of Coromandel Town and Waihi. From left: Cathedral Cove (p84); Hot Water Beach (p87)

PICHUGIN DMITRY/SHUTTERSTOCK ©

PETER UNGER/GETTY IMAGES ©

Christchurch

Go-getting city leads to looming peaks

Christchurch (p190) is recovering with creativity and community spirit after the city's 2010 and 2011 earthquakes. On Banks Peninsula, the charming harbour town of Akaroa combines a French colonial heritage with marine wildlife including NZ's smallest dolphin species. Lake Tekapo, southwest of Christchurch, is the improbably scenic gateway to the Mackenzie Country and Aoraki/Mt Cook, the country's highest peak. Top: Lake Tekapo (p210); Bottom: Re:START Mall, Christchurch (p195)

Rotorua

Centre of Māori culture and steaming thrills

Geothermal activity is what you're here to see: gushing geysers, bubbling mud and boiling pools of mineral-rich water. Māori culture is also strong in Rotorua (p116) – take time to attend a *hangi* and Māori concert – and enjoy the region's exciting array of adventure activities including zip-lining, river rafting and mountain biking. Slow things down with a leisurely walk through the the beautiful Redwoods Whakarewarewa Forest.

Wellington

Harbourside setting for up-to-the-minute drinking and dining

GERARD WALKER/GETTY IMAGES ©

One of the coolest little capitals in the world, windy Wellington (p152) keeps things hip and diverse. It's long famed for a vibrant arts and music scene, fuelled by excellent cafes, restaurants and craft beer bars. Te Papa, the country's national museum, is a brilliant showcase of all things NZ, and a short trip up the coast, Kapiti Island offers great walking and bird-watching. Bottom right: *Solace in the Wind* sculpture by Max Patté

OLIVER STREWE/GETTY IMAGES ©

Waitomo Caves & Hamilton

Beaut caves and hobbits, too

Waitomo Caves (p102) are a must-see: a maze of subterranean caverns, canyons and rivers. Black-water rafting is the big lure here (like white-water rafting but through a dark cave), plus glowworm grottoes, underground abseiling and hidden stalactites and sta- lagmites. With good museums and an enviable eating and drinking scene, riverside Hamilton (p108) is also a centrally located base to visit Middle-earth cinematic highlights at Hobbiton (p106).

11

BO TORNVIG/GETTY IMAGES ©

West Coast

Powerful glaciers grind towards wild, windswept coasts

Hemmed in by the Tasman Sea and the Southern Alps, the West Coast (p212) is like nowhere else in New Zealand with a remote, end- of-the-road vibe, There's an alluring combination of wild coastline, rich wilderness, and must-see sights like Punakaiki's Pancake Rocks, and the Franz Josef and Fox Glaciers. Sleepy Hokitika is all about heritage and a spectacular hinterland. Fox Glacier (p220)

12

Plan Your Trip
Need to Know

When to Go

Auckland
GO Feb–Apr

Rotorua
GO Oct–Dec

Wellington
GO Dec–Feb

Christchurch
GO Jan–Mar

Queenstown
GO Jun–Aug

High Season (Dec–Feb)

○ Summer: busy beaches, festivals and sporting events.

○ Big-city accommodation prices rise.

○ High season in the ski towns is winter (Jun–Aug).

Shoulder (Mar & Apr)

○ Prime travelling time: fine weather, short queues, kids in school and warm(ish) ocean.

○ Long evenings sipping Kiwi wines and craft beers.

○ Spring (Sep–Nov) is shoulder season, too.

Low Season (May–Aug)

○ Head for the slopes of the Southern Alps for some brilliant southern-hemisphere skiing.

○ No crowds, good accommodation deals.

○ Warm-weather beach towns may be half asleep.

Currency
New Zealand dollar ($)

Languages
English, Māori and New Zealand Sign Language

Visas
Citizens of Australia, the UK and 58 other countries don't need visas for NZ (length-of-stay allowances vary). See www.immigration. govt.nz.

Money
ATMs are widely available in cities and larger towns. Credit cards accepted in most hotels and restaurants.

Mobile Phones
European phones will work on NZ's network, but most US or Japanese phones will not. Use global roaming or a local SIM card and prepaid account.

Time
GMT/UTC plus 12 hours (two hours ahead of Australian Eastern Standard Time)

Daily Costs

Budget: Less than $150

- Dorm beds or campsites: $25–38

- Main course in a budget eatery: less than $15

- Naked Bus or InterCity bus pass: five trips from $15

Midrange: $150–250

- Double room in a midrange hotel/motel: $120–200

- Main course in a midrange restaurant: $15–32

- Car hire from $30 per day

Top End: More than $250

- Double room in a top-end hotel: from $200

- Three-course meal in a classy restaurant: $80

- Flight Auckland to Christchurch: from $100

Websites

100% Pure New Zealand (www.new zealand.com) Official tourism site.
Department of Conservation (DOC: www.doc.govt.nz) Parks and camping info.
Lonely Planet (www.lonelyplanet.com/new-zealand) Destination information, hotel bookings, traveller forum and more.
Destination New Zealand (www.destination-nz.com) Resourceful tourism site.
DineOut (www.dineout.co.nz) Restaurant reviews.
Te Ara (www.teara.govt.nz) Online encyclopedia of NZ.

Opening Hours

Opening hours vary seasonally, but these are a general guide. Note that most places close on Christmas Day and Good Friday.

Banks 9.30am–4.30pm Monday to Friday, some also 9am–noon Saturday

Cafes 7am–4pm
Post offices 8.30am–5pm Monday to Friday; larger branches also 9.30am–1pm Saturday
Pubs & bars noon–late ('late' varies by region and day)
Restaurants noon–2.30pm and 6.30–9pm
Shops & businesses 9am–5.30pm Monday to Friday and 9am to noon or 5pm Saturday
Supermarkets 8am–7pm, often 9pm or later in cities

Arriving in New Zealand

Auckland Airport (p305) Airbus Express buses run into the city every 10 to 30 minutes around the clock. Door-to-door shuttle buses also run 24 hours. A taxi into the city costs $75 to $90 (45 minutes).
Wellington Airport (p306) Airport Flyer buses run into the city every 10 to 20 minutes from 6.30am to 9.30pm. Door-to-door shuttle buses run 24 hours. A taxi into the city costs around $30 (20 minutes).
Christchurch Airport (p305) Christchurch Metro Purple Line runs into the city regularly from 6.45am to 11pm. Door-to-door shuttles run 24 hours. A taxi into the city costs around $50 (20 minutes).

Getting Around

New Zealand is long and skinny and many roads are two-lane country byways: getting from A to B requires some patience.

Car Travel at your own tempo, explore remote areas and visit regions with no public transport. Hire cars in major towns.

Bus Reliable, frequent services around the country (usually cheaper than flying).

Plane Fast-track your holiday with affordable, frequent and fast internal flights.

Train Reliable, regular services (if not fast or cheap) along specific routes on both islands.

For more on getting around, see p306

Plan Your Trip
If You Like...

Cities

Auckland Sydney for beginners? We prefer Seattle minus the rain, infused with vibrant Pacific Islander culture. (p34)

Wellington All the lures you'd expect in a capital city, packed into a compact CBD. (p152)

Christchurch Re-emerging post-earthquakes with energy and verve, largely due to the determination and resilience of proud locals. (p190)

Hamilton With a big student population, Hamilton's bars, restaurants and museums all deserve a look. (p108)

Queenstown Combining the relaxed ease of a lakeside town with an energetic international vibe. (p232)

Adventure Activities

Queenstown Strap yourself into the astonishing Shotover Canyon Swing or Nevis Bungy. (p236)

Ohakune Old Coach Road Bounce along on two wheels on NZ's finest oneday mountain-bike ride. (p149)

Waitomo Black-Water Rafting Don a wet suit, a life vest and a helmet with a torch attached and rampage along an underground river. (p102)

Extreme Auckland Check out the SkyWalk and SkyJump at the Sky Tower. (p53)

Eco-rafting West Coast rafting trips including a helicopter ride. How much adrenaline can you pack into one day? (p219)

History

Waitangi Treaty Grounds Where Māori chiefs and the British Crown signed the contentious Treaty of Waitangi. (p68)

Rotorua Museum Excellent exhibitions on the Te Arawa people of the region and the cataclysmic Tarawera eruption in 1886. (p128)

Te Papa Wellington's vibrant treasure-trove museum, where history – both Māori and Pākehā – speaks, sparkles and shakes. (p156)

Auckland Museum Crowning Auckland Domain, and featuring excellent Pacific Island culture galleries. (p38)

Waihi Explore fascinating gold-mining heritage. (p88)

LLOYD PARK/GETTY IMAGES ©

Māori Culture

Rotorua Catch a cultural performance including a *haka* (war dance) and a *hangi* (Māori feast). (p116)

Maori Made Contemporary Māori apparel and homewares feature at this Rotorua store. (p130)

Hokitika Home to master carvers of *pounamu* (greenstone), stone, bone and paua in traditional Māori designs. (p228)

Toi Hauāuru Studio Visit this Raglan studio for contemporary Māori carving, visual arts and *ta moko* (tattooing). (p114)

Te Wharewaka o Pōneke Waka Tours Combine cultural insights with a two-hour paddle tour in a Māori *waka* (canoe). (p165)

Pubs, Bars & Beer

Wellington craft beer Garage Project and the Fork & Brewer are hoppy highlights. (p158)

Queenstown The only place in NZ where you can head out for a big Monday night and not be the only one there. (p252)

Auckland Seek out superb small bars like Mo's, Golden Dawn and Freida Margolis. (p60)

Nelson craft beer Home of NZ hops, Nelson boasts its own craft beer trail featuring a host of breweries and legendary inns. (p185)

Pomeroy's Old Brewery Inn Hands down, the best pub in Christchurch. (p205)

Foodie Experiences

Eating in Auckland New restaurants, ethnic cuisine enclaves and food trucks make Auckland NZ's eating capital. (p57)

Central Otago vineyard restaurants Eye-popping scenery combined with the best of NZ food and wine. (p238)

Christchurch city scene The big southern CBD restaurant and bar scene is burgeoning once more. (p203)

West Coast whitebait Have a patty and a pint at a country pub, or buy a half-pound from an old-timer's back door.

From left: Kawarau Gorge, near Queenstown (p232); Whitebait

Plan Your Trip
Month by Month

January

✿ World Buskers Festival

Christchurch hosts a gaggle of jugglers, musos, tricksters, puppeteers, mime artists and dancers throughout this 10-day summertime festival (www.worldbuskers festival.com). Shoulder into the crowd, see who's making a scene in the middle and maybe leave a few dollars.

February

✿ Waitangi Day

On 6 February 1840 the Treaty of Waitangi (www.nzhistory.net.nz) was first signed between Māori and the British Crown. The day remains a public holiday across NZ, but in Waitangi itself (the Bay of Islands) there's a lot happening: guided tours, concerts, market stalls and family entertainment.

⚲ Marlborough Wine & Food Festival

NZ's biggest and best wine festival (www. wine-marlborough-festival.co.nz) features tastings from around 50 Marlborough wineries (also NZ's biggest and best), plus fine food and entertainment. The mandatory over-indulgence usually happens on a Saturday early in the month.

✿ New Zealand Festival

Feeling artsy? This month-long spectacular (www.festival.co.nz) happens in Wellington in February to March every even-numbered year, and is sure to spark your imagination. NZ's cultural capital exudes artistic enthusiasm with theatre, dance, music, writing and visual arts. International acts aplenty.

✿ Fringe NZ

Wellington simmers with music, theatre, comedy, dance, visual arts...but not the mainstream stuff that makes it into the New Zealand Festival. These are the fringe-dwelling, unusual, emerging, controversial, low-budget and/or downright weird

Above: *Poi* dance performed during Waitangi Day celebrations

CHAMELEONSEYE/SHUTTERSTOCK ©

acts that don't seem to fit in anywhere else (www.fringe.co.nz).

☆ Hamilton Gardens Arts Festival

Across the last two weeks of February, music, comedy, theatre, dance and movies are all served up alfresco amid the verdant and fragrant surroundings of the Hamilton Gardens (www.hgaf.co.nz).

🎉 Splore

Explore Splore (www.splore.net), a cutting-edge, three-day outdoor summer fest in Tapapakanga Regional Park on the coast 70km southeast of Auckland. Contemporary live music, performance, visual arts, safe swimming, pohutukawa trees... If we were feeling parental, we'd tell you to take sunscreen, a hat and a water bottle.

March

✖ Wildfoods Festival

Eat some worms, hare testicles or crabs at Hokitika's comfort-zone-challenging food fest (www.wildfoods.co.nz). Not for the

★ Best Festivals

Waitangi Day

Wildfoods Festival

Pasifika Festival

Beervana (p24)

World of WearableArt Show (p24)

mild-mannered or weak-stomached – but even if you are, it's still fun to watch! There are usually plenty of quality NZ brews available, too, which help subdue the more difficult tastes.

🎉 Pasifika Festival

With upwards of 140,000 Māori and notable communities of Tongans, Samoans, Cook Islanders, Niueans, Fijians and other South Pacific Islanders, Auckland has the largest Polynesian community in the world. These vibrant island cultures

Above: Hamilton Gardens, venue for the Hamilton Gardens Arts Festival

come together at this annual fiesta (www.aucklandnz.com/pasifika) in Western Springs Park.

☆ Auckland City Limits

Time to get yer rocks off! Auckland City Limits (www.aucklandcitylimits.com) is a new international indie-rock festival loosely modelled on Austin City Limits in the US. The NZ version occupies four stages at Western Springs Stadium for one day in March.

May

☆ New Zealand International Comedy Festival

A three-week laugh-fest (www.comedyfestival.co.nz) with venues across Auckland, Wellington and various regional centres. International gag-merchants (Arj Barker, Danny Bhoy) line up next to homegrown talent (anyone seen that Rhys Darby guy lately?).

June

🎊 Matariki

Māori New Year is heralded by the rise of Matariki (aka Pleiades star cluster) in May and the sighting of the new moon in June. Three days of remembrance, education, music, film, community days and tree planting take place, mainly around Auckland and Northland (www.teara.govt.nz/en/matariki-maori-new-year).

July

🎊 Queenstown Winter Festival

This southern snow-fest (www.winterfestival.co.nz) has been running since 1975, and now attracts around 45,000 snow-bunnies. It's a 10-day party with fireworks, jazz, street parades, comedy, a Mardi Gras, masquerade ball and lots of snow-centric activities on the mountain slopes. Sometimes starts in late June.

August

☆ Bay of Islands Jazz & Blues Festival

You might think that the Bay of Islands is all about sunning yourself on a yacht while dolphins splash saltwater on your stomach. And you'd be right. But in the depths of winter, this jazzy little festival (www.jazz-blues.co.nz) will give you something else to do.

🍺 Beervana

Attain beery nirvana at this annual craft beer guzzle fest (www.beervana.co.nz) in Wellington. It's freezing outside – what else is there to do? But seriously, the NZ craft beer scene is booming – here's your chance to sample the best of it.

September

🎊 World of WearableArt Show

A bizarre (in the best possible way) two-week Wellington event (www.worldofwearableart.com) featuring amazing hand-crafted garments. Entries from the show are displayed at the World of WearableArt & Classic Cars Museum in Nelson after the event (Cadillacs and corsetry?). Sometimes spills over into October.

October

✖ Kaikoura Seafest

Kaikoura is a town built on crayfish. Well, not literally, but there sure are plenty of crustaceans in the sea here, many of which find themselves on plates during Seafest (www.seafest.co.nz). Also a great excuse to drink a lot and dance around.

🎊 Nelson Arts Festival

Sure, Nelson is distractingly sunny, but that doesn't mean the artsy good stuff isn't happening inside and out. Get a taste of the local output over two weeks in October (www.nelsonartsfestival.co.nz).

Plan Your Trip
Get Inspired

Hobbiton (p106), Matamata

Read

The Luminaries (Eleanor Catton, 2013) New Zealand goldfield epic set in the 1860s. Man Booker Prize–winner.

Mister Pip (Lloyd Jones, 2007) Reflections of *Great Expectations* in an isolated Bougainville community. Another great Kiwi writer to be Man Booker Prize–shortlisted.

In My Father's Den (Maurice Gee, 1972) A harrowing homecoming; made into a film in 2004.

The Bone People (Keri Hulme, 1984) Māori legends, isolation and violence: Man Booker Prize–winner, exploring traumatic family interactions.

Watch

Once Were Warriors (director Lee Tamahori, 1994) Brutal, tragic, gritty: Jake 'the Muss' Heke in urban Auckland.

The Lord of the Rings trilogy (director Peter Jackson, 2001–03) *The Fellowship of the Ring*, *The Two Towers* and the Oscar-winning *The Return of the King*. Then came *The Hobbit*...

Whale Rider (director Niki Caro, 2002) Māori on the East Coast are torn between tradition and today's world.

Boy (director Taika Waititi, 2010) Coming-of-age poignancy and self-deprecation. The highest-grossing NZ-made film of all time!

Listen

Don't Dream it's Over (Crowded House, 1986) Neil Finn catches a deluge in a paper cup – timeless melancholia.

Pink Frost (The Chills, 1984) Flying Nun's finest evoke huge southern landscapes.

Anchor Me (The Mutton Birds, 1994) Marine metaphors for love and longing from NZ's most underrated band.

Royals (Lorde, 2013) Schoolyard-chant-evoking, worldwide hit from 16-year-old Ella Yelich-O'Connor.

Not Many (Scribe, 2003) Hot Kiwi hip-hop.

Home Again (Shihad, 1997) Riff-driven power from NZ's guitar-rock kings.

Plan Your Trip
One-Week Itinerary

Southern Scene

Starting amid Christchurch's urban energy, this spectacle-packed journey traverses NZ's Southern Alps, travels down to the West Coast glaciers, then to exciting Queenstown. The iconic natural wonders of Fiordland are the trip's final highlights.

3 Franz Josef Glacier (p216) Discover the leviathan river of ice on a thrilling helicopter ride followed by a three-hour guided walk. 🚗 4½ hrs to Queenstown

4 Queenstown (p232) Spectacular lake and mountain scenery, extreme sports, a vibrant restaurant and bar scene, and superb wine country nearby. 🚗 2 hrs to Te Anau

5 Te Anau (p268) Explore the remote landscapes of Fiordland by hiking and getting out on the water at Milford Sound or Doubtful Sound.

PETER UNGER/GETTY IMAGES ©

1 Christchurch (p190) Witness the spirit and creativity driving the re-emergence of NZ's second-largest city after powerful earthquakes in 2010 and 2011. 🚗 1½ hrs to Akaroa

2 Akaroa (p206) Charming Akaroa has wildlife-watching, including NZ's smallest species of dolphin, and an interesting French colonial heritage. 🚗 5 hrs to Franz Josef Glacier

Plan Your Trip
10-Day Itinerary

North Explorer

The North Island's volcanic heart offers active ways to offset the city delights of Auckland, Hamilton and Wellington. Mountain bike in Rotorua, hike around volcanoes near Taupo, or abseil into caves at Waitomo.

1 Auckland (p34)
Soak up the cosmopolitan harbourside vibe, sail on the harbour and combine art, wine and vineyard dining across on Waiheke Island. 🚗 2 hrs to Hamilton

2 Hamilton (p108) A base to explore the Waitomo Caves, visit the cinematic Hobbiton, and trip to the surf town of Raglan. 🚗 1½ hrs to Rotorua

3 Rotorua (p116)
A steaming wonderland of geothermal activity and a heartland of NZ's indigenous Māori culture. 🚗 1 hr to Taupo

4 Taupo (p134)
Enjoy boat trips on Lake Taupo, trout fishing at Turangi and an eyeful of geothermal and volcanic activity. 🚗 1¾ hrs to Ohakune

5 Ohakune (p149)
Gateway to the spectacular Tongariro Alpine Crossing day hike, or bike the Old Coach Road. 🚗 3½ hrs to Wellington

6 Wellington (p152)
End in NZ's capital, with the country's national museum, spectacular harbour views, and cafes, restaurants and bars.

Plan Your Trip
10-Day Itinerary

Coast & Culture

From Auckland journey north to the Bay of Islands for history and spectacular islands before negotiating the meandering roads of the Coromandel Peninsula to hidden beaches and the region's gold-mining past.

2 Paihia (p77)
The heart of the spectacular Bay of Islands gives an understanding of NZ's bicultural history at the Waitangi Treaty Grounds.
🚗 3¼ hrs to Auckland

4 Coromandel Town (p92) Gateway to the rugged beauty of Far North Coromandel, this heritage town is steeped in gold mining.
🚗 45 min to Whitianga

1 Auckland (p34) Combine a visit to Auckland's West Coast surf beaches like Muriwai and Piha with the best of the region's vineyards.
🚗 3¼ hrs to Paihia

5 Whitianga (p94) More stunning Coromandel coastline is squeezed into this short hop. 🚗 1¾ hrs to Waihi

3 Auckland (p34) Overnight in Auckland before heading for the coastal roads of the Coromandel Peninsula.
🚗 3¼ hrs to Coromandel Town

6 Waihi (p88) See spectacular Cathedral Cove at Hahei, dig a natural spa pool at Hot Water Beach, then tour into the massive Martha Mine at Waihi.

Plan Your Trip
Family Travel

New Zealand for Kids

NZ is a terrific place to travel with kids: safe and affordable, with loads of playgrounds, kid-centric activities and a moderate climate.

Planning

Lonely Planet's *Travel with Children* contains buckets of useful information for travel with little'uns. Handy family websites:

o www.kidspot.co.nz

o www.kidsnewzealand.com

o www.kidsfriendlytravel.com

When to Go

NZ is a winner during summer, but summer means peak season and school-holiday time: expect pricey accommodation and booking ahead for family-sized rooms. Recommended are the shoulder months of March, April (sidestepping Easter) and November, when the weather is still good and the tourism sector is less busy.

Need to Know

Admission & discounts Kids' and family rates are often available for accommodation, tours, attractions and transport. Toddlers (under four years old) usually get free admission and transport.

Breastfeeding & nappy changing Most Kiwis are relaxed about public breastfeeding and nappy (diaper) changing. Alternatively, most major towns have public rooms where parents can go to feed their baby or change a nappy.

Babysitting For specialised child care, try www.rockmybaby.co.nz, or look under 'babysitters' and 'childcare centres' in the Yellow Pages (www.yellow.co.nz).

What to pack New Zealand's weather can be fickle, even in summer: a wardrobe with lots of layers is recommended. Definitely pack beach gear for your summer, but also throw in long-sleeve tops and jackets.

Sun protection New Zealand has some of the strongest levels of ultraviolet (UV) radiation, which can lead to sunburn even on a cloudy day. Be sure the kids cover up with loose clothing, hats, sunglasses and high-factor sunscreen.

MATTHEW MICAH WRIGHT/GETTY IMAGES ©

Travel times New Zealand might not look big on the map, but getting from A to B might take longer than you think; roads are narrow and winding, and there are often mountains (or at least hills) to navigate. But there are plenty of places to break a journey for toilet stops, snacks and time for the kids to run around.

Eating Out

Cafes are kid-friendly, and you'll see families in pub dining rooms. Most places can supply high chairs. Dedicated kids' menus are common, but selections are usually uninspiring.

Getting Around

For families, hiring a campervan is a good-value and flexible option, and there are holiday parks with playgrounds and children's facilities throughout the country.

★ Best Destinations for Kids
Bay of Islands (p64)
Rotorua (p116)
Waitomo Caves (p102)
Coromandel Peninsula (p80)
Queenstown (p232)

If your kids are little, check that your car-hire company can supply and fit the right-sized car seat for your child. Some companies legally require you to fit car seats yourself.

From left: Surf school, Coromandel Peninsula; Camping in Far North Coromandel (p90)

Climb or jump off Auckland
Harbour Bridge (p53)

Hauraki Gulf

City Centre
Newly energised with Britomart and Wynyard Quarter for dining, shopping and waterfront strolling

Devonport
Well-preserved Victorian and Edwardian buildings and loads of cafes, all just a short ferry ride from the city

Waitemata Harbour

Ponsonby
Buzzing restaurants and bars and fashion in Auckland's hippest suburb

AUCKLAND MUSEUM

Parnell
One of Auckland's oldest areas, with cafes, restaurants and fancy retailers

Mt Eden
Cool villagey feel nestled below Auckland's highest volcanic cone

Manukau Harbour

N 0 [2 km / 1 miles]

City Centre & Ponsonby Map (p50)
Mt Eden, Newmarket & One Tree Hill Map (p56)

Auckland at a glance...

New Zealand's most international city is an exciting urban centre sprawling across the slender isthmus dividing the Manukau and Waitemata harbours. Proximity to the sea is a constant, either on the beaches along meandering Tamaki Drive, the regular ferries crossing to islands in the Hauraki Gulf, and the vineyards, galleries and beaches of Waiheke Island that are firm favourites with Aucklanders. To the west, surf beaches provide a forested escape easily reached from the city.

Auckland in two days

Begin with breakfast at **Best Ugly Bagels** (p57) in the City Works Depot before visiting the **Auckland Museum** (p38). The Māori and Pacific galleries are especially interesting. In the afternoon go sailing on the Hauraki Gulf with **Explore** (p53), before joining the locals for dinner in the **Wynyard Quarter** or trendy **Ponsonby**. The following day get a first taste of New Zealand extreme adventure on the **SkyWalk** (p53) or **SkyJump** (p53).

Auckland in four days

Follow our two-day itinerary before self-driving or taking a tour to Auckland's **west coast beaches** (p44). Highlights include bush-clad scenery, wineries and the Takapu Refuge gannet colony at **Muriwai**. On day four catch the ferry to **Waiheke Island** (p40) for excellent vineyard restaurants and more great beaches, and try to squeeze in an overnight stay on this relaxed Hauraki Gulf highlight.

AUCKLAND

Get great views from the
Sky Tower (p49)

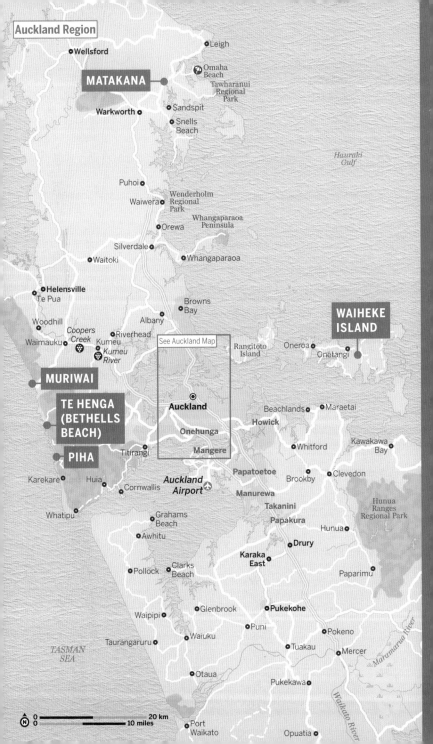

Auckland Region

Wellsford

Leigh

MATAKANA

Omaha Beach

Tawharanui Regional Park

Warkworth

Sandspit

Snells Beach

Hauraki Gulf

Puhoi

Wenderholm Regional Park

Waiwera

Orewa

Whangaparaoa Peninsula

Silverdale

Whangaparaoa

Waitoki

Helensville

Te Pua

Browns Bay

Woodhill

Albany

Coopers Creek

Riverhead

WAIHEKE ISLAND

Waimauku

Kumeu

Kumeu River

Oneroa

Rangitoto Island

Onetangi

See Auckland Map

MURIWAI

TE HENGA (BETHELLS BEACH)

Auckland

Beachlands

Maraetai

Howick

Onehunga

PIHA

Titirangi

Mangere

Whitford

Kawakawa Bay

Karekare

Huia

Cornwallis

Auckland Airport

Papatoetoe

Brookby

Clevedon

Manurewa

Whatipu

Grahams Beach

Takanini

Papakura

Hunua Ranges Regional Park

Awhitu

Drury

Hunua

Karaka East

Paparimu

Pollock

Clarks Beach

Waipipi

Glenbrook

Pukekohe

Tasman Sea

Taurangaruru

Waiuku

Puni

Pokeno

Tuakau

Mercer

Otaua

Pukekawa

Waikato River

Maramarua River

0 20 km
0 10 miles

N

Port Waikato

Opuatia

Sail or kayak on
Waitemata Harbour (p53)

Visit a volcano at
Mt Eden (p49)

Auckland Harbour Bridge

Arriving in Auckland

Auckland International Airport
Located 21km south of the city with domestic flights around the country and to/from Australia, Asia, the Pacific, and North and South America.

172 Quay Street Buses and shuttles depart opposite the Ferry Building to destinations around the North Island.

Auckland Strand Railway Station
The terminus for the *Northern Explorer* linking Auckland and Wellington via Hamilton, Otorohanga and Tongariro National Park.

What's on

Auckland Anniversary Day Regatta
The 'City of Sails' fulfils its name; Monday closest to 29 January.

Music in Parks (www.musicinparks. co.nz) Free gigs across summer across the city.

Silo Cinema & Markets (www.silopark. co.nz; Dec-Easter) Classic movies screened outdoors on Friday nights, and food trucks, DJs and craft stalls on Friday nights and weekend afternoons.

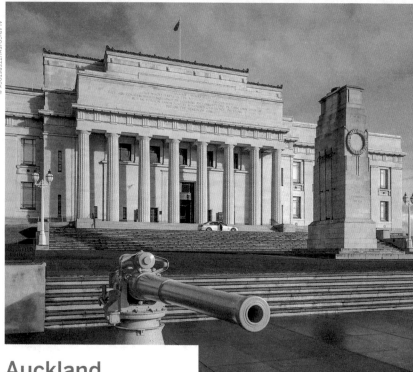

Auckland Museum

Auckland Museum

One of Auckland's more distinctive buildings, the Auckland Museum sits proudly amid Auckland Domain. Auckland is the world's biggest Polynesian city, and the museum's Pacific Island displays are compelling viewing.

Great For...

☑ **Don't Miss**

The views across the harbour and central Auckland from the museum's front entrance.

This imposing neoclassical temple (1929), capped with an impressive copper-and-glass dome (2007), dominates the Auckland Domain and is a prominent part of the Auckland skyline, especially when viewed from the harbour.

The displays of Pacific Island and Māori artefacts on the museum's ground floor are essential viewing. Highlights include a 25m canoe – carved from a giant totara tree, it is the last great war canoe used in battle – and a carved meeting house (remove your shoes before entering). There's also a fascinating display on Auckland's volcanic field, including an eruption simulation. The upper floors showcase military displays, fulfilling the building's dual role as a war memorial, with many displays telling the personal stories of both the armed forces and the New Zealanders who remained at

Carved wall panel in Hotunui meeting house

PAUL KENNEDY/GETTY IMAGES ©

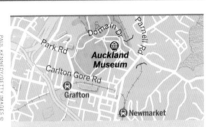

ⓘ Need to Know

Map p51; ☏09-309 0443; www.auckland museum.com; Auckland Domain, Parnell; adult/child $25/10; ⊙10am-5pm

✕ Take a Break

From the museum, it's 1.4km to excellent eating at Parnell's **Woodpecker Hill** (p59).

★ Top Tip

Check the museum website for concerts, shows and events, often featuring local musicians.

home. Auckland's main Anzac commemorations take place at dawn on 25 April at the cenotaph in the museum's forecourt.

Visiting Auckland Museum

Admission packages can be purchased that incorporate a highlights tour and a Māori cultural performance ($45 to $55). This performance is your chance to see twirling *poi* dances, a hair-raising *haka* (the Māori ceremonial war dance) and to meet and chat with the performers.

What's Nearby?

Around 1.5km south of the museum, Newmarket is a bustling retail district with some of Auckland's best fashion and design shopping, especially around Teed and Nuffield Streets. Karen Walker (p55) is a world-renowned designer whose cool (but pricey) threads have been worn by Madonna and Kirsten Dunst; Zambesi (p55) is another iconic NZ label much sought after by local and international celebs. For interesting art and design from a collective of 100 local artists, visit **Texan Art Schools** (www.texanartschools.co.nz; 366 Broadway).

Newmarket also offers good cafes and restaurants. The cosy **Basque Kitchen Bar** (www.basquekitchenbar.co.nz; 61 Davies Cres) serves delectable tapas accompanied by Spanish wine, beer and sherry. At the **Teed St Larder** (www.teedstreetlarder.co.nz; 7 Teed St) it's hard to go past the delicious sandwiches and tarts.

Waiheke Island

World-class wineries, superb dining with spectacular ocean views and a few of the region's best beaches all combine to make Waiheke Island a favourite destination of Aucklanders.

Great For...

❶ Need to Know

Waiheke Island (www.aucklandnz.com) is reached from downtown Auckland by passenger ferry (around 40 minutes). Check www.fullers.co.nz for discounted 'Hot Seat Deals' for selected ferry departures.

★ **Top Tip**

The *Waiheke Art Map* brochure, free from the i-SITE in Oneroa village, lists galleries and craft stores.

Tantalisingly close to Auckland and blessed with its own warm, dry microclimate, blissful Waiheke Island has long been a favourite escape for city dwellers and visitors alike. On the island's landward side, emerald waters lap at rocky coves, while its ocean flank offers arcing sandy beaches.

While beaches are Waiheke's biggest drawcard, wine is a close second. There are around 30 boutique wineries scattered about, many with tasting rooms, swanky restaurants and breathtaking views. The island also boasts plenty of quirky galleries and craft stores, a lasting legacy of its hippyish past.

When you've had enough of supping, dining, lazing on the sand and splashing in the surf, there are plenty of other pursuits to engage in. A network of walking trails leads through nature reserves and past the clifftop holiday homes of the Auckland elite. The kayaking is excellent and there are ziplines to whizz along and clay pigeons to shoot. All in all, it's a magical place.

Beaches

Waiheke's two best beaches are Onetangi, a long stretch of white sand at the centre of the island, and Palm Beach, a pretty little horseshoe bay between Oneroa and Onetangi. Both have nudist sections; head west just past some rocks in both cases. Oneroa and neighbouring Little Oneroa are also excellent, but you'll be sharing the waters with moored yachts in summer. Reached by an unsealed road through farmland, Man O' War Bay is a compact sheltered beach that's excellent for swimming.

Waiheke Island vineyard

Vineyard Restaurants

Shed at Te Motu   Modern NZ $$

(09-372 6884; www.temotu.co.nz/the-shed; 76 Onetangi Rd; shared plates small $12-18, large $22-36; noon-3pm daily, 6pm-late Fri & Sat Nov-Apr, reduced hours in winter) Secure a table shaded by umbrellas in the Shed's rustic courtyard for shared plates imbued with global culinary influences and served by the restaurant's savvy and equally inter-national staff. Highlights include shiitake pancakes with kimchi and black garlic, or the wonderfully slow-cooked lamb shoulder

---

> ★ **Top Tip**
>
> As well as the very helpful **Waiheke Island i-SITE** (116 Ocean View Rd, Oneroa), there's a (usually unstaffed) i-SITE counter in the ferry terminal at Matiatia Wharf.

---

partnered with a delicate biryani-spiced pilaf. Te Motu's standout wines are its stellar Bordeaux-style blends.

Cable Bay   Modern NZ $$$

(09-372 5889; www.cablebay.co.nz; 12 Nick Johnstone Dr; mains $42-44; noon-3pm Tue-Sun, 6pm-late Tue-Sat;) Impressive ubermodern architecture, interesting sculpture and beautiful views set the scene for this acclaimed restaurant. The food is sublime, but if the budget won't stretch to a meal, stop in for a wine tasting ($10 for five wines, refundable with a purchase; 11am to 5pm daily) or platters and shared plates at the Verandah bar.

Te Whau   Modern NZ $$$

(09-372 7191; www.tewhau.com; 218 Te Whau Dr; mains $40-42; 11am-5pm daily & 6.30-11pm Thu-Sat Dec & Jan, 11am-5pm Wed-Mon & 6.30-11pm Sat Feb-Easter, 11am-4.30pm Fri-Sun & 6.30-11pm Sat Easter-Nov) Perched on the end of Te Whau peninsula, this winery restaurant has exceptional views, food and service, and one of the finest wine lists you'll see in the country. The attached tasting room offers samples of its own impressive Bordeaux blends (11am to 5pm; four tastes for $12).

Walks

Ask at the i-SITE about the island's beauti-ful coastal walks (ranging from one to three hours) and the 3km Cross Island Walkway (from Onetangi to Rocky Bay). Other tracks traverse Whakanewha Regional Park, a haven for rare coastal birds and geckos, and the Royal Forest & Bird Protection So-ciety's three reserves: Onetangi (Waiheke Rd), Te Haahi-Goodwin (Orapiu Rd) and Atawhai Whenua (Ocean View Rd).

Nesting gannets, Muriwai

SHAUN JEFFERS/SHUTTERSTOCK ©

West Coast Beaches

Shrouded in the native forest of the Waitakere Ranges Regional Park, Auckland's west coast beaches are a rugged counter-point to the urban attractions of the big city just 40km away.

Great For...

☑ Don't Miss

Work by more than 200 local artists is sold at Piha's **West Coast Gallery** (☎09-812 8029; www.westcoastgallery.co.nz; Seaview Rd; ☺10am-5pm).

Wild black-sand surf beaches and the up-close and personal experience of viewing a gannet colony combine on the coast west of Auckland. There's also excellent bushwalking in the nearby Waitakere Ranges Regional Park (www.regionalparks.aucklandcouncil.govt.nz), and en route from Auckland, the area's Croatian heritage lingers in vineyards and other fine eating and drinking venues (p60).

Muriwai

A rugged black-sand surf beach, Muriwai's main claim to fame is the Takapu Refuge gannet colony, spread over the southern headland and outlying rock stacks. Viewing platforms get you close enough to watch (and smell) these fascinating seabirds. Every August hundreds of adult birds return to this spot to hook up with their regular partners and get busy – expect lots

MANCHAN/GETTY IMAGES ©

ⓘ Need to Know

There's no public transport to the beaches, so rent a car or join a tour.

✕ Take a Break

Big-city standards mesh seamlessly with beachy informality at the eco-friendly **Piha Cafe** (📞09-812 8808; www.pihacafe.com; 20 Seaview Rd; mains $14-27; ⏲8.30am-3.30pm Mon-Wed, to 10pm Thu-Sat, to 5pm Sun).

★ Top Tip

Auckland's west coast surf beaches can be dangerous, so always swim between the flags.

of outrageously cute neck-rubbing, bill-touching and general snuggling. The net result is a single chick per season; December and January are the best times to see the little birds testing their wings before embarking on an impressive odyssey.

Nearby, a couple of short tracks will take you through beautiful native bush to a lookout that offers views along the 60km length of the beach. Wild surf and treacherous rips mean that swimming is safe only when the beach is patrolled (always swim between the flags). Apart from surfing, Muriwai is a popular spot for hang gliding, parapunting, kiteboarding and horse riding.

Piha

The view of the coast as you drive down Piha Rd is spectacular. Perched on its

haunches near the centre of the beach is Lion Rock (101m), whose 'mane' glows golden in the evening light. It's actually the eroded core of an ancient volcano and a Māori *pa* (fortified village) site. A path at the southern end of the beach takes you to some great lookouts. At low tide you can walk south along the beach and watch the surf shooting through a ravine in another large rock known as the Camel. A little further along, the waves crash through the Gap and form a safe swimming hole. A small colony of little penguins nests at the beach's northern end.

Te Henga (Bethells Beach)

Breathtaking Bethells Beach is reached by taking Te Henga Rd at the northern end of Scenic Dr. It's a raw, black-sand beach with surf, windswept dunes and walks, such as the popular one that takes you over giant sand dunes to Lake Wainamu (starting near the bridge on the approach to the beach).

Matakana

Once a sleepy rural village, Matakana (67km north of Auckland) is now the hub of an excellent local food and wine scene, plus there's great snorkelling nearby.

Great For...

☑ **Don't Miss**

Leigh Sawmill Cafe (☎09-422 6019; www.sawmillcafe.co.nz; 142 Pakiri Rd) for local craft beer and wood-fired pizza.

The excellent **Matakana Village Farmers Market** (www.matakanavillage.co.nz; Matakana Sq, 2 Matakana Valley Rd; ⊙8am-1pm Sat) lures Aucklanders north up the highway, and the **Mahurangi River Winery & Restaurant** (☎09-425 0306; www.mahurangiriver.co.nz; 162 Hamilton Rd; mains $28-34; ⊙11am-4pm Thu-Mon), a rural spot off Sandspit Rd, has a relaxed ambience, savvy food and expansive vineyard views. Matakana wines and decent bistro food including local Mahurangi oysters all feature at the pub, **The Matakana** (☎09-422 7518; www.matakana.co.nz; 11 Matakana Valley Rd; mains $17-25; ⊙noon-12.30am). To explore the local vineyards by bike, contact **Matakana Bicycle Hire** (☎09-423 0076; www.matakanabicyclehire. co.nz; 951 Matakana Rd; half-/full-day hire from $30/40, tours from $70).

PHIL WALTER/GETTY IMAGES ©

Hauraki Gulf

Matakana

Warkworth ● ● Sandspit
● Snells
Beach

ℹ️ Need to Know

Get all the info at **Matakana Information Centre** (📞09-422 7433; www.matakanainfo.org.nz; 2 Matakana Valley Rd; ⏰10am-1pm).

✕ Take a Break

Superb sorbet and gelato made from fresh fruit feature at **Charlie's Gelato Garden** (📞09-422 7942; www.charliesgelato.co.nz; 17 Sharp Rd; ⏰9am-5pm Nov-Mar, 10am-4pm Fri-Sun Apr-Oct).

★ Top Tip

Pick up the *Matakana Wine Trail* (www.matakanawine.com) brochures at the Matakana Information Centre.

Sights

Goat Island Marine Reserve
Wildlife Reserve

(www.doc.govt.nz; Goat Island Rd) Only 16km northeast of Matakana, this 547-hectare aquatic area was established in 1975 as the country's first marine reserve. In less than 40 years the sea has reverted to a giant aquarium, giving an impression of what the NZ coast must have been like before humans arrived. You only need step knee-deep into the water to see snapper (the big fish with blue dots and fins), blue maomao and stripy parore swimming around. Rent gear or book a tour with **Octopus Hideaway** (📞09-422 6212; www.theoctopushideaway.nz; 7 Goat Island Rd; ⏰10am-5pm).

Excellent interpretive panels explain the area's Māori significance (it was the landing place of one of the ancestral canoes) and pictures of the local species.

Omaha Beach
Beach

The nearest swimming beach to Matakana, Omaha has a long stretch of white sand, good surf and ritzy holiday homes. **Blue Adventures** (📞022 630 5705; www.blueadventures.co.nz; 331 Omaha Flats Rd, Omaha; lessons per hour $40-80) will get you kitesurfing, paddle boarding and wakeboarding.

Tawharanui Regional Park
Beach

(📞09-366 2000; http://regionalparks.auckland-council.govt.nz/tawharanui; 1181 Takatu Rd) A partly unsealed road leads to this 588-hectare reserve at the end of a peninsula. This special place is an open sanctuary for native birds, protected by a pest-proof fence, while the northern coast is a marine park (bring a snorkel). There are plenty of walking tracks (1½ to four hours) but the main attraction is Anchor Bay, one of the region's finest white-sand beaches.

Auckland

It's hard to imagine a more geographically blessed city than Auckland. Its two harbours frame a narrow isthmus punctuated by volcanic cones and surrounded by fertile farmland. From any of its numerous vantage points you'll be surprised how close the Tasman Sea and Pacific Ocean come to kissing and forming a new island.

Whether it's the ruggedly beautiful west coast surf beaches, or the glistening Hauraki Gulf with its myriad islands, the water's never far away. And within an hour's drive from the city's high-rise heart, there are dense tracts of rainforest, thermal springs, wineries and wildlife reserves. No wonder Auckland is regularly rated one of the world's top cities for quality of life and liveability.

◎ SIGHTS

Auckland Art Gallery   Gallery
(Map p50; ☑09-379 1349; www.auckland artgallery.com; cnr Kitchener & Wellesley Sts; ☺10am-5pm) **FREE** Following a significant 2011 refurbishment, Auckland's premier art repository now has a striking glass-and-wood atrium grafted onto its 1887 French-chateau frame. It showcases the best of NZ art, along with important works by Pieter Bruegel the Younger, Guido Reni, Picasso, Cézanne, Gauguin and Matisse. Highlights include the intimate 19th-century portraits of tattooed Māori subjects by Charles Goldie and the starkly dramatic text-scrawled canvases of Colin McCahon. Free tours depart from the foyer daily at 11.30am and 1.30pm.

One Tree Hill   Volcano, Park
(Maungakiekie; Map p56) This volcanic cone was the isthmus' key *pa* and the greatest fortress in the country. From the top (182m) there are 360-degree views and the grave of John Logan Campbell, who gifted the land to the city in 1901 and requested that a memorial be built to the Māori people on the summit. Nearby is the stump of the last 'one tree'. Allow time to explore surrounding Cornwall Park with its mature trees and historic Acacia Cottage (1841).

Auckland Art Gallery

ROBIN BUSH/GETTY IMAGES ©

The **Cornwall Park Information Centre** (Map p56; ☎09-630 8485; www.cornwallpark.co.nz; Huia Lodge; ⏰10am-4pm) has fascinating interactive displays illustrating what the *pa* would have looked like when 5000 people lived here. Near the excellent children's playground, the **Stardome** (Map p56; ☎09-624 1246; www.stardome.org.nz; 670 Manukau Rd; shows adult/child $15/12; ⏰10am-5pm Mon, to 9.30pm Tue-Thu, to 11pm Fri-Sun) FREE offers regular stargazing and planetarium shows that aren't dependent on Auckland's fickle weather (usually 7pm and 8pm Wednesday to Sunday, with extra shows on weekends).

To get to One Tree Hill from the city take a train to Greenlane and walk 1km along Green Lane West. By car, take the Greenlane exit of the Southern Motorway and turn right into Green Lane West.

Mt Eden — Volcano

(Maungawhau; Map p56; 250 Mt Eden Rd)

From the top of Auckland's highest volcanic cone (196m), the entire isthmus and both harbours are laid bare. The symmetrical crater (50m deep) is known as Te Ipu Kai a Mataaho (the Food Bowl of Mataaho, the god of things hidden in the ground) and is considered highly *tapu* (sacred). Do not enter it, but feel free to explore the remainder of the mountain. The remains of *pa* terraces and food storage pits are clearly visible.

Until recently it was possible to drive right up to the summit but concerns over erosion have led to restricted vehicle access. Paths lead up the mountain from six different directions and the walk only takes around 10 minutes, depending on your fitness.

Sky Tower — Tower

(Map p50; ☎09-363 6000; www.skycityauckland.co.nz; cnr Federal & Victoria Sts; adult/child $28/11; ⏰8.30am-10.30pm) The impossible-to-miss Sky Tower looks like a giant hypodermic giving a fix to the heavens. Spectacular lighting renders it space age at night and the colours change for special events. At 328m it is the

Exploring Tamaki Drive

This scenic, pohutukawa-lined road heads east from the city, hugging the waterfront. In summer it's a jogging, cycling and rollerblading blur. The friendly team at Fergs Kayaks (p53) at Okahu Bay can help with rollerblade and bike hire.

A succession of child-friendly, peaceful swimming beaches starts nearby at Okahu Bay. Around the headland is Mission Bay, a popular beach with an art-deco fountain, historic mission house, restaurants and bars. Safe swimming beaches Kohimarama and St Heliers follow. Further east along Cliff Rd, the Achilles Point lookout offers panoramic views and Māori carvings.

Stop in at the excellent **St Heliers Bay Bistro** (www.sthelierbaybistro.co.nz; 387 Tamaki Dr, St Heliers; brunch $16-27, dinner $25-27; ⏰7am-11pm), a classy eatery with views of the harbour and Rangitoto Island. Look forward to upmarket takes on the classics (fish and chips, burgers, beef pie), along with cooked breakfasts, tasty salads and lots of Mediterranean influences. It also does terrific ice creams. Combine a walk along the beach with the salted caramel or licorice flavour.

Buses 767 and 769, departing from behind Britomart station in central Auckland, follow this route all the way to St Heliers, while buses 745 to 757 go as far as Mission Bay.

Competitors in the Round the Bays fun run
SANDRA MU/GETTY IMAGES ©

City Centre & Ponsonby

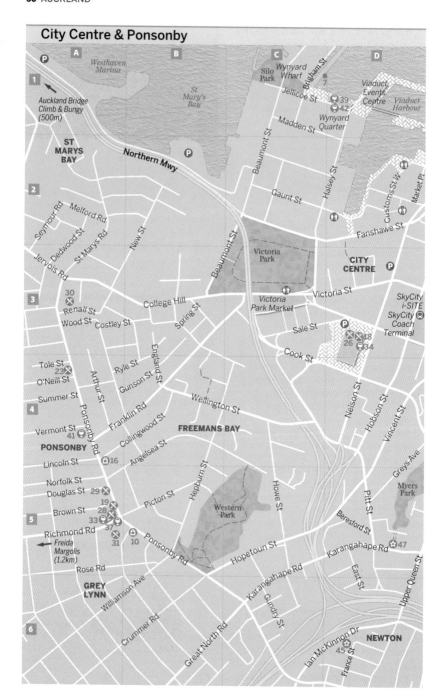

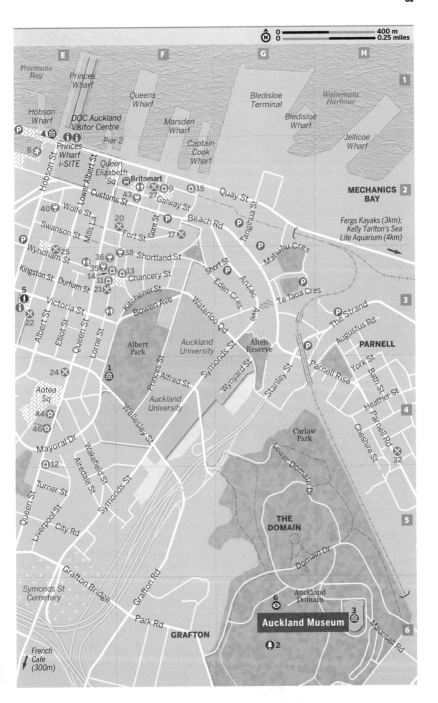

City Centre & Ponsonby

Sights

1	Auckland Art Gallery	E4
2	Auckland Domain	G6
3	Auckland Museum	H6
4	New Zealand Maritime Museum	E1
5	Sky Tower	E3
6	Wintergarden	G6

Activities, Courses & Tours

7	Auckland Seaplanes	C1
8	Explore	E2
	SkyJump	(see 5)
	SkyWalk	(see 5)

Shopping

9	Karen Walker (Britomart)	F2
10	Karen Walker (Ponsonby)	B5
11	Pauanesia	E3
12	Real Groovy	E4
13	Strangely Normal	F3
14	Unity Books	E3
15	Zambesi (Britomart)	F2
16	Zambesi (Ponsonby)	A4

Eating

17	Beirut	F2
18	Best Ugly Bagels	D3
19	Blue Breeze Inn	A5
20	Cassia	F2
21	Chuffed	E3
22	Depot	E3
23	Dizengoff	A4
24	Giapo	E4
25	Grove	E3
26	Odette's	D3
27	Ortolana	F2
28	Ponsonby Central	A5
29	Saan	A5
30	Sidart	A3
31	Street Food Collective	A5
	Sugar Club	(see 5)
32	Woodpecker Hill	H4

Drinking & Nightlife

33	Bedford Soda & Liquor	A5
34	Brothers Beer	D3
35	Cassette Nine	E3
36	Gin Room	E3
37	Golden Dawn	A5
38	Hotel DeBrett	F3
39	Jack Tar	D1
40	Mo's	E2
41	Shanghai Lil's	A4
42	Sixteen Tun	D1
43	Xuxu	F2

Entertainment

44	Auckland Town Hall	E4
45	Kings Arms Tavern	D6
46	Q Theatre	E4
47	Whammy Bar	D5

southern hemisphere's tallest structure. A lift takes you up to the observation decks in 40 stomach-lurching seconds; look down through the glass floor panels if you're after an extra kick. Consider visiting at sunset and having a drink in the Sky Lounge Cafe & Bar.

The Sky Tower is also home to the SkyWalk (p53) and SkyJump (p53).

Auckland Domain — Park

(Map p50; Domain Dr, Parnell; ⌚24hr) Covering about 80 hectares, this green swathe contains the Auckland Museum (p38), sports fields, interesting sculpture, formal gardens, wild corners and the **Wintergarden** (Map p50; Wintergarden Rd, Parnell; ⌚9am-5.30pm Mon-Sat, to 7.30pm Sun Nov-Mar, 9am-4.30pm Apr-Oct) FREE, with its fernery, tropical house, cool house, cute cat statue, coffee kiosk and neighbouring cafe. The mound in the centre of the park is all that remains of Pukekaroa, one of Auckland's volcanoes. At its humble peak, a totara tree surrounded by a palisade honours the first Māori king.

Auckland Zoo — Zoo

(Map p56; ☎09-360 3805; www.aucklandzoo.co.nz; Motions Rd; adult/child $28/12; ⌚9.30am-5pm, last entry 4.15pm) At this modern, spacious zoo, the big foreigners tend to steal the attention from the timid natives, but if you can wrestle the kids away from the tigers and orangutans, there's a well-presented NZ section. Called Te Wao Nui, it's divided into six ecological zones: Coast (seals, penguins), Islands (mainly lizards, including NZ's pint-sized dinosaur, the tuatara), Wetlands (ducks, herons, eels), Night (kiwi, naturally, along with frogs, native owls and weta), Forest (birds) and High Country (cheekier birds and lizards).

Frequent buses (adult/child $4.50/2.50) run from 99 Albert St in the city to bus stop 8124 on Great North Rd, where it is a 700m walk to the zoo's entrance.

Kelly Tarlton's Sea Life Aquarium
Aquarium

(☑09-531 5065; www.kellytarltons.co.nz; 23 Tamaki Dr, Orakei; adult/child $39/22; ☺9.30am-5pm) ✎ In this topsy-turvy aquarium sharks and stingrays swim over and around you in transparent tunnels that were once storm-water tanks. You can also enter the tanks in a shark cage with a snorkel ($124), or dive straight into the tanks ($265). Other attractions include the Penguin Discovery tour (10.30am Tuesday to Sunday, $199 per person) where just four visitors per day can get up close with Antarctic penguins. For all tickets, there are significant discounts online.

A free shark-shaped shuttle bus departs from 172 Quay St (opposite the Ferry Building) hourly on the half-hour from 9.30am to 3.30pm.

New Zealand Maritime Museum
Museum

(Map p50; ☑09-373 0800; www.maritime museum.co.nz; 149-159 Quay St; adult/child $20/10, incl harbour cruise $50/25; ☺9am-5pm, free tours 10.30am & 1pm Mon-Fri) This museum traces NZ's seafaring history, from Māori voyaging canoes to the America's Cup. Recreations include a tilting 19th-century steerage-class cabin and a 1950s beach store and bach (holiday home). Blue Water Black Magic is a tribute to Sir Peter Blake, the Whitbread Round the World– and America's Cup–winning yachtsman who was murdered in 2001 on an environmental monitoring trip in the Amazon. Packages including an optional one-hour harbour cruise on a heritage boat are also available.

⊕ ACTIVITIES

Nothing gets you closer to the heart and soul of Auckland than sailing on the Hauraki Gulf. If you don't want to fork out on a yacht cruise, catch a ferry to Waiheke Island instead. Trading on the country's action-packed reputation, Auckland has sprouted its own set of thrill-inducing activities.

Auckland Bridge Climb & Bungy
Adventure Sports

(☑09-360 7748; www.bungy.co.nz; 105 Curran St, Westhaven; adult/child climb $125/85, bungy $160/130, both $230) Climb up or jump off the Auckland Harbour Bridge.

SkyJump
Adventure Sports

(Map p50; ☑0800 759 586; www.skyjump. co.nz; Sky Tower, cnr Federal & Victoria Sts; adult/child $225/175; ☺10am-5.15pm) This thrilling 11-second, 85km/h base wire leap from the observation deck of the Sky Tower is more like a parachute jump than a bungy. Combine it with the **SkyWalk** in the Look & Leap package ($290).

SkyWalk
Adventure Sports

(Map p50; ☑0800 759 925; www.skywalk. co.nz; Sky Tower, cnr Federal & Victoria Sts; adult/child $145/115; ☺10am-4.30pm) The SkyWalk involves circling the 192m-high, 1.2m-wide outside halo of the Sky Tower without rails or a balcony. Don't worry, it's not completely crazy – there is a safety harness.

Explore
Boating

(Map p50; ☑0800 397 567; www.explorenz. co.nz; Viaduct Harbour) Shoot the breeze for two hours on a genuine America's Cup yacht (adult/child $170/120), take a 90-minute cruise on a glamorous large yacht (adult/child $75/55) or tuck into a 2½-hour Harbour Dinner Cruise ($120/85).

Fergs Kayaks
Kayaking

(☑09-529 2230; www.fergskayaks.co.nz; 12 Tamaki Dr, Orakei; ☺9am-5pm) Hires kayaks (per hour/day from $20/80), paddleboards ($25/70), bikes ($20/80) and inline skates ($15/45). Guided kayak trips head to Devonport ($100, 8km, three hours) or Rangitoto ($140, 13km, six hours).

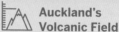

Auckland's Volcanic Field

Some cities think they're tough just by living in the shadow of a volcano. Auckland's built on 50 of them and, no, they're not all extinct. The last one to erupt was Rangitoto about 600 years ago and no one can predict when the next eruption will occur. Auckland's quite literally a hot spot – with a reservoir of magma 100km below, waiting to bubble to the surface. But relax: this has only happened 19 times in the last 20,000 years.

Some of Auckland's volcanoes are cones, some are filled with water and some have been completely quarried away. Moves are afoot to register the field as a World Heritage Site and protect what remains. Most of the surviving cones show evidence of terracing from when they formed a formidable series of Māori *pa* (fortified villages). The most interesting to explore are Mt Eden, One Tree Hill, North Head and Rangitoto, but Mt Victoria, Mt Wellington (Maungarei), Mt Albert (Owairaka), Mt Roskill (Puketāpapa), Lake Pupuke, Mt Mangere and Mt Hobson (Remuera) are all worth a visit.

One Tree Hill (p48)
PATRIKSTEDRAK/GETTY IMAGES ©

🅖 TOURS

Auckland Wine Trail Tours Wine
(☑09-630 1540; www.winetrailtours.co.nz) Small-group tours around West Auckland wineries and the Waitakere Ranges (half-/full day $125/255); further afield to Matakana ($265); or a combo of the two ($265).

Auckland Seaplanes Scenic Flights
(Map p50; ☑09-390 1121; www.aucklandsea planes.com; 11 Brigham St, Wynyard Quarter; per person from $200) Flights in a cool 1960s floatplane that explore Auckland's harbour and islands.

Bush & Beach Walking
(☑09-837 4130; www.bushandbeach.co.nz) 🥾 Tours including guided walks in the Waitakere Ranges and along west-coast beaches ($150 to $235); three-hour city minibus tours ($78); and food and wine tours in either Kumeu or Matakana (half-/full day $235/325).

Big Foody Food Tour Food
(☑021 481 177, 0800 366 386; www.thebigfoody. com; per person $125-185) Small-group city tours, including market visits, visits to artisan producers and lots of tastings.

TIME Unlimited Cultural
(☑09-846 3469; www.newzealandtours.travel) Cultural, walking and sightseeing tours from a Māori perspective.

Toru Tours Bus
(☑027 457 0011; www.torutours.com; per person $79) The three-hour Express Tour will depart with just one booking – ideal for solo travellers.

Tāmaki Hikoi Cultural
(☑021 146 9593; www.tamakihikoi.co.nz; 1/3hr $40/95) Guides from the Ngāti Whātua *iwi* (tribe) lead various Māori cultural tours, including walking and interpretation of sites such as Mt Eden and the Auckland Domain.

🔒 SHOPPING

Followers of fashion should head to the Britomart precinct, Newmarket and Ponsonby Rd. For vintage clothing and secondhand boutiques try Karangahape Rd (K Rd) or Ponsonby Rd.

Karen Walker — Clothing

(Map p50; 📞09-309 6299; www.karenwalker.
com; 18 Te Ara Tahuhu Walkway, Britomart;
🕙10am-6pm) Join Madonna and Kirsten
Dunst in wearing Walker's cool (but pricey)
threads. Also in Ponsonby Rd (Map p50;
📞09-361 6723; 128a Ponsonby Rd, Grey Lynn;
🕙10am-5.30pm Mon-Sat, 11am-4pm Sun) and
Newmarket (Map p56; 📞09-522 4286;
6 Balm St, Newmarket; 🕙10am-6pm).

Pauanesia — Gifts

(Map p50; 📞09-366 7282; www.pauanesia.
co.nz; 35 High St; 🕙9.30am-6.30pm Mon-Fri,
10am-4.30pm Sat & Sun) Homewares and gifts
with a Polynesian and Kiwiana influence.

Zambesi — Clothing

(Map p50; 📞09-303 1701; www.zambesi.
co.nz; 56 Tyler St; 🕙9.30am-6pm Mon-Sat,
11am-4pm Sun) Iconic NZ label much sought
after by local and international A-listers.
Also in Ponsonby (Map p50; 📞09-360 7391;
169 Ponsonby Rd, Ponsonby; 🕙9.30am-6pm
Mon-Sat, 11am-4pm Sun) and Newmarket (Map
p56; 📞09-523 1000; 38 Osborne St, Newmarket; 🕙9.30am-6pm Mon-Sat, 11am-4pm Sun).

Royal Jewellery Studio — Jewellery

(Map p56; 📞09-846 0200; www.
royaljewellerystudio.com; 486 New North Rd,
Kingsland; 🕙10am-4pm Tue-Sun) Work by local
artisans, including beautiful Māori designs
and authentic *pounamu* (greenstone)
jewellery.

Otara Flea Market — Market

(📞09-274 0830; www.otarafleamarket.co.nz;
Newbury St; 🕙6am-noon Sat) Held in the car
park between the Manukau Polytech and
the Otara town centre, this market has a
palpable Polynesian atmosphere and is
good for South Pacific food, music and
fashions. Take bus 472, 487 or 497 from 55
Customs St in the city ($6.50, 50 minutes).

Real Groovy — Music

(📞09-302 3940; www.realgroovy.co.nz; 369
Queen St; 🕙9am-7pm Sat-Wed, to 9pm Thu &
Fri) Masses of new, secondhand and rare
releases in vinyl and CD format, as well as

*no one can predict when the next
eruption will occur*

SkyJumper at the Sky Tower (p49)

MATTASCAUSA/SHUTTERSTOCK/GETTY IMAGES ©

Mt Eden, Newmarket & One Tree Hill

concert tickets, giant posters, DVDs, books, magazines and clothes.

Unity Books
Books

(☑09-307 0731; www.unitybooks.co.nz; 19 High St; ⊗8.30am-7pm Mon-Sat, 10am-6pm Sun) The inner city's best independent bookshop.

Strangely Normal
Clothing

(☑09-309 0600; www.strangelynormal.com; 19 O'Connell St; ⊗10am-6pm Mon-Sat, 11am-4pm Sun) Quality, NZ-made, men's tailored shirts

straight out of *Blue Hawaii* sit alongside hipster hats, sharp shoes and cufflinks.

✖ EATING

Because of its size and ethnic diversity, Auckland tops the country when it comes to dining options and quality. The hippest new foodie enclaves are Britomart (the blocks above the train station) and Federal St (under the Sky Tower), and recent openings have resurrected and reinforced the culinary reputation of Ponsonby. The Wynyard Quarter and the former City Works Depot on the corner of Wellesley and Nelson Sts are also up-and-coming areas.

🏙 City Centre

Best Ugly Bagels
Bakery, Cafe $

(Map p50; 📞09-366 3926; www.bestugly. co.nz; City Works Depot, 90 Wellesley St; filled bagels $5-12; ⏰7am-3am; 🖋) Hand rolled, boiled and wood-fired, Best Ugly's bagels are a thing of beauty. Call into its super-hip bakery in a converted heavy vehicle workshop and order one stuffed with pastrami, bacon, smoked salmon or a variety of vegetarian fillings. Or just ask for a cinnamon bagel slathered with cream cheese and jam. The coffee is killer too.

Chuffed
Cafe $

(📞09-367 6801; www.chuffedcoffee.co.nz; 43 High St; mains $6.50-18; ⏰7am-5pm Mon-Fri, 9am-5pm Sat & Sun) Tucked away in a lightwell at the rear of a building, this hip little place, liberally coated in street art, is a definite contender for the inner city's best cafe. Grab a seat on the indoor-outdoor terrace and tuck into cooked breakfasts, Wagyu burgers, lamb shanks or flavour-packed toasted sandwiches.

Depot
Modern NZ $$

(Map p50; www.eatatdepot.co.nz; 86 Federal St; dishes $16-34; ⏰7am-late) TV chef Al Brown's popular eatery offers first-rate comfort food in informal surrounds (communal tables, butcher tiles and a constant buzz). Dishes are designed to be shared, and a pair of clever shuckers serve up the city's freshest clams and oysters. It doesn't take bookings, so get there early or expect to wait.

Beirut
Lebanese $$

(Map p50; 📞09-367 6882; www.beirut.co.nz; 85 Fort St; mains $26-29; ⏰7am-late Mon-Fri, 5pm-late Sat) Sacking curtains and industrial decor don't necessarily scream out Lebanese, but the sophisticated, punchy flavours bursting from the plates at this wonderful new restaurant certainly do.

The cocktails are nearly as exciting as the food – and that's saying something.

Cassia
Indian $$

(Map p50; 📞09-379 9702; 5 Fort Lane; www. cassiarestaurant.co.nz; 5 Fort Lane; mains $28-34; ⏰noon-3pm Wed-Fri, 5.30pm-late Tue-Sat) Occupying a moodily lit basement off an access lane, Cassia serves quality modern Indian food with plenty of punch and panache. Start with a *pani puri,* a bite-sized crispy shell bursting with flavour, before settling into a decadently rich curry. The Delhi duck is excellent, as is the piquant Goan fish curry.

Odette's
Modern NZ $$

(Map p50; 📞09-309 0304; www.odettes. co.nz; Shed 5, City Works Depot, 90 Wellesley St; mains $17-25; ⏰8am-3pm Sun & Mon, 7am-11pm Tue-Sat) Nothing about Odette's is run of the mill. Not the bubbly light fixtures or the quirky photography, and certainly not the menu. How about octopus or spicy short ribs for brunch? Or spongy wild mushrooms served with doughnuts and Persian feta? In the evening the more cafe-ish items are replaced with dishes for sharing. It gets hectic on weekends.

Giapo
Ice Cream $$

(Map p50; 📞09-550 3677; www.giapo.com; 279 Queen St; ice cream $10-22; ⏰noon-10.30pm Sun-Thu, to 11.45pm Fri & Sat) That there are queues outside this boutique ice-cream shop even in the middle of winter says a lot about the magical confections that it conjures up. These are no simple scoops in cones, rather expect elaborate constructions of ice-cream art topped with all manner of goodies.

Ortolana
Italian $$

(www.ortolana.co.nz; 33 Tyler St, Britomart; mains $25-29; ⏰7am-11pm) Mediterranean and regional Italian flavours are showcased at this stylish restaurant. Dishes are as artfully arranged as they are delicious, and much of the produce comes from the owners' small farm in rural west Auckland. Some of the sweets come from its sister patisserie, the very fabulous Milse, next door. It doesn't take bookings.

Sugar Club · Modern NZ $$$

(☏09-363 6365; www.thesugarclub.co.nz; L53 Sky Tower, Federal St; 2-/3-/4-/5-course lunch $56/70/84/98, 3-/4-/5-/6-course dinner $90/108/118/128; ☺noon-2.30pm Wed-Sun & 5.30-9.30pm daily) It pays not to expect too much from restaurants stuck up towers, but when the executive chef is NZ's most famous culinary son, Peter Gordon, heralded in the UK as the 'godfather of fusion cuisine', you can comfortably raise your expectations. Gordon's meticulously constructed, flavour-filled dishes compete with the stupendous views and come out on top.

Grove · Modern NZ $$$

(☏09-368 4129; www.thegroverestaurant.co.nz; St Patrick's Sq, Wyndham St; 5-/9-course degustation $89/145; ☺noon-3pm Thu & Fri, 6pm-late Mon-Sat) Romantic fine dining: the room is moodily lit, the menu encourages sensual experimentation and the service is effortless. If you can't find anything to break the ice from the extensive wine list, give it up, mate – it's never going to happen.

✖ Ponsonby & Grey Lynn

Street Food Collective · Fast Food $

(Map p50; ☏021 206 4503; www.thestreetfoodcollective.co.nz; Rear, 130 Ponsonby Rd, Grey Lynn; dishes $5-15; ☺11am-3pm & 5-10pm) A great concept this: 14 different food trucks take turns to occupy four spots in a courtyard accessed from a narrow back lane running between Richmond Rd and Mackelvie St (look for the wrought-iron gates). The roster's posted online and there's a separate bar truck too.

Dizengoff · Cafe $

(Map p50; ☏09-360 0108; www.facebook.com/dizengoff.ponsonby; 256 Ponsonby Rd, Ponsonby; mains $6.50-20; ☺6.45am-4.30pm) This stylish shoebox crams in a disparate crowd of corporate and fashion types, Ponsonby denizens and travellers. There's a Jewish influence to the food, with tasty Israeli platters, chopped liver, bagels and chicken salads, along with tempting baking,

Dizengoff

heart-starting coffee and a great stack of reading material.

Saan
Thai $$

(Map p50; ☎09-320 4237; www.saan.co.nz; 160 Ponsonby Rd, Ponsonby; dishes $14-28; ⏱5pm-late Mon & Tue, noon-late Wed-Sun) Hot in both senses of the word, this super-fashionable restaurant focuses on the fiery cuisine of the Isaan and Lanna regions of Northern Thailand. The menu is conveniently sorted from least to most spicy, and split into smaller and larger dishes for sharing. Be sure to order the soft-shell crab; it's truly exceptional.

Blue Breeze Inn
Chinese $$

(Map p50; ☎09-360 0303; www.theblue breezeinn.co.nz; Ponsonby Central, 146 Ponsonby Rd, Ponsonby; mains $26-32; ⏱noon-late) Regional Chinese flavours combine with a funky retro Pacific ambience at this so-hip-it-hurts eatery. The staff are sassy, the rum cocktails are deliciously strong, and menu standouts include pork belly and pickled cucumber steamed buns, and cumin-spiced lamb.

Ponsonby Central
Cafe $$

(Map p50; www.ponsonbycentral.co.nz; 136-138 Ponsonby Rd, Ponsonby; mains $15-35; ⏱7am-10.30pm Sun-Wed, to midnight Thu-Sat) From Auckland's best pizza to Argentinean, Thai and Japanese – loads of flavour-filled restaurants, cafes, bars and gourmet food shops fill this upmarket former warehouse space.

Sidart
Modern NZ $$$

(Map p50; ☎09-360 2122; www.sidart.co.nz; Three Lamps Plaza, 283 Ponsonby Rd, Ponsonby; 8-course lunch $50, 5-9 course dinner $85-150; ⏱noon-2.30pm Fri, 6-11pm Tue-Sat) No one in Auckland produces creative degustations quite like Sid Sahrawat. It's food as art, food as science but, more importantly, food to fire up your taste buds, delight the brain, satisfy the stomach and put a smile on your face. The restaurant is a little hard to find, tucked away at the rear of what was once the Alhambra cinema.

Parnell

Woodpecker Hill
Asian, Fusion $$$

(Map p50; ☎09-309 5055; www.woodpecker hill.co.nz; 196 Parnell Rd, Parnell; large dishes $32-37; ⏱noon-late) Marrying the flavours and shared dining style of Southeast Asian cuisine with an American approach to meat (smoky slow-cooked brisket, sticky short ribs etc), this odd bird has pecked out a unique place on the Auckland dining scene. The decor is as eclectic as the food, a riotous mishmash of tartan, faux fur, copper bells and potted plants.

Mt Eden

Bolaven
Cafe $$

(Map p56; ☎09-631 7520; www.bolaven. co.nz; 597 Mt Eden Rd, Mt Eden; mains $11-26; ⏱8am-3pm Tue-Sun, 6-10pm Wed-Sat; ☎) Cafe fare with a heavy Lao accent is the big attraction at this stylish but informal eatery. Alongside the bagels and bircher muesli you'll find the likes of 'Grandpa's *pho*' (noodle soup), sticky rice with fried eggs, and *mok pa* (steamed fish parcels). Come dinnertime the menu is more decidedly Lao, featuring vegetable curry, pork skewers and pan-fried squid.

Merediths
Modern NZ $$$

(Map p56; ☎09-623 3140; www.merediths. co.nz; 365 Dominion Rd, Mt Eden; 5-/8-/9-course degustation $80/120/140; ⏱noon-3pm Fri, 6pm-late Tue-Sat) Dining at Merediths is the culinary equivalent of black-water rafting – tastes surprise you at every turn, you never know what's coming next and you're left with a sense of breathless exhilaration. There's no *à la carte* option and only the nine-course tasting is offered on Saturdays.

Newton

French Cafe
French $$$

(Map p56; ☎09-377 1911; www.thefrenchcafe. co.nz; 210 Symonds St, Newton; mains $46, tasting menu $145; ⏱noon-3pm Fri, 6pm-late Tue-Sat) The legendary French Cafe has been rated as one of Auckland's top restaurants for more than 20 years and it still continues to excel. The cuisine is French-influenced, but chef Simon Wright sneaks in lots of tasty Asian and Pacific Rim touches. The service is impeccable.

West Auckland's Wine, Food & Beer

West Auckland's main wine-producing area still has some vineyards owned by the original Croatian families who kick-started NZ's wine industry. The fancy eateries that have mushroomed in recent years have done little to dint the relaxed farmland feel to the region, but everything to encourage an afternoon's indulgence on the way back from the beach. Most cellars offer free tastings, and there's even a great craft brewery.

Coopers Creek (☑09-412 8560; www. cooperscreek.co.nz; 601 SH16, Huapai; ☉10.30am-5.30pm) Buy a bottle and spread out a picnic in the attractive gardens. From January to Easter, enjoy Sunday-afternoon jazz sessions.

Kumeu River (☑09-412 8415; www. kumeuriver.co.nz; 550 SH16; ☉9am-4.30pm Mon-Fri, 11am-4.30pm Sat) Owned by the Brajkovich family, this winery produces one of NZ's best chardonnays.

Soljans Estate (☑09-412 5858; www.soljans. co.nz; 366 SH16; ☉tastings 9am-5pm, cafe 10am-3pm) One of the pioneering Croat–Kiwi family vineyards, Soljans has a wonderful cafe (mains $19 to $33) offering brunch and vintner's platters crammed with Mediterranean treats.

Tasting Shed (☑09-412 6454; www. thetastingshed.co.nz; 609 SH16, Huapai; dishes $14-26; ☉4-10pm Wed & Thu, noon-11pm Fri-Sun) Complementing its rural aspect with rustic chic decor, this slick eatery conjures up delicious dishes designed to be shared.

Hallertau (☑09-412 5555; www.hallertau. co.nz; 1171 Coatesville–Riverhead Hwy, Riverhead; ☉11am-midnight) Offers tasting paddles ($14) of its craft beers served on a vine-covered terrace edging the restaurant. Occasional weekend DJs and live music.

 DRINKING & NIGHTLIFE

Auckland's nightlife is quiet during the week – for some vital signs, head to Ponsonby Rd, Britomart or the Viaduct. Karangahape Rd (K Rd) wakes up late on Friday and Saturday; don't even bother staggering this way before 11pm. Along Ponsonby Rd, the line between cafe, restaurant, bar and club gets blurred. A lot of eateries also have live music or become clubs later on.

City Centre

Brothers Beer   Craft Beer

(Map p50; ☑09-366 6100; www.brothers beer.co.nz; City Works Depot, 90 Wellesley St; ☉noon-10pm) Our favourite Auckland beer bar combines industrial decor with 18 taps crammed with the Brothers' own brews and guest beers from NZ and further afield. Hundreds more bottled beers await chilling in the fridges, and bar food includes top-notch pizza. It also offers tasting flights (five small glasses for $25).

Mo's   Bar

(Map p50; ☑09-366 6066; www.mosbar. co.nz; cnr Wolfe & Federal Sts; ☉3pm-late Mon-Fri, 6pm-late Sat; ☎) There's something about this tiny corner bar that makes you want to invent problems just so the bartender can solve them with soothing words and an expertly poured martini.

Gin Room   Bar

(Map p50; www.ginroom.co.nz; L1, 12 Vulcan Lane; ☉5pm-midnight Tue & Wed, 5pm-2am Thu, 4pm-4am Fri, 6pm-4am Sat) There's a slightly dishevelled colonial charm to this bar, which is completely in keeping with its latest incarnation as a gin palace. There are at least 50 ways to ruin mother here – ask the bar staff for advice – and that's not even counting the juniper-sozzled cocktails.

Xuxu
Cocktail Bar

(Map p50; ☑09-309 5529; www.xuxu. co.nz; cnr Galway & Commerce Sts, Britomart; ☺noon-late Mon-Fri, 5pm-late Sat) A winning combination of Asian-tinged cocktails and tasty dumplings. DJs kick in on weekends.

Hotel DeBrett
Bar

(www.hoteldebrett.com; 2 High St; ☺noon-late) Grab a beer in the colourful Cornerbar or a cocktail in the art-deco Housebar at the very heart of this chic hotel.

Cassette Nine
Club

(☑09-366 0196; www.cassettenine.com; 9 Vulcan Lane; ☺4pm-late Tue-Fri, 6pm-late Sat) Hipsters gravitate to this eccentric bar-club for music ranging from live indie to international DJ sets.

 Grey Lynn

Golden Dawn
Bar

(Map p50; ☑09-376 9929; www.gold-endawn.co.nz; 134b Ponsonby Rd, Grey Lynn; ☺4pm-midnight Tue-Fri, noon-midnight Sat & Sun) Occupying an old shopfront and an inviting stables yard, this hip drinking den regularly hosts happenings including DJs and live bands. There's also excellent food on offer, including pulled-pork rolls, and prawn buns with Japanese mayo and chilli. The entrance is via the unmarked door just around the corner on Richmond Rd.

Freida Margolis
Bar

(☑09-378 6625; www.facebook.com/freida margolis; 440 Richmond Rd, Grey Lynn; ☺4pm-late) Formerly a butchers – look for the Westlynn Organic Meats sign – this corner location is now a great little neighbour-hood bar with a backstreets-of-Bogota ambience. Loyal locals sit outside supping on sangria, wine and craft beer, and enjoy-ing eclectic sounds on vinyl.

 Ponsonby

Bedford Soda & Liquor
Cocktail Bar

(☑09-378 7362; www.bedfordsodaliquor.co.nz; Ponsonby Central, Richmond Rd, Ponsonby; ☺noon-midnight) Candlelight and a semi-industrial fit-out set the scene for a New York–style bar devoted to the American drinking culture. The cocktails are pricey but worth it: some come wreathed in smoke, others in the alcoholic equivalent of a snow globe, while the 'salted caramel Malteaser whisky milkshake' is exactly as decadent as it sounds.

Shanghai Lil's
Cocktail Bar

(☑09-360 0396; www.facebook.com/lils ponsonby; 212 Ponsonby Rd, Ponsonby; ☺5pm-late Tue-Sat) A louche old-world Shanghai vibe pervades this small bar, where the owner dispenses charm in a silk Mandarin jacket and octogenarian musicians play for satin-voiced jazz singers. It attracts a widely varied and eclectic crowd, with a healthy quotient of gay men in the mix.

 Wynyard Quarter

Sixteen Tun
Craft Beer

(Map p50; ☑09-368 7712; www.16tun.co.nz; 10-26 Jellicoe St, Wynyard Quarter; tasting 4/6/8 beers $12/18/24; ☺11.30am-late) The glister of burnished copper perfectly com-plements the liquid amber on offer here in the form of dozens of NZ craft beer by the bottle and a score on tap. If you can't decide, go for a tasting 'crate' of 200ml serves.

Jack Tar
Pub

(Map p50; ☑09-303 1002; www.jacktar. co.nz; North Wharf, 34-37 Jellicoe St, Wyn-yard Quarter; ☺7am-late) A top spot for a late-afternoon/early-evening beer or wine and pub grub amid the relaxed vibe of the waterfront Wynyard Quarter.

 Newton

Galbraith's Alehouse
Brewery, Pub

(Map p56; ☑09-379 3557; http://alehouse. co.nz; 2 Mt Eden Rd, Newton; ☺noon-11pm) Brewing real ales and lagers on-site, this cosy English-style pub in a grand heritage building offers bliss on tap. There are always more craft beers on the guest taps, and the food's also very good.

ENTERTAINMENT

Auckland Live   Performing Arts
(☑09-309 2677; www.aucklandlive.co.nz)
Auckland's main arts and entertainment
complex is grouped around Aotea Sq. It's
comprised of the Auckland Town Hall, Civic
Theatre and Aotea Centre, along with the
Bruce Mason Centre in Takapuna.

Auckland Town Hall   Classical Music
(Map p50; ☑09-309 2677; www.aucklandlive.
co.nz; 305 Queen St) This elegant Edwardian
venue (1911) hosts the NZ Symphony
Orchestra (www.nzso.co.nz) and Auckland
Philharmonia (www.apo.co.nz), among
others.

Q Theatre   Theatre
(Map p50; ☑09-309 9771; www.qtheatre.
co.nz; 305 Queen St) Theatre by various companies and intimate live music. Silo Theatre
(www.silotheatre.co.nz) often performs
here.

Kings Arms Tavern   Live Music
(☑09-373 3240; www.kingsarms.co.nz; 59
France St, Newton) This heritage pub with a
great beer garden is Auckland's leading
small venue for local and up-and-coming
international bands.

Whammy Bar   Live Music
(www.facebook.com/thewhammybar; 183
Karangahape Rd, Newton; ☺8.30pm-4am Wed-
Sat) Small, but a stalwart on the live indie
music scene nonetheless.

❶ INFORMATION

Princes Wharf i-SITE (Map p50; ☑09-365
9914; www.aucklandnz.com; 139 Quay St; ☺9am-
5pm) Auckland's main official information centre,
incorporating the **DOC Auckland Visitor Centre**
(Map p50; ☑09-379 6476; www.doc.govt.nz;
137 Quay St, Princes Wharf; ☺9am-5pm Mon-Fri,
extended in summer).

SkyCity i-SITE (Map p50; ☑09-365 9918;
www.aucklandnz.com; SkyCity Atrium, cnr Victoria & Federal Sts; ☺9am-5pm)

Auckland International Airport i-SITE (☑09-
365 9925; www.aucklandnz.com; International
Arrivals Hall; ☺6.30am-10.30pm)

GETTING THERE & AWAY

AIR

Auckland Airport (p305) is 21km south of the
city centre. It is the main international gateway
to NZ, and a hub for domestic flights.There are
separate international and domestic terminals, a
10-minute walk apart via a signposted footpath;
a free shuttle service operates every 15 minutes
(5am to 10.30pm). The city is linked to domestic
NZ destinations, major Australian cities, Asia, the
Pacific, and North and South America.

BUS

Buses and shuttles for destinations around the
North Island depart from 172 Quay St, opposite
the Ferry Building, except for InterCity services,
which depart from the **SkyCity Coach Terminal**
(Map p50; 102 Hobson St). Many southbound
services also stop at the airport.

TRAIN

The **Northern Explorer** (☑0800 872 467; www.
kiwirailscenic.co.nz) from KiwiRail Scenic travels
between Auckland and Wellington, stopping at
Tongariro National Park and Ohakune en route.

❶ GETTING AROUND

The most useful bus services are the environ-
mentally friendly Link Buses that loop in both
directions around three routes (taking in many
of the major sights) from 7am to 11pm:

City Link (adult/child 50¢/30¢ every seven to 10
minutes) Wynyard Quarter, Britomart, Queen St
and Karangahape Rd.

Inner Link (adult/child $2.50/1.50, every 10 to
15 minutes) Queen St, SkyCity, Victoria Park, Ponsonby Rd, Karangahape Rd, Museum, Newmarket,
Parnell and Britomart.

Outer Link (maximum $4.50, every 15 minutes)
Art Gallery, Ponsonby, Herne Bay, Westmere,
MOTAT 2, Pt Chevalier, Mt Albert, St Lukes Mall,
Mt Eden, Newmarket, Museum, Parnell and
University.

Where to Stay

Befitting a burgeoning international city, Auckland has a wide range of accommodation. Booking ahead can secure better deals. Keep an eye out for when international concerts and big rugby games are scheduled as accommodation around the city can fill up.

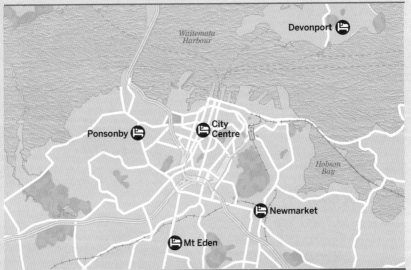

Neighbourhood	Atmosphere
City Centre	Luxury hotels, international chains and hostels feature in the CBD. Convenient but lacking character.
Ponsonby	Near to good restaurants and bars with a good selection of B&Bs and hostels. A short distance from central Auckland.
Mt Eden	A leafy suburb on the fringe of the city with good hostels and B&Bs. Good transport links to the CBD and harbour ferries.
Devonport	A seaside suburb reached by ferry from downtown Auckland with beautiful Edwardian B&Bs.
Newmarket	Good-value motels along Great South Rd and near to good shopping. An easy bus ride into central Auckland.

BAY OF ISLANDS

Bay of Islands at a glance...

Part of the 'winterless north' – the upper reaches of the North Island are always a few degrees warmer than further south – the Bay of Islands offers the opportunity to take boat trips around the bay, often seeing dolphins and other marine mammals. The Waitangi Treaty Grounds showcase New Zealand's bicultural history, blending the stories of the indigenous Māori and the Pākehā (European New Zealanders) and the new Musuem of Waitangi is innovative and interactive.

The Bay of Islands in two days

After looking around historic **Russell** (p74) in the morning, catch the passenger or vehicle ferry across to **Paihia** (p77) and spend the afternoon understanding the impact of the Treaty of Waitangi at the **Waitangi Treaty Grounds** (p68). Head to dinner at **Provenir** (p78) in Paihia, and the following morning hook up with an exciting boat trip exploring the Bay of Islands. After your marine excursion, relax with absolute waterfront drinks at **Alongside** (p78).

The Bay of Islands in three days

Kick off the following morning with great coffee and a breakfast burrito at **El Cafe** (p78) in Paihia before continuing to more foodie treats around **Kerikeri** (p72). Take your pick from fudge, wine-tasting and local macadamias, before revelling in Thai flavours at **Food at Wharepuke** (p73).

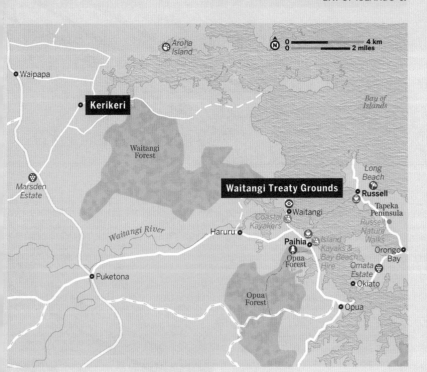

Arriving in the Bay of Islands

Kerikeri Airport Around 23km west of Paihia with regular Air New Zealand flights to/from Auckland. Super Shuttle operates a shuttle service from the airport to Kerikeri, Paihia, Opua and Kawakawa.

InterCity Bus Terminate at the Paihia i-SITE and on Cobham Rd opposite the Kerikeri Library.

Where to Stay

Russell has more atmosphere, but Paihia is definitely more convenient and has motels, apartments and B&Bs on the waterfront and around the surrounding hills. Paihia also has an excellent range of hostels, and Kings Rd is the main 'backpackers' row.' Russell has a few decent midrange options and there are several small budget lodges, but you'll need to book ahead at busy times. If budget is not a consideration, Russell does luxury B&Bs very well.

Kapa haka group at Waitangi Day celebrations

Waitangi Treaty Grounds

With a wonderful coastal location, including immaculate lawns offering views across the bay, the Waitangi Treaty Grounds are an essential destination for visitors wishing to understand New Zealand history.

Great For...

☑ **Don't Miss**

The beautiful carvings and *tukutuku* (woven panels) at Waitangi's *whare runanga* (meeting house).

The birthplace of modern NZ, Waitangi inhabits a special, somewhat complex place in the national psyche – aptly demonstrated by the mixture of celebration, commemoration, protest and apathy that accompanies the nation's birthday (Waitangi Day, 6 February).

Occupying a headland draped in lawns and bush, this is NZ's most significant historic site. It was here that the long-neglected and much-contested Treaty of Waitangi was first signed, on 6 February 1840, between the first 43 Māori chiefs and the British Crown, establishing British sovereignty or something a bit like it, depending on whether you're reading the English or Māori version of the document. Eventually, over 500 chiefs would sign it. If you're interested in coming to grips with

Meeting house, Waitangi Treaty Grounds

❶ Need to Know

☎09-402 7437; www.waitangi.org.nz; 1 Tau Henare Dr; adult/child $40/20; 9am-5pm Mar-24 Dec, 9am-6pm 26 Dec-Feb

✗ Take a Break

Overlooking the Treaty Grounds, the **Whare Waka** (Waitangi Treaty Grounds; snacks & mains $7-18; ⊙9am-5pm) offers good cafe fare.

★ Top Tip

Experience a *hangi* dinner and concert at **Whare Waka**; Tuesday and Thursday evenings, December to March.

NZ's history and race relations, this is the place to start.

The importance of the treaty is well understood by a NZ audience, but visitors might find it surprising that there's not more information displayed here about the role it has played in the nation's history: the long litany of breaches by the Crown, the wars and land confiscations that followed, and the protest movement that led to the current process of redress for historic injustices.

The **Treaty House** was built in 1832 as the four-room home of British resident James Busby. It's now preserved as a memorial and museum containing displays, including a copy of the treaty. Just across

the lawn, the magnificently detailed *whare runanga* (meeting house) was completed in 1940 to mark the centenary of the treaty. The fine carvings represent the major Māori tribes. Near the cove is the 35m *waka taua* (war canoe), also built for the centenary. A photographic exhibit details how it was fashioned from gigantic kauri logs.

Admission incorporates entry to the Treaty Grounds, a guided tour and cultural performance, and also entry to the new **Museum of Waitangi** (☎09-402 7437; www.waitangi.org.nz; 1 Tau Henare Dr; adult/child $40/20; ⊙9am-5pm Mar-24 Dec, 9am-6pm 26 Dec-Feb). Admission for NZ residents is $20 upon presentation of a passport or driver's licence.

A walking track (one way 1½ hours, 5km) leads from the Treaty Grounds to beautiful horseshoe-shaped Haruru Falls.

Hole in the Rock

Bay of Islands Marine Adventures

Being on the water is the best way to experience the Bay of Islands. Spectacular scenery combines with sea kayaking and marine mammals, including the opportunity to swim with dolphins.

Great For...

☑ Don't Miss

Fine subtropical diving at the wreck of the *Rainbow Warrior* off the Cavalli Islands, about 1 hour north of Paihia by boat.

Options to explore the Bay of Islands include sailing boats, jetboats and large launches. Boats leave from either Paihia or Russell, calling into the other town as their first stop.

One of the bay's most striking islands is Piercy Island (Motukokako) off Cape Brett, at the bay's eastern edge. This steep-walled rock fortress features a vast natural arch – the famous Hole in the Rock. If conditions are right, most boat tours pass right through the heart of the island. En route it's likely you'll encounter bottlenose and common dolphins, and you may see orcas, other whales and penguins.

A great way to explore the bay is under sail. Either help crew the boat (no experience required), or spend the afternoon island-hopping, swimming and snorkelling.

R Tucker Thompson sailing ship

ROBERT ARMSTRONG/GETTY IMAGES ©

to see dolphins en route to the Hole in the Rock, and stopping at Urupukapuka Island on the way back. The four-hour **Dolphin Eco Experience** (adult/child $117/58, ⊘departs 8am and 12.30pm) is focused on finding dolphins to swim with.

R Tucker Thompson — Boating

(☑09-402 8430; www.tucker.co.nz; ⊘Nov-Apr) Run by a charitable trust with an education focus, the *Tucker* is a majestic tall ship offering day sails (adult/child $145/73, including a barbecue lunch) and late-afternoon cruises (adult/child $65/33).

Carino — Boating

(☑09-402 8040; www.sailingdolphins.co.nz; adult/child $119/74) ⚑ This 50ft catamaran is licensed by NZ's Department of Conservation (DOC) for swimming with dolphins and it adheres to NZ's Marine Mammal Protection Act of 1978. A barbecue lunch is available for $6.

Mack Attack — Boating

(☑0800 622 528; www.mackattack.co.nz; 9 Williams Rd, Paihia; adult/child $99/49) An exhilarating, high-speed 1½-hour jetboat trip to the Hole in the Rock. Another option is an Inner Bay of Islands tour (adult/child $85/49).

Tours

Explore NZ — Cruise

(☑09-402 8234; www.explorenz.co.nz; cnr Marsden & Williams Rds, Paihia) The four-hour Swim with the Dolphins Cruise (adult/child $95/50, additional $15 to swim) departs Paihia at 8am and 12.30pm from November to April. The four-hour Discover the Bay Cruise (adult/child $115/65) departs at 9am and 1.30pm, heading to the Hole in the Rock and stopping at Urupukapuka Island.

Fullers Great Sights — Cruise

(☑0800 653 339; www.dolphincruises.co.nz; Paihia Wharf) The four-hour Dolphin Cruise (adult/child $105/53) departs Paihia daily at 9am and 1.30pm, offering the chance

Stone Store

Kerikeri

A snapshot of early Māori and Pākehā interaction is showcased at the historic sites arrayed around Kerikeri's picturesque river basin. There's also a good local food scene.

Great For

☑ Don't Miss

Partnering local wine and food on the deck at **Marsden Estate** (☏09-407 9398; www.marsdenestate.co.nz; 56 Wiroa Rd; ☉10am-5pm).

In 1819 the powerful Ngāpuhi chief Hongi Hika allowed Reverend Samuel Marsden to start a mission under the shadow of his Kororipo Pa. There's an ongoing campaign to have the area now incorporating the Stone Store and the Mission House recognised as a Unesco World Heritage Site.

Sights

Stone Store   Historic Building

(☏09-407 9236; www.historic.org.nz; 246 Kerikeri Rd; ☉10am-4pm) Dating from 1836, the Stone Store is NZ's oldest stone building. It sells interesting Kiwiana gifts as well as the type of goods that used to be sold in the store. Tours of the wooden Mission House NZ's oldest building (1822), depart from here.

❶ Need to Know

There is a handy information centre at Kerikeri's **Procter Library** (Cobham Rd; ⊘8am-5pm Mon-Fri, 9am-2pm Sat; 🛜).

✕ Take a Break

Try the *shakshuka* (baked eggs in a spicy tomato sauce) at **Cafe Jerusalem** (✐09-407 1001; www.facebook.com/cafe jerusalem; Village Mall, 85 Kerikeri Rd; snacks & mains $9-18; ⊘11am-late Mon-Sat).

> ★ **Top Tip**
>
> For information on Kerikeri's burgeoning wine scene, visit www. northlandwinegrowers.co.nz.

Mission House   Historic Building

(www.historic.org.nz; tours $10) Take a tour of the wooden Mission House, NZ's oldest building (1822). Tours leave from the Stone Store and include admission to The Soul Trade exhibition on the 1st floor of the store.

Aroha Island   Wildlife Reserve

(✐09-407 5243; www.arohaisland.co.nz; 177 Rangitane Rd; ⊘9.30am-5.30pm) ✐**FREE** This 5-hectare island provides a haven for the North Island brown kiwi and other native birds, as well as a pleasant picnic spot for their nonfeathered admirers. It has a visitor centre, kayaks for rent, and after-dark walks to spy kiwi in the wild (per person $35) can also be arranged. You've got around a 50% chance of seeing a kiwi, and booking ahead is essential. Aroha Island is 12km northeast of Kerikeri.

What's Nearby

Between Kerikeri and Paihia there are lots of craft and artisan shops, Our picks for the best local flavours include:

Kerikeri Farmers Market (www.boifm.org.nz; Hobson Ave; ⊘8.30am-noon Sun) From gourmet sausages to limoncello.

The Old Packhouse Market (✐09-401 9588; www.theoldpackhousemarket.co.nz; 505 Kerikeri Rd; ⊘8am-1.30pm Sat) Every Saturday morning.

Get Fudged & Keriblue Ceramics (✐09-407 1111; www.keriblueceramics.co.nz; 560 Kerikeri Rd; ⊘9am-5pm) An unusual pairing of ceramics and big, decadent slabs of fudge.

Makana Confections (✐09-407 6800; www. makana.co.nz; 504 Kerikeri Rd; ⊘9am-5.30pm) Artisanal chocolate factory with lots of sampling.

Food at Wharepuke (✐09-407 8936; www.food atwharepuke.co.nz; 190 Kerikeri Rd; breakfast $14-22, lunch & dinner $24-39; ⊘10am-10.30pm Tue-Sun) Excellent Thai food and cafe classics surrounded by lush sub-tropical gardens.

 Historic Russell

In the early 19th century, Russell's sleepy cove was New Zealand's first European settlement, and it quickly became a magnet for fleeing convicts, whalers and drunken sailors. By the 1830s dozens of whaling ships were anchored in the harbour, and Charles Darwin described it as full of 'the refuse of society.'

Those coming to Russell for debauchery in the 21st century will be sadly disappointed: they've missed the orgies on the beach by 180 years. Instead Russell is now a historic town with gift shops, good restaurants and B&Bs.

Christ Church
ULRICH HOLLMANN/GETTY IMAGES ©

Russell

Once known as 'the hellhole of the Pacific,' Russell is a sleepy town filled with historical echoes of raffish colonial times, and a quieter bookend to Paihia across the bay. During summer, you can rent kayaks and dinghies along the Strand, and the town's pebble-beached esplanade is a pleasant place to stroll.

⊙ SIGHTS

Pompallier Mission　Historic Building
(☏09-403 9015; www.pompallier.co.nz; The Strand; tours adult/child $10/free; ⊙10am-4pm) Built in 1842 to house the Catholic mission's printing press, this rammed-earth building is the mission's last remaining building in the Western Pacific. A staggering

40,000 books were printed here in Māori. In the 1870s it was converted into a private home, but it is now restored to its original state, complete with tannery and printing workshop.

Christ Church　Church
(Church St) English naturalist Charles Darwin made a donation towards the cost of building the country's oldest church (1836). The graveyard's biggest memorial commemorates Tamati Waka Nene, a powerful Ngāpuhi chief from Hokianga who sided against Hone Heke in the Northland War. The church's exterior has musket and cannonball holes dating from the 1845 battle.

Haratu　Museum
(www.kororarekanz.com; cnr The Strand & Pitt St; ⊙gallery 10am-4pm Mon-Sat) Run by the local *marae* society, Haratu has Māori art and craft, mostly available for purchase. There are also audiovisual displays and information boards. Check the website to download an app (US$4.99) providing a one-hour walking tour of Russell based around local Māori legends and stories. The centre is volunteer-run, so opening times can vary.

Russell Museum　Museum
(☏09-403 7701; www.russellmuseum.org. nz; 2 York St; adult/child $10/3; ⊙10am-4pm) This small, modern museum has a well-presented Māori section, a large 1:5-scale model of Captain Cook's *Endeavour*, and a 10-minute video on the town's history.

Long Beach　Beach
(Long Beach Rd) About 1.5km behind Russell (an easy walk or cycle) is this placid, child-friendly beach. Turn left (facing the sea) to visit **Donkey Bay**, a small cove that is an unofficial nudist beach.

Omata Estate　Winery
(☏09-403 8007; www.omata.co.nz; Aucks Rd; ⊙tastings & food 10am-5pm Nov-Mar, tastings only 11am-5pm Wed-Sun Apr-Oct) With a growing reputation for red wines – especially its old-growth syrah – Omata Estate is one of

Northland's finest wineries. To complement the tastings and stunning sea views, shared platters ($40) are available. Phone ahead from April to October to confirm it's open. The winery is on the road from Russell to the car ferry at Okiato.

ACTIVITIES

Russell Nature Walks   Ecotour

(✆027 908 2334; www.russellnaturewalks.co.nz; 6080 Russell Whakapara Rd; day walk adult/child $38/20, night walk $45/20; ☺day walk 10am, night walk varies depending on sunset) Located in privately owned native forest 2.5km south of Russell, guided day and night tours provide the opportunity to see native birds, including the weka and tui, and insects such as the weta. Glow-worms softly illuminate night tours, and after dark there's the opportunity to hear (and very occasionally see) NZ's national bird, the kiwi. Walks last 1½ to two hours.

Owners Eion and Lisette also run a kiwi nesting program.

TOURS

Russell Mini Tours   Bus

(✆09-403 7866; www.russellminitours.com; cnr The Strand & Cass St; adult/child $29/15; ☺tours 11am, 1pm, 2pm & 3pm, also 10am & 4pm Oct-Apr) Minibus tour around historic Russell with commentary. Tours depart opposite Russell Wharf.

EATING

Newport Chocolates   Cafe $

(✆09-403 8402; www.newportchocolates.co.nz; 3 Cass St; chocolates around $3-4 each; ☺10am-6pm Tue-Thu, 10am-7.30pm Fri-Sat) Delicious artisan chocolates – handmade on site – with flavours including raspberry, lime and chilli, and, our favourite, caramel and sea salt. Also a top spot for rich hot chocolate and refreshing frappes.

Hell Hole   Cafe $

(✆022 604 1374; www.facebook.com/hell-holecoffee; 16 York St; snacks $6-12; ☺7am-5pm mid-Dec–Feb, 8am-3pm Mar, Apr & Oct–mid-Dec) Bagels, baguettes and croissants all feature

Gables restaurant (p76)

Paihia

with the best coffee in town at this compact spot one block back from the waterfront. Beans are locally roasted and organic soft drinks and artisan ice blocks all combine to make Hell Hole a hugely popular place, especially during Russell's peak season from mid-December to February.

Duke   Pub Food $$

(☏09-403 7829; www.theduke.co.nz; 35 The Strand; lunch $15-25, dinner $25-38; ⊙11am-late) There's no better spot in Russell to while away a few hours, glass in hand, than the Duke's sunny deck. Thankfully the upmarket bistro food matches the views, plus there's an excellent wine list and a great selection of NZ craft beers.

Hone's Garden   Pizza $$

(☏022 466 3710; www.facebook.com/hones garden; York St; pizza $18-25, wraps & salads $14-16; ⊙noon-late summer only) Head out to Hone's pebbled courtyard for wood-fired pizza (with 11 different varieties), cold craft beer on tap and a thoroughly easygoing Kiwi vibe. An expanded menu now also features tasty wraps and healthy salads.

Antipasto platters ($29 to $45) are good for groups and indecisive diners.

Gables   Modern NZ $$

(☏09-403 7670; www.thegablesrestaurant. co.nz; 19 The Strand; lunch $23-29, dinner $27-34; ⊙noon-3pm Fri-Mon, from 6pm Thu-Mon) Serving an imaginative take on Kiwi classics (lamb, venison, seafood), the Gables occupies an 1847 building on the waterfront, built using whale vertebrae for foundations. Ask for a table by the windows for maritime views and look forward to local produce, including oysters and cheese. Cocktails are summery and there's a decent selection of NZ beer and wine.

🍷 DRINKING & NIGHTLIFE

Duke of Marlborough Tavern   Pub

(☏09-403 7831; www.duketavern.co.nz; 19 York St; ⊙noon-late) A cool, cosy tavern with pool tables and a local vibe. Pub quiz on a Tuesday night (from 7pm) is always good fun, and there are well-priced burgers and fish and chips.

INFORMATION

Russell Booking & Information Centre (☑09-403 8020, 0800 633 255; www.russellinfo.co.nz; Russell Pier; ☉8am-5pm, extended hours summer) Loads of ideas on how to explore the area.

GETTING THERE & AWAY

A car ferry (car/motorcycle/passenger $11/5.50/1) runs every 10 minutes from Opua (5km from Paihia) to Okiato (8km from Russell), between 6.40am and 10pm. Buy your tickets on board; cash only.

On foot, the easiest way to reach Russell is on a passenger ferry from Paihia (adult/child one way $7/3, return $12/6). They run from 7am to 7pm (until 10pm October to May), generally every 20 minutes, but hourly in the evenings. Buy tickets on board.

Paihia

Joined to Waitangi by a bridge, and to Russell by a passenger ferry across the harbour, Paihia is the most central base from which to explore the Bay of Islands. Many boat trips and other marine excursions depart from its main jetty, and it has a good selection of restaurants, bars and accommodation.

SIGHTS

St Paul's Church   Church
(Marsden Rd) The characterful St Paul's was constructed of Kawakawa stone in 1925, and stands on the site of NZ's first church, a simple *raupo* (bulrush) hut erected in 1823. Look for the native birds in the stained glass above the altar – the kotare (kingfisher) represents Jesus (the king plus 'fisher of men'), while the tui (parson bird) and kereru (wood pigeon) portray the personalities of the Williams brothers (one scholarly, one forceful), who set up the mission station here.

Opua Forest   Forest
Just behind Paihia, this regenerating forest has walking trails ranging from 10

Kawakawa's Lovely Loos

Kawakawa is just an ordinary Kiwi town, located on SH1 south of Paihia, but the public toilets (60 Gillies St) are anything but. They were designed by Austrian-born artist and eco-architect Friedensreich Hundertwasser, who lived near Kawakawa in an isolated house without electricity from 1973 until his death in 2000. The most photographed toilets in NZ are typical Hundertwasser – lots of organic wavy lines decorated with ceramic mosaics and brightly coloured bottles, and with grass and plants on the roof. Other examples of his work can be seen in Vienna and Osaka.

Interior of Kawakawa's public toilets
ANDREW BAIN/GETTY IMAGES ©

minutes to five hours. A few large trees have escaped axe and fire, including some big kauri. Walk up from School Rd for about 30 minutes to good lookouts. Information on Opua Forest walks is available from the i-SITE. Drive into the forest by taking Oromahoe Rd west from Opua.

ACTIVITIES

Coastal Kayakers   Kayaking
(☑0800 334 661; www.coastalkayakers.co.nz; Te Karuwha Pde, Paihia) Runs guided tours (half-/full day $89/139, minimum two people) and multiday adventures. Kayaks (half-/full day $40/50) can also be rented for independent exploration.

Swimming with Dolphins

Cruises offering the opportunity to interact with wild dolphins operate year-round. They have a high success rate and you're generally offered a free trip if dolphins aren't sighted. Dolphin swims are subject to weather and sea conditions, with restrictions if calves are present.

It's totally up to the dolphins as to whether they choose to swim with you or not. You'll need to be a strong swimmer to keep abreast with them – even when they're humouring you by cruising along at half-speed. Those concerned with the welfare of dolphins should be aware that swimming with dolphins in the wild is considered by some to be disruptive to the habitat and behaviour of the animals.

Only three operators are licensed for dolphin swimming: Explore NZ (p71), Fullers Great Sights (p71) and the yacht Carino (p71). All pay a portion of the cost towards marine research, via DOC.

TOURS

Taiamai Tours Heritage Journeys   Cultural, Canoeing
(☑09-405 9990; www.taiamaitours.co.nz; 2½hr tour $135; ◷10am & 1pm Oct-Apr) ✔ Paddle a traditional 50ft carved *waka* (canoe) from the Waitangi bridge to the Haruru Falls. The Ngapuhi hosts wear traditional garb, and perform the proper *karakia* (incantations) and share stories.

✪ EATING

El Cafe   Cafe, South American $
(☑09-402 7637; www.facebook.com/elcafe paihia; 2 Kings Rd; snacks & mains $5-15; ◷8am-4pm Tue-Thu, to 9.30pm Fri-Sun; ☎) Excellent Chilean-owned cafe with the best coffee in town and terrific breakfast burritos, tacos and baked egg dishes, like spicy huevos

rancheros. Say *hola* to owner Javier for us. His Cuban pulled-pork sandwich is truly a wonderful thing. The fruit smoothies are also great on a warm Bay of Islands day.

35 Degrees South   Seafood $$
(☑09-402 6220; www.35south.co.nz; 69 Marsden Rd; shared plates $15-18, mains $28-26; ◷11.30am-late) Service can be a bit disorganised, but you can't beat the over-the-water location in central Paihia. The menu is at its best with local oysters from nearby Orongo Bay, local seafood and the shared small plates. Try the salt-and-pepper squid and pan-fried scallops, and maybe share a dessert of Dutch raisin doughnuts.

Provenir   Modern NZ $$$
(☑09-402 0111; www.paihiabeach.co.nz; 130 Marsden Rd, Paihia Beach Resort & Spa; mains $32-34; ◷8-10.30am & 6pm-late) A concise seasonal menu of main dishes showcases local seafood and regional NZ produce, and subtle Asian influences underpin smaller plates, including scallops and plump oysters from nearby Orongo Bay. The wine list is one of Northland's best, and during summer dining poolside is where you want to be.

Provenir is also open for 'Revive at Five' from 5pm to 7pm for a combination of classy bar snacks, beer and wine, all at a well-priced $8 each.

◉ DRINKING & NIGHTLIFE

Alongside   Bar
(☑09-402 6220; www.alongside35.co.nz; 69 Marsden Rd; ◷8am-10pm) Quite possibly the biggest deck in all of Northland extends over the water, and a versatile approach to entertaining begins with coffee and bagels for breakfast before the inevitable transformation of Alongside into a very enjoyable bar. There are good bar snacks and meals on offer, and lots of comfy lounges are ready for conversations fuelled by cocktails or cold beer.

Sauce   Craft Beer
(☑09-402 7590; www.facebook.com/sauce pizzaandcraft; Marsden Rd; ◷11am-10pm)

Haruru Falls (p69)

Design-your-own pizzas (pizza $12 to $22), plus the added attraction of excellent craft beer on tap from Hamilton's Good George Brewery, and a few well-chosen bottles from other smaller Kiwi breweries.

ℹ️ INFORMATION

Bay of Islands i-SITE (☑09-402 7345; www. northlandnz.com; Marsden Rd; ☺8am-5pm Mar–mid-Dec, 8am-7pm mid-Dec–Feb) Information and bookings.

ℹ️ GETTING THERE & AWAY

All buses serving Paihia stop at the Maritime Building by the wharf.

Passenger ferries depart regularly for Russell. A car ferry (car/motorcycle/passenger $11/5.50/1) runs every 10 minutes from Opua (5km from Paihia) to Okiato (8km from Russell), between 6.40am and 10pm. Buy your tickets on board. Only cash is accepted for tickets.

ℹ️ GETTING AROUND

For bikes, visit Island **Kayaks & Bay Beach Hire** (☑09-402 6078; www.baybeachhire.co.nz; Marsden Rd, Paihia; half-day kayaking tour $79; ☺9am-5.30pm).

COROMANDEL PENINSULA

Coromandel Peninsula at a glance...

Jutting into the Pacific east of Auckland, the Coromandel Peninsula's east coast has some of the North Island's best white-sand beaches. Visit in summer to see beaches and coves illuminated by the scarlet bloom of pohutukawa trees. Popular destinations are Hahei and the natural arch of Cathedral Cove, while Whitianga is a good base for boat trips exploring the Te Whanganui-A-Hei Marine Reserve. This is also gold-mining country, and this comes to life in the heritage town of Waihi.

The Coromandel Peninsula in two days

From your base in **Whitianga** (p94), make your way to **Hahei** (p84) and walk down to explore the graceful arch of **Cathedral Cove** (p86). If the tides are right the following day – tide times are posted at local i-SITEs – continue to **Hot Water Beach** (p87) before quaffing a Coromandel craft beer at **The Pour House** (p87) or **Hot Water Brewing Co** (p87).

The Coromandel Peninsula in four days

Consider incorporating a boat trip around the **Te Whanganui-A-Hei Marine Reserve** (p96) in the two-day itinerary, before continuing south to explore the Coromandel's fascinating gold-mining heritage in **Waihi** (p88). Stop in at **Waihi Bicycle Hire** (p89) to rent a bike and get details on the **Goldfields Railway** (p89) for a leisurely discovery of the **Hauraki Rail Trail** (p89) on your fourth and final day.

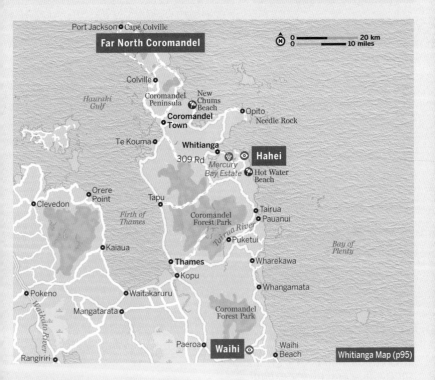

Arriving in the Coromandel Peninsula

Whitianga Airport Sunair has regular flights to/from Auckland.

Bus From destinations including Auckland and Hamilton; they stop outside the Whitianga i-SITE, Waihi i-SITE and in Coromandel Town.

Shuttle Go Kiwi links Auckland – both downtown and the airport – to Hahei and Whitianga.

Where to Stay

Whitianga has accommodation in all categories, and the town's location makes it a good base to explore the region. Other well-placed accommodation options include Hahei and Hot Water Beach. Coromandel Town has a good range of accommodation, from hostels to motels and B&Bs. Enquire at **Coromandel Accommodation Solutions** (www.accommodation coromandel.co.nz) about renting a house at one of the nearby beaches.

Cathedral Cove

Hahei

Hahei's Cathedral Cove is one of NZ's most spectacular natural attractions, and boat trips and snorkelling and diving expeditions make it easy to explore the surrounding Te Whanganui-A-Hei Marine Reserve.

Whitianga ○
Cooks Beach ○
◉ *Hahei*
Hot Water Beach

Great For...

ⓘ Need to Know

See www.hahei.co.nz for local information on activities, dining and accommodation.

★ **Top Tip**

Hire a bike from **Hahei Beach Bikes** (☎ 021 701 093; www.haheibeach bikes.co.nz; 2 Margot Pl; bike hire half-/full day $35/45) and ride the rolling 8km to Hot Water Beach.

Beachy Hahei balloons to bursting in summer, but it's almost abandoned otherwise – apart from the busloads of tourists stopping off at Cathedral Cove. It's a charming spot and a great place to unwind for a few days, especially in the quieter months. The town takes its name from Hei, the eponymous ancestor of the Ngāti Hei people, who arrived in the 14th century on the Te Arawa canoe.

Beautiful **Cathedral Cove**, with its famous gigantic stone arch and natural waterfall shower, is best enjoyed early or late in the day – avoiding the worst of the hordes. On the way there's rocky **Gemstone Bay**, which has a snorkelling trail where you're likely to see big snapper, crayfish and stingrays, and sandy **Stingray Bay**. **Cathedral Cove Dive & Snorkel** (☏07-866 3955; www.hahei.co.nz/diving; 48

Hahei Beach Rd; dives from $90) offers daily dive trips and rents diving gear, snorkelling gear ($25) and boogie boards ($20). **Hahei Explorer** (☏07-866 3910; www.haheiexplorer. co.nz; adult/child $85/50) offers hour-long jetboat rides touring the coast. Other boat operators are included in our Whitianga coverage (p94).

Walking from Hahei Beach to Cathedral Cove takes a little over an hour. From the car park, a kilometre north of Hahei, it's a rolling walk of around 30 to 40 minutes. Other options are to take the 10-minute **Cathedral Cove Water Taxi** (☏027 919 0563; www.cathedralcovewatertaxi.co.nz; one-way/return adult $15/25, child $10/15; ☉every 30min) or jump aboard Go Kiwi's summer-only **Beach Bus** (☏0800 446 549; www.go-kiwi.co.nz; adult/child/family $10/5/22, adult/family day pass $28/50; ☉9.15am-5.15pm

Hahei Beach

late Dec-Easter). Note that over the peak summer months both the car park and the cove itself can be exceptionally busy.

What's Nearby

Hot Water Beach, 8km south of Hahei, is quite extraordinary. For two hours either side of low tide, you can access an area of sand in front of a rocky outcrop at the middle of the beach where hot water oozes up from beneath the surface. Bring along a spade – or hire one ($5) from local businesses – dig a hole and, voila, you've got a personal spa pool. Tide times are posted at **Hot Waves** (07-866 3887; 8 Pye Pl; mains $12-26; 8.30am-4pm Mon-Thu & Sun, to 8.30pm Fri & Sat), the excellent local cafe.

Note that Hot Water Beach has dangerous rips, especially directly in front of the main thermal section, and swimming here is not safe if the lifeguards aren't on patrol.

Craft Beer

The craft beer scene washing over New Zealand has also reached the Coromandel Peninsula, and these two brewpubs are both perfect for a cold one after exploring Cathedral Cove or being immersed in a natural spa pool at Hot Water Beach.

The Pour House   Craft Beer

(www.coromandel brewingcompany.co.nz; 7 Grange Rd; 11am-11pm) Home base for the Coromandel Brewing Company, this modern Hahei pub and bistro regularly features around five of its beers. Platters of meat, cheese and local seafood, as well as decent pizzas, are served in the beer garden. Our favourite brew is the Code Red Irish Ale.

Hot Water Brewing Co   Craft Beer

(07-866 3830; www.hotwaterbrewingco.com; Sea Breeze Holiday Park, 1043 SH25, Whenuakite; 11am-late) This modern craft brewery has lots of outdoor seating. Standout brews include the hoppy Kauri Falls Pale Ale and the robust Walkers Porter. Platters and pizzas make it easy to order another beer, and the lamb burger is deservedly famous around these parts. Ask if the superb Barley Wine is available. You'll find all the hoppy goodness in Whenuakite.

> ★ **Top Tip**
>
> Though thronged in summer, come off-season the area really does have a laid back, 'gone fishing' vibe.

> ✕ **Take a Break**
>
> Housed in an ultra-charming wooden church, **The Church** (07-866 3797; www.thechurchhahei.co.nz; 87 Hahei Beach Rd; 5.30pm-late Mon-Sat) is Hahei's swankiest eatery with excellent Spanish- and North African–inspired dishes made to be shared, as well as a stellar, if pricey, selection of Kiwi craft beers.

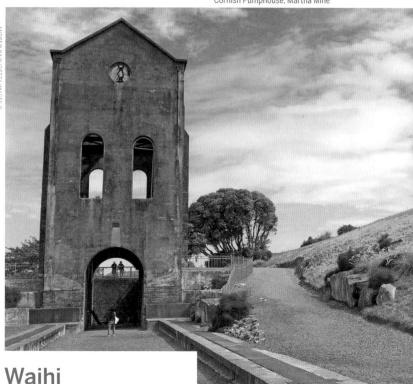

Cornish Pumphouse, Martha Mine

Waihi

Waihi is a good place to learn about the history of prospecting and gold-mining throughout the Coromandel Peninsula. Modern-day diversions include a great beach and a brilliant biking trail.

Great For...

☑ Don't Miss

Being surprised how heavy a gold bar is at the Gold Discovery Centre.

Gold and silver have been dragged out of Waihi's Martha Mine, NZ's richest, since 1878. The town's main drag, Seddon St, has grand buildings and sculptures, and information panels about Waihi's golden past.

Atmospherically lit at night, the skeleton of a derelict Cornish Pumphouse (1904) is Waihi's main landmark. From here the Pit Rim Walkway has fascinating views into the 250m-deep Martha Mine. The *Historic Hauraki Gold Towns* pamphlet (free from the Waihi i-SITE) outlines walking tours of Waihi.

Waihi's superb new **Gold Discovery Centre** (☏07-863 9015; www.golddiscovery centre.co.nz; 126 Seddon St, Waihi; adult/child $25/12; ◷9am-5pm, to 4pm in winter) tells the area's gold-mining past, present and future through personal and poignant interactive displays. Holograms and short movies both inform and entertain visitors. Good luck in

ℹ Need to Know

Waihi i-SITE (☐07-863 9015; www.waihi.
org.nz; 126 Seddon St, Waihi; ⊙9am-5pm, to
4pm winter)

✖ Take a Break

Treat yourself to a salted-caramel ice
cream from the store at the **Waihi
Beach Hotel** (☐07-863 5402; www.waihi-
beachhotel.co.nz; 60 Wilson Rd, Waihi Beach;
mains $20-32).

★ Top Tip

Waihi's German Bakery (☐07-863
6431; www.thegermanbakery.co.nz;
54a Seddon St, Waihi; snacks & mains
$10-20; h8am-3pm Wed-Fri, to 1pm
Sat & Sun) is a brilliant place to stock
up for picnics.

taking on the grizzled miner at 'virtual' Two-
Up (a gambling game using coins).

To get down into the spectacular Martha
Mine, join a 1½-hour **Waihi Gold Mine Tour**
(☐07-863 9015; www.golddiscoverycentre.co.nz/
tours; 126 Seddon St, Gold Discovery Centre, Waihi;
adult/child $34/17; ⊙10am & 12.30pm daily,
additional tours in summer) departing from the
Gold Discovery Centre.

Separated from Waihi by 11km of farmland, Waihi Beach offers great swimming
and stretches 9km to Bowentown. Waihi
Beach also has a growing foodie scene with
excellent cafes.

What's Nearby

From Waihi township, an excellent day
excursion is to combine a train ride on the
heritage **Goldfields Railway** (☐07-863 8251;
www.waihirail.co.nz; 30 Wrigley St, Waihi; adult/
child return $18/10, bikes $2 extra per route;
⊙departs Waihi 10am, 11.45am & 1.45pm Sat, Sun
& public holidays) with a few hours riding part
of the popular **Hauraki Rail Trail** through
the scenic Karangahake Gorge. Bikes can be
rented at **Waihi Bicycle Hire** (☐07-863 8418;
www.waihibicyclehire.co.nz; 25 Seddon St, Waihi;
bike hire half-/full day from $30/40; ⊙8am-5pm)
and carried on the train.

This spectacular part of the Hauraki Rail
Trail winds through a beautiful river valley.
Book ahead for lunch at **Bistro at the Falls
Retreat** (☐07-863 8770; www.fallsretreat.co.nz;
25 Waitawheta Rd; pizzas $20-24, mains $25-28;
⊙10am-10pm) in the heart of the sun-dappled
forest. Gourmet pizzas and rustic meat
dishes emerge from the wood-fired oven
and there's a playground for children.

See www.haurakirailtrail.co.nz for detailed
information, including trail maps.

Colville General Store

DAVID WALL PHOTO/GETTY IMAGES ©

Far North Coromandel

Supremely isolated and gob-smackingly beautiful, the rugged tip of the Coromandel Peninsula is well worth the effort required to reach it. Some roads are unsealed but the scenery is stunning.

Great For

☑ **Don't Miss**

The surprising white stupa of the **Mahamudra Centre** (☎07-866 6851; www.mahamudra.org.nz; RD4, Main Rd, Colville), a Buddhist retreat near Colville.

Heading north from Coromandel Town, the stunning drive rolls past brilliant coastal scenery. The first stop after 26km is at sleepy Colville, a remote rural community that's a magnet for alternative lifestylers. The 1260-hectare **Colville Farm** (☎07-866 6820; www.colvillefarmholidays.co.nz; 2140 Colville Rd; d $75-130; @🛜) has a range of interesting accommodation and guests can try their hand at farm work (including milking) or go on horse treks ($40 to $150, one to five hours). Organic food is available at the **Colville General Store** (☎07-866 6805; Colville Rd; ⊗8.30am-5pm).

Three kilometres north of Colville, at Whangaahei, the sealed road turns to gravel and splits to straddle each side of the peninsula. Following the west coast, ancient pohutukawa spread overhead as you past turquoise waters and stony

Waitete Bay, between Coromandel Town and Colville

ⓘ Need to Know

Camping is the best option for accommodation. Fill up with petrol before leaving Coromandel Town.

✗ Take a Break

Stop in Colville at **Hereford 'n' a Pickle** (☐021 136 8952; www.facebook.com/hereford.n.a.pickle; Colville Town; pies $4-6; ☺9am-4pm; 🕾) for locally made sausages and smoked meats.

★ Top Tip

Visit in summer when the gravel roads are dry and pohutukawa trees are blooming.

beaches with some lovely campsites. There's a spectacular lookout about 4km further on, where a metal dish identifies the various islands on the horizon. Great Barrier Island is only 20km away, looking every part the extension of the Coromandel Peninsula that it once was.

The road stops at Fletcher Bay – a magical land's end. Although it's only 37km from Colville, allow an hour for the drive. Note there is no road linking Fletcher Bay with the east coast of the peninsula, so you need to return to Whangaahei before branching left to return to Coromandel Town via a spectacular east coast road taking in Waikawau Bay and Kennedy Bay.

The Coromandel Coastal Walkway is a scenic, 3½-hour one-way hike between Fletcher Bay and Stony Bay. It's a relatively easy walk with great coastal views and an ambling section across farmland. If you're not keen on walking all the way back, Coromandel Discovery (www.coromandeldiscovery.co.nz) will drive you from Coromandel Town up to Fletcher Bay and pick you up from Stony Bay four hours later.

Heading south from Stony Bay, where the east coast road terminates, there are a couple of nice beaches peppered with baches (holiday homes) on the way to the slightly larger settlement of Port Charles.

Be aware that sections of this road are unsealed gravel. For the entire journey north from Colville to Fletcher Bay, back south to Whangaahei, and then around the east coast back to Coromandel Town, allow around four to five hours of driving time. For the Coromandel Town north to Colville section, add around 30 minutes.

There is no public transport up here.

Coromandel Town

Crammed with heritage buildings, Coromandel Town is a thoroughly quaint little place. Its natty cafes, interesting art stores, excellent sleeping options and delicious smoked mussels could keep you here longer than you expected.

◎ SIGHTS

Coromandel Goldfield Centre & Stamper Battery   Historic Building

(☑021 0232 8262; www.coromandelstamper battery.weebly.com; 360 Buffalo Rd; adult/child $10/5; ◎10am-4pm, tours hourly 10am-3pm, closed Fri in winter) The rock-crushing machine clatters into life during the informative tours of this 1899 plant. You can also try panning for gold ($5) and stop to see NZ's largest working waterwheel. Ask about the special summertime tours by lamplight at 5pm daily.

Coromandel Mining & Historic Museum   Museum

(☑07-866 8987; 841 Rings Rd; adult/child $5/ free; ◎10am-1pm Sat & Sun Feb–mid-Dec, 10am-4pm daily mid-Dec–Jan) Small museum with glimpses of pioneer life.

✪ ACTIVITIES

Driving Creek Railway & Potteries   Railway

(☑07-866 8703; www.drivingcreekrailway. co.nz; 380 Driving Creek Rd; adult/child $35/13; ◎10.15am & 2pm, additional times in summer) ✔ A lifelong labour of love for its conservationist owner, this unique train runs up steep grades, across four trestle bridges, along two spirals and a double switchback, and through two tunnels, finishing at the 'Eye-full Tower'. The one-hour trip passes artworks and regenerating native forest – more than 17,000 natives have been planted, including 9000 kauri. Booking ahead is recommended in summer.

Coromandel Town harbour

CREATIVENATURE.NL/GETTY IMAGES ©

It's worth lingering for the video about the extraordinary guy behind it all, well-known potter, the late Barry Brickell.

Mussel Barge Snapper Safaris
Fishing

(☑07-866 7667; www.musselbargesafaris. co.nz; adult/child $55/30) Fishing trips with a local flavour and lots of laughs. Pick-up available.

 TOURS

Coromandel Adventures
Driving

(☑07-866 7014; www.coromandeladventures. co.nz; 480 Driving Creek Rd; 1-day tour adult/ child $80/50) Various tours around Coromandel Town and the peninsula, plus shuttles to Whitianga and Auckland.

 SHOPPING

The Source
Arts & Crafts

(☑07-866 7345; 31 Kapanaga Rd; ⊙10am-4pm) Creative showcase of more than 30 local artists.

 EATING

Coromandel Oyster Company
Seafood $

(☑07-866 8028; 1611 Tiki Rd; snacks & meals $5-25; ⊙10am-5.30pm Sat-Thu, to 6.30pm Fri) Briny-fresh mussels, scallops, oysters and cooked fish and chips and flounder. Coming north from Thames you'll find it on the hill around 7km before you reach Coromandel Town.

Chai Tea House
Cafe $

(☑021 893 055; www.facebook.com/chaitea house; 24 Wharf Rd; snacks $6-12; ⊙10am-5pm Tue-Sun; ☑) ✿ Welcoming cafe with a bohemian New Age bent serving up lots of organic, vegan and vegetarian goodies. The outdoor garden is a very relaxing space and is occasionally used for live-music gigs. Shorter hours outside of summer.

 From Coromandel Town to Whitianga

From Coromandel Town to Whitianga it's 32km on meandering SH25, and a few stops make it worthy of a leisurely journey. Around 13km from Coromandel Town, the turn-off at Te Rerenga follows the harbour to **Whangapoua**. Walk along the rocky foreshore for 30 minutes to the remote, beautiful, undeveloped and often-deserted **New Chum's Beach**, regarded as one of the most beautiful in the country.

Continuing east on SH25 you soon reach **Kuaotunu**, a more interesting holiday village on a beautiful stretch of white-sand beach, with a cafe-gallery, a store and an ancient petrol pump. In Kuaotunu village, **Luke's Kitchen & Cafe** (☑07 866 4420; www.lukeskitchen. co.nz; 20 Blackjack Rd, Kuaotunu; mains & pizza $15-28; ⊙cafe & gallery 8.30am-3.30pm, restaurant & bar 11am-10pm, shorter hours in winter) has a rustic surf-shack ambience, cold brews (including craft beers from around NZ) and excellent wood-fired pizza. Occasional live music, local seafood and fruit smoothies make Luke's an essential stop.

Heading off the highway at Kuaotunu takes you (via an unsealed road) to a couple of Coromandel's best-kept secrets. First, the long stretch of **Otama Beach** comes into view – deserted but for a few houses and farms. Continuing along the narrowing road, the sealed road finally starts again and you reach the beautiful sandy arc of **Opito**. Returning back to Kuaotunu, it's a further 15km south to Whitianga.

Driving Creek Cafe
Vegetarian $

(☑07-866 7066; www.drivingcreekcafe.com; 180 Driving Creek Rd; mains $9-18; ⊙9.30am-5pm; ☑☑) ✿ Vegetarian, vegan, gluten-free, organic and fair-trade delights await at this funky mudbrick cafe. The food is beautifully presented, fresh and healthy. Once sated, the kids can play in the sandpit while the adults check their email with the free wi-fi. Don't miss ordering a terrific juice or smoothie.

Coromandel Mussel Kitchen
Seafood $$

(☑07-866 7245; www.musselkitchen.co.nz; cnr SH25 & 309 Rd; mains $18-21; ☺9am-3.30pm, plus dinner late Dec-Feb) This cool cafe-bar sits among fields 3km south of town. Mussels are served with Thai- and Mediterranean sauces or grilled on the half-shell. In summer the garden bar is perfect for a mussel-fritter stack and a frosty craft beer from MK Brewing Co, the on-site microbrewery. Smoked and chilli mussels and bottles of beer are all available for takeaway.

Pepper Tree
Modern NZ $$

(☑07-866 8211; www.peppertreerestaurant. co.nz; 31 Kapanga Rd; mains lunch $16-28, dinner $25-39; ☺10am-9pm; ☎) Coromandel Town's most upmarket option dishes up generously proportioned meals with an emphasis on local seafood. On a summer evening, the courtyard tables under the shady tree are the place to be.

Umu
Cafe $$

(www.facebook.com/umucafe; 22 Wharf Rd; breakfast $11-18, lunch $12-25, dinner $14-32; ☺9am-9pm; ☎) Classy cafe fare including pizza, counter food (tarts and quiches around $7), superb coffee and tummy-taming breakfasts.

🍷 DRINKING & NIGHTLIFE

Star & Garter Hotel
Pub

(☑07-866 8503; www.starandgarter.co.nz; 5 Kapanga Rd; ☺11am-late) Making the most of the simple kauri interior of an 1873 building, this smart pub has pool tables, decent sounds and a roster of live music and DJs on weekends. The beer garden is smartly clad in corrugated iron.

ℹ️ INFORMATION

Coromandel Town Information Centre
(☑07-866 8598; www.coromandeltown.co.nz; 85 Kapanga Rd; ☺10am-4pm; ☎) Good maps and local information. Pick up the Historic Places Trust's *Coromandel Town* pamphlet here.

ℹ️ GETTING THERE & AWAY

InterCity (☑09-583 5780; www.intercity.co.nz) has buses linking Coromandel Town to Hamilton ($40, 3½ hours) and **Go Kiwi** (☑0800 446 549; www.go-kiwi.co.nz) heads to Thames and Auckland ($59, 4½ hours).

Whitianga

Whitianga's big attractions are the sandy beaches of Mercury Bay and the diving, boating and kayaking opportunities afforded by the craggy coast and nearby Te Whanganui-A-Hei Marine Reserve. The pretty harbour is a renowned base for game fishing (especially marlin and tuna between January and March).

The legendary Polynesian explorer and seafarer Kupe is believed to have landed near here sometime around AD 950. The name Whitianga is a contraction of Te Whitianga a Kupe (the Crossing Place of Kupe).

◉ SIGHTS

Buffalo Beach stretches along Mercury Bay, north of Whitianga Harbour. A five-minute passenger ferry (☑021 025 10169; www.whitiangaferry.co.nz; adult/child/bicycle $4/2/1.50; ☺7.30am-7.30pm & 8.30-10.30pm) ride will take you across the harbour to Ferry Landing. From here you can walk to local sights like Whitianga Rock Scenic & Historical Reserve, a park with great views over the ocean, and the Shakespeare Cliff Lookout.

Further afield are Hahei Beach (13km), Cathedral Cove (15km) and Hot Water Beach (18km, one hour by bike). Look forward to relatively flat terrain if you're keen on riding from Ferry Landing to these other destinations. **Cathedral Cove Shuttles**

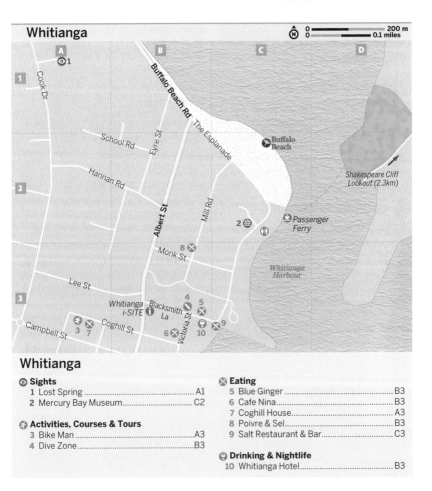

Whitianga

◉ Sights
1 Lost Spring	A1
2 Mercury Bay Museum	C2

⊕ Activities, Courses & Tours
3 Bike Man	A3
4 Dive Zone	B3

⊗ Eating
5 Blue Ginger	B3
6 Cafe Nina	B3
7 Coghill House	A3
8 Poivre & Sel	B3
9 Salt Restaurant & Bar	C3

⊖ Drinking & Nightlife
10 Whitianga Hotel	B3

(☏027 422 5899; www.catheralcoveshuttles. co.nz; per person $40) runs a handy service from Ferry Landing to these destinations, and in summer from late December to March, Go Kiwi shuttles also run the convenient Beach Bus (p86) starting from Ferry Landing.

Lost Spring   Spring
(☏07-866 0456; www.thelostspring.co.nz; 121a Cook Dr; per 90min/day $38/68; ⊙10.30am-6pm Sun-Fri, to 8pm Sat) This expensive but intriguing Disney-meets-Polynesia thermal complex comprises a series of hot pools in

a lush jungle-like setting complete with an erupting volcano. It's the ideal spot to relax in tropical tranquillity, with a cocktail in hand. Children under 14 must be accompanied by an adult in the pools.

Mercury Bay Museum   Museum
(☏07-866 0730; www.mercurybaymuseum. co.nz; 11a The Esplanade; adult/child $7.50/50¢; ⊙10am-4pm) A small but interesting museum focusing on local history – especially Whitianga's most famous visitors, Kupe and Cook.

Te Whanganui-A-Hei Marine Reserve

There are a baffling number of tours to Te Whanganui-A-Hei Marine Reserve where you'll see interesting rock formations and, if you're lucky, dolphins, fur seals, penguins and orcas. Some are straight-out cruises while others offer optional swims and snorkelling. Ask at the Whitianga i-SITE.

 TOURS & ACTIVITIES

Ocean Leopard Boating

(☏0800 843 8687; www.oceanleopardtours. co.nz; adult/child $80/45; ☺10.30pm, 1.30pm & 4pm) Two-hour trips taking in coastal scenery, naturally including Cathedral Cove. A one-hour Whirlwind Tour (adult/child $60/35) is also on offer.

Cave Cruzer Boating

(☏07-866 0611; www.cavecruzer.co.nz; adult/child 1hr $50/30, 2hr $75/40) Tours on a rigid-hull inflatable.

Glass Bottom Boat Boating

(☏07-867 1962; www.glassbottomboat whitianga.co.nz; adult/child $95/50) Two-hour bottom-gazing tours exploring the Te Whanganui-A-Hei Marine Reserve.

Windborne Boating

(☏027 475 2411; www.windborne.co.nz; day sail $95; ☺Dec-Apr) Day sails in a 19m 1928 schooner from December to April, and departures to the Mercury Islands ($150) in February and March.

Whitianga Adventures Boating

(☏0800 806 060; www.whitianga-adventures. co.nz; adult/child $75/45) A two-hour Sea Cave Adventure in an inflatable.

Bike Man Cycling

(☏07-866 0745; thebikeman@xtra.co.nz; 16 Coghill St; per day $25; ☺9am-5pm Mon-Fri, to 1pm Sat) Rent a bike to take across on the ferry and journey to Hahei and Hot Water Beach.

Dive Zone Diving

(☏07-867 1580; www.divezonewhitianga.co.nz; 7 Blacksmith Lane; trips $150-225) Shore, kayak and boat dives.

 EATING

Cafe Nina Cafe $

(☏07-866 5440; www.facebook.com/cafe ninawhitianga; 20 Victoria St; mains $8-20; ☺8am-3pm) Barbecue for breakfast? Why the hell not. Too cool to be confined within four walls, the kitchen grills bacon and eggs on an outdoor hotplate while the punters spill out onto tables in the park. Other dishes include robust Greek salads and tasty quesadillas.

Coghill House Cafe $

(☏07-866 0592; www.thecog.co.nz; 10 Coghill St; mains $10-18; ☺8am-3pm) On the sunny terrace of this side-street cafe good counter food is partnered with huge pancake stacks and plump tortilla wraps.

Mercury Bay Estate Winery $$

(☏07-866 4066; www.mercurybayestate. co.nz; 761a Purangi Rd, Cooks Beach; platters $18-48, wine tasting $8-15; ☺10am-5pm Mon-Fri, 9am-6pm Sat & Sun) Repurposed timber and corrugated iron feature at this rustic but chic vineyard en route from Ferry Landing to Cooks Beach. Seafood, cheese and charcuterie platters team well with wines like the excellent Lonely Bay chardonnay. It's 35km from Whitianga town.

Blue Ginger Southeast Asian $$

(☏07-867 1777; www.blueginger.co.nz; 1/10 Blacksmith Lane; shared plates $9-14, mains $22-28; ☺11am-2pm Tue-Fri & 5pm-late Tue-Sat) Southeast Asian flavours infuse the menu at this relaxed spot with shared tables. Highlights include Indonesian-style beef rendang, pad thai noodles and a great roast duck red curry.

Salt Restaurant & Bar Seafood $$$

(☏07-866 5818; www.salt-whitianga.co.nz; 2 Blacksmith Lane; shared plates $12-30, mains

Ferry Landing (p94), near Whitianga

$28-38; ⊘11.30am-late) Views of the Whitianga marina – including the sleepy ferry crossing to Ferry Landing – provide the backdrop for relaxed but stylish dining at this restaurant. In summer the place to be is out on the deck, combining local wines with pan-seared fish with Cloudy Bay clams or Coromandel oysters from the raw bar.

Poivre & Sel Modern NZ **$$$**
(☑07-866 0053; www.poivresel.co.nz; 2 Mill Rd; mains $35-40; ⊘6pm-late Tue-Sat) This Mediterranean-style villa – complete with a garden shaded by palm trees – is the most stylish eatery in town. Begin with crab and black garlic in an avocado and grapefruit parfait before moving on to delicate porcini-stuffed quail with asparagus. Happy hour $5 drinks from 5pm to 6pm are a good way to kick things off.

🍷 DRINKING & NIGHTLIFE

Whitianga Hotel Pub
(☑07-866 5818; www.whitiangahotel.co.nz; 1 Blacksmith Lane; ⊘11am-late) Good value pub food, lots of frosty beers on tap and a

relaxed garden bar equal a classic Kiwi pub experience. Challenge the locals on the pool table and return on weekend nights for DJs and cover bands.

ℹ️ INFORMATION

Whitianga i-SITE (☑07-866 5555; www.whitianga.co.nz; 66 Albert St; ⊘9am-5pm Mon-Fri, to 4pm Sat & Sun) Information and internet access. Hours are extended in summer.

ℹ️ GETTING THERE & AWAY

Sunair (☑0800 786 247; www.sunair.co.nz) operates flights linking Whitianga to Auckland.

Bus and shuttle services include Auckland, Hamilton and Coromandel Town.

ℹ️ GETTING AROUND

From Ferry Landing across Whitianga Harbour, shuttles run to Hahei, Cathedral Cove and Hot Water Beach. Services are usually restricted to summer and holiday weekends.

Mangapohue Natural Bridge (p105)

WAITOMO CAVES, HAMILTON & AROUND

Waitomo Caves, Hamilton & Around at a glance...

At the hub of this area punctuated by rolling dairy pastures, the riverside city of Hamilton is enlivened by excellent restaurants and a lively after-dark scene fuelled by an energetic student population. Options to explore the Waitomo Caves to the south include a boat ride on an underground river, or more challenging zip-lining and abseiling. The caves may resemble Middle-earth, but Hobbiton is where the true movie buffs are most thrilled.

Waitomo Caves & Hamilton in two days

From **Hamilton** (p108), head west to **Raglan** (p114) and spend the day beach-hopping around **Ngarunui** and **Manu Bay**. Make time for Raglan's excellent cafes before dinner at **Gothenburg** (p111) back in Hamilton. The following day continue to the **Waitomo Caves** (p102; 75km) and discover the area's subterranean surprises with a spot of black-water rafting.

Waitomo Caves & Hamilton in four days

On day three it's back to Hamilton to combine a trip to the **Hamilton Gardens** (p108) with the **Waikato River Explorer** (p109). Have a riverside dinner at **Chim Choo Ree** (p111) followed by New Zealand craft beer in the bars along Hood St. On your fourth day, make your way to **Matamata** (p106; 65km east of Hamilton), and indulge all your Middle-earth fan fantasies at **Hobbiton**.

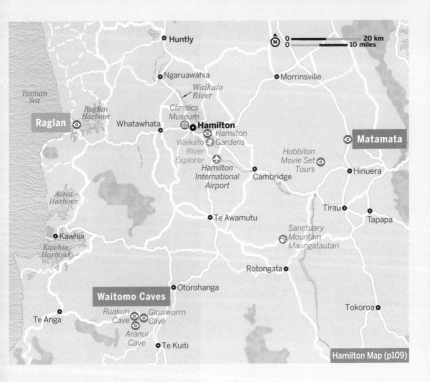

Arriving in Hamilton

Hamilton Airport Around 12km south of the city with regular flights to/from Auckland, Wellington, Christchurch and Nelson.

Hamilton Transport Centre Terminus for InterCity buses and also local Busit! departures to Raglan.

Frankton Railway Station The *Northern Explorer* linking Auckland and Wellington stops in Hamilton before continuing south to Otorohanga where there are shuttles to the Waitomo Caves (15km).

Where to Stay

Hamilton has the biggest choice of accommodation in the area and hotels in the city centre provide good access to cafes, restaurants and bars.

Accommodation at Waitomo Caves ranges from an excellent holiday park and hostels through to good B&Bs, but during summer the village can be booked out.

Matamata has a selection of motels along its main drag, but for most visitors it's a day destination.

Lost World Cave

Waitomo Caves

The Waitomo Caves are the ultimate destination for travellers seeking subterranean stimulation. Accessible to all is the Glowworm Cave, and for adventurous types, action aplenty awaits in other cave systems.

Great For...

❶ Need to Know

Waitomo Shuttle (07-873 8279, 0800 808 279; www.waitomo.org.nz/transport-to-waitomo; one-way adult/child $12/7) links with Otorohanga (14km) five times a day, coordinating with bus and train arrivals.

★ **Top Tip**

Adventure operators offer a discount for prebooking online. During summer this strategy is recommended.

CHRIS MCLENNAN/ALAMY ©

Even if damp, dark tunnels are your idea of hell, head to Waitomo anyway. The area's limestone caves are one of the North Island's premier attractions.

The name Waitomo comes from *wai* (water) and *tomo* (hole or shaft): dotted across this region are numerous shafts dropping into underground cave systems and streams. There are 300-plus mapped caves in the area: the three main caves – Glowworm, Ruakuri and Aranui – have been bewitching visitors for over 100 years.

Your Waitomo experience needn't be claustrophobic: the electrically lit, cathedral-like Glowworm Cave is far from squeezy. But if it's excitement you're after, Waitomo can definitely oblige.

Caves

Glowworm Cave   Cave

(☏0800 456 922; www.waitomo.com/waitomo-glowworm-caves; adult/child $49/22; ☻45min tours half-hourly 9am-5pm) The guided tour of the Glowworm Cave, which is behind the visitor centre, leads past impressive stalactites and stalagmites into a large cavern known as the Cathedral. The highlight comes at the tour's end when you board a boat and swing off onto the river. As your eyes grow accustomed to the dark you'll see a Milky Way of little lights surrounding you – these are the glowworms. Book your tour at the visitor centre and ask about combo deals incorporating the Glowworm Cave, Aranui Cave and Ruakiri.

Aranui Cave

Ruakuri Cave
Cave

(☎0800 782 587, 07-878 6219; www.waitomo.com/ruakuri-cave; adult/child $71/27; ⏱2hr tours 9am, 10am, 11am, 12.30pm, 1.30pm, 2.30pm & 3.30pm) Ruakuri Cave has an impressive 15m-high spiral staircase, bypassing a Māori burial site at the cave entrance. Tours lead through 1.6km of the 7.5km system, taking in caverns with glowworms, subterranean streams and waterfalls. Visitors have described it as spiritual – some claim it's haunted – and it's customary to wash your hands when leaving to remove the *tapu* (taboo).

> ### ★ Top Tip
> **Waitomo i-SITE** (☎07-878 7640; www.waitomocaves.com; 21 Waitomo Caves Rd; ⏱9am-5.30pm) has internet access, a post office and a booking agent.

Aranui Cave
Cave

(☎0800 456 922; www.waitomo.com/aranui-cave; adult/child $49/22; ⏱1hr tours depart 9am-4pm) This cave is dry (hence no glowworms) but compensates with an incredible array of limestone formations. Thousands of tiny 'straw' stalactites hang from the ceiling. Book tours at the visitor centre, from where there is also transport to the cave entrance. A 15-minute bush walk is also included.

Going Underground

Waitomo excels with challenging and unique ways to explore the area's subterranean wonders.

Legendary Black Water Rafting Company
(☎0800 782 5874; www.waitomo.com/black-water-rafting; 585 Waitomo Caves Rd; ⏱Black Labyrinth tour 9am, 10.30am, noon, 1.30pm & 3pm, Black Abyss tour 9am & 2pm, Black Odyssey tour 10am & 3pm) Don a wet suit and float down an underground river in an inner tube. Options incorporate a flying fox and negotiating high wires.

CaveWorld (☎0800 228 338, 07-878 6577; www.caveworld.co.nz; cnr Waitomo Caves Rd & Hotel Access Rd) Black-water rafting on inner tubes through glowworm-filled Te Anaroa.

Waitomo Adventures (☎0800 924 866, 07-878 7788; www.waitomo.co.nz; 654 Waitomo Caves Rd) An adventurous combination of abseiling, tubing, caving and rock climbing. Ask about the 'Lost World.'

What's Nearby

The Mangapohue Natural Bridge Scenic Reserve, 26km west of Waitomo, is a 5.5-hectare reserve with a giant natural limestone arch. On the far side, big rocks full of 35-million-year-old oyster fossils jut up from the grass, and at night you'll see glowworms.

> ### ✕ Take a Break
> The general store in Waitomo sells the basics, but it's cheaper to stock up at supermarkets in Otorohanga or Te Kuiti before you visit. Waitomo Caves village has several good cafes and restaurants.

Hobbit hole, Hobbiton

Matamata

Rolling green hills, a pretty lake and well-kept gardens around compact Hobbit holes all make it very easy to suspend reality in Matamata's make-believe Middle-earth world of Hobbiton.

Great For

☑ **Don't Miss**

Having an Oak Barton Brew or Sackville Cider at Hobbiton's Green Dragon Inn.

Matamata was just one of those pleasant, horsey country towns you drove through until Peter Jackson's epic film trilogy *The Lord of the Rings* put it on the map. During filming, 300 locals got work as extras (hairy feet weren't a prerequisite). Following the subsequent filming of *The Hobbit*, the town has now ardently embraced its Middle-earth credentials, including a spooky statue of Gollum, and given the local **i-SITE** (☏07-888 7260; www.matamatanz. co.nz; 45 Broadway; ◷9am-5pm) an appropriate extreme makeover.

Due to copyright, all the movie sets around NZ were actually dismantled after the filming of *The Lord of the Rings*, but Hobbiton's owners negotiated to keep their hobbit holes, which were then rebuilt for the filming of *The Hobbit*. **Tours** (☏0508 446 224 866, 07-888 1505; www.hobbitontours.

● Hamilton   ◉ *Matamata*
       Hobbiton ●
                    ● Hinuera
     Cambridge
                 ● Tirau

ⓘ Need to Know

Free bus transfers leave from the Matamata i-SITE – check timings on the Hobbiton website.

✕ Take a Break

Matamata's **Redoubt Bar & Eatery** (☏07-888 8585; www.redoubtbarandeatery. co.nz; 48 Broadway; ⊙11am-2pm & 5-9pm Mon-Fri, 11am-9pm Sat & Sun) serves thin-crust pizzas named after *LOTR* characters.

★ Top Tip

Booking ahead is recommended, especially for Hobbiton's Evening Banquet Tours on Wednesday and Sunday.

com; 501 Buckland Rd, Hinuera; adult/child $79/39.50, dinner tours $190/100 Sun & Wed; ⊙10am-4.30pm) include a drink at the wonderful Green Dragon Inn, and are packed full of interesting stories from the clued-up guides about the making of the films. To get to Hobbiton with your own transport, head towards Cambridge from Matamata, turn right into Puketutu Rd and then left into Buckland Rd, stopping at the Shire's Rest Cafe.

Most tourists who come to Matamata are dedicated Hobbit-botherers, but there are other worthy attractions while you are in the area. **Firth Tower** (☏07-888 8369; www.firthtower.co.nz; Tower Rd; grounds free, tours adult/child $5/1; ⊙grounds 10am-4pm daily, buildings 10am-4pm Thu-Mon) was built by Auckland businessman Josiah Firth in 1882. The 18m concrete tower was then a fashionable status symbol; now it's filled with Māori and pioneer artefacts. Ten other historic buildings are set around the tower, including a school room, church and jail. It's 3km east of town. About 15km northeast of Matamata are the spectacular 153m Wairere Falls, the highest on the North Island. From the car park it's a 45-minute walk through native bush to the lookout or a steep 1½-hour climb to the summit.

For a bite to eat, stop in at **Workman's Cafe Bar** (☏07-888 5498; 52 Broadway; mains $12-30; ⊙7.30am-late). Truly eccentric (old transistor radios dangling from the ceiling; a wall-full of art-deco mirrors; Johnny Cash on the stereo), this funky eatery has built itself a reputation that extends beyond Matamata. It's also a decent bar later at night.

From Hamilton, it is 65km east to Matamata.

Hamilton

At the heart of dairy farming country, fast-growing Hamilton – now officially New Zealand's fourth-largest city – is a convenient base for exploring the compact Waikato and King Country region. Destinations including Raglan, the Waitomo Caves and Matamata (for Hobbiton) are easily reached on day trips, and the city's cosmopolitan eating and drinking scene offers entertaining distractions at day's end.

◉ SIGHTS

Hamilton Gardens　　　　　　Gardens

(☏07-838 6782; www.hamiltongardens.co.nz; Cobham Dr; guided tour adult/child $15/8; ⊙gardens 7.30am-5pm, info centre 9am-5pm, guided tours 11am Sep-Apr) FREE Spread over 50 hectares southeast of the city centre, Hamilton Gardens incorporates a large park, cafe, restaurant and extravagant themed enclosed gardens. There are separate Italian Renaissance, Chinese, Japanese, English, American and Indian gardens complete with colonnades, pagodas and a mini Taj Mahal. Equally interesting are the sustainable Productive Garden Collection, fragrant herb garden and precolonisation Māori Te Parapara garden. Look for the impressive *Nga Uri O Hinetuparimaunga* (Earth Blanket) sculpture at the main gates.

Recent additions include a Tudor-style garden and a tropical garden with more than 200 different warm climate species. Booking ahead for the guided tours is recommended.

Waikato Museum　　　　　　Museum

(www.waikatomuseum.co.nz; 1 Grantham St; admission by donation; ⊙10am-4.30pm) The excellent Waikato Museum has five main areas: an art gallery; interactive science galleries; Tainui galleries housing Māori treasures, including the magnificently carved *waka taua* (war canoe), *Te Winikawaka;* a WWI exhibition entitled 'For Us They Fell'; and a Waikato River exhibition. The museum also runs a rigorous program

of public events. Admission is charged for some exhibits.

Classics Museum　　　　　　Museum

(www.classicsmuseum.co.nz; 11 Railside Pl, Frankton; adult/child $20/8; ⊙9am-4pm) Travel in time amid this collection of over 100 classic cars from the first half of the 20th century. Even if you're not a motorhead, you'll still be dazzled by the crazy Amphicar and the cool Maserati and Corvette sports cars. The museum is just off SH1, northwest of central Hamilton.

Zealong Tea Estate　　　　Tea Estate

(☏0800 932 566; www.zealong.com; 495 Gordonton Rd, Gordonton; tea experience adult/child $25/13; ⊙10am-5pm Tue-Sun, tours 9.30am & 2.30pm) Interesting tours learning about the only tea plantation in New Zealand, located around 10km northeast of Hamilton. For an extra $35, partner the tea experience with a tiffin-style high tea spread of sweet and savoury snacks. There's also a good on-site cafe serving high tea without the tour ($42) and offering tea tastings (per person $9) and main dishes.

Riff Raff　　　　　　　　Monument

(www.riffraffstatue.org; Victoria St) One of Hamilton's more unusual public artworks is a life-sized statue of *Rocky Horror Picture Show* writer Richard O'Brien, aka Riff Raff, the time-warping alien from the planet Transsexual. It looks over a small park on the site of the former Embassy Theatre where O'Brien worked as a hairdresser, though it's hard to imagine 1960s Hamilton inspired the tale of bisexual alien decadence. Free wi-fi emanates from Riff Raff's three-pronged stun gun.

ArtsPost　　　　　　　　　Gallery

(www.waikatomuseum.co.nz/artspost; 120 Victoria St; ⊙10am-4.30pm) FREE This contemporary gallery and gift shop is housed in a grand, former post office. It focuses on the best of local art: paintings, glass, prints, textiles and photography.

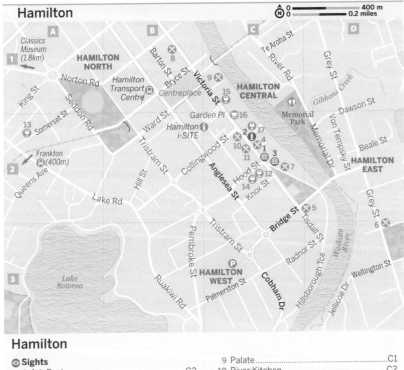

Hamilton

⊙ Sights
1	ArtsPost	C2
2	Riff Raff	C2
3	Waikato Museum	C2

⊗ Eating
4	Banh Mi Caphe	C2
5	Chim Choo Ree	D2
6	Duck Island Ice Cream	D3
7	Gothenburg	C2
8	Hazel Hayes	B1

9	Palate	C1
10	River Kitchen	C2
11	Scott's Epicurean	C2

⊙ Drinking & Nightlife
12	Craft	C2
13	Good George Brewing	A2
14	Little George	C2
15	Local Taphouse	C1
16	SL28	C2
17	Wonderhorse	C2

🟢 ACTIVITIES

Waikato River Explorer   Cruise
(☏0800 139 756; www.waikatoexplorer.co.nz;
Hamilton Gardens Jetty; adult/child $29/15;
☺Wed-Sun, daily 26 Dec-6 Feb) Scenic 1½-hour
cruises along the Waikato River depart
from the Hamilton Gardens jetty. On
Sunday at 11am, the boat cruises (adult/
child $79/40) to the Vilagrad Winery for

wine tasting and a Mediterranean-style spit
roast lunch. On Saturday from 2pm, there's
more wine tasting and a cheese platter at
the nearby Mystery Creek area (adult/child
$79/35).

Kiwi Balloon Company   Ballooning
(☏07-843 8538, 021 912 679; www.kiwiballoon
company.co.nz; per person $350) Floating
above lush Waikato countryside, the whole

experience takes about four hours and includes a champagne breakfast and an hour's flying time.

EATING

Befitting its status as one of the North Island's biggest cities, Hamilton has a tasty selection of cafes and restaurants. Around Victoria and Hood Sts you'll find the greatest diversity of eateries. Across the river, Hamilton East is also developing as a dining destination.

Duck Island Ice Cream   Ice Cream $

(☑07-856 5948; 300 Grey St; ice cream from $4; ☺11am-6pm Tue-Thu & Sun, to 8pm Fri & Sat) A dazzling array of ever-changing flavours – how does crab apple crumble or coconut and kaffir lime sound – make Duck Island quite probably NZ's best ice cream parlour. The sunny corner location is infused with a hip retro vibe, and the refreshing house-made sodas and ice cream floats are other worthy reasons to cross the river to Hamilton East.

Scott's Epicurean   International $

(☑07-839 6680; www.scottsepicurean.co.nz; 181 Victoria St; mains $11-20; ☺7am-3pm Mon-Fri, 8.30am-4pm Sat & Sun) This gorgeous joint features swanky leather banquettes, pressed-tin ceilings, great coffee and an interesting and affordable menu: try the *pytti panna* (Swedish bubble-and-squeak) for breakfast or the ever-popular *spaghetti aglio e olio* (spaghetti with garlic and oil) for a quick lunch. Friendly service and fully licensed.

Hamilton Farmers Market   Market $

(☑022 639 1995; www.waikatofarmersmarkets. co.nz; Te Rapa Racecourse; ☺8am-noon Sun) Around 4km north of central Hamilton at the Te Rapa Racecourse, this farmers market is a veritable Sunday-morning feast of local cheeses, baked goods and produce. A coffee from the Rocket caravan and a flash hot dog from Bangin Bangaz is our recommended breakfast combo.

Hamilton Gardens (p108)

CHAMELEONSEYE/SHUTTERSTOCK ©

Banh Mi Caphe
Vietnamese $

(☏07-839 1141; www.facebook.com/banh
micaphe; 198/2 Victoria St; snacks & mains
$10-17; ⊙11am-4pm Tue-Wed, to 9pm Thu-Sat)
Fresh spring rolls, Vietnamese *banh mi*
(sandwiches) and steaming bowls of *pho*
(noodle soup) all feature at this hip spot
channelling the backstreets of Hanoi.

Gothenburg
Tapas $$

(☏07-834 3562; www.gothenburg.co.nz; ANZ
Centre, 21 Grantham St; shared plates $7-24;
⊙9am-11pm Mon-Fri, 11.30am-late Sat) In a
scenic riverside spot with high ceilings
and a summer-friendly deck, Gothenburg
has morphed from a bar into our favourite
Hamilton restaurant. The menu of shared
plates effortlessly spans the globe – try
the pork and kimchi dumplings or the beef
and chorizo meatballs – and the beer list
features rotating taps from local Waikato
craft brewers. The range of wine and
cocktails is equally stellar – especially the
pomegranate mojito – and the dessert
of coconut and lime panna cotta is fast
becoming a Gothenburg classic.

Hazel Hayes
Cafe $$

(☏07-839 1953; www.hazelhayes.co.nz; 587
Victoria St; mains $10-23; ⊙7am-4pm Mon-Fri,
8am-2pm Sat) This mash-up of country
kitchen decor showcases inventive cafe
fare. Free-range and organic options punc-
tuate the short, focused menu, and both
the service and coffee are very good. Try
the homemade hash browns with salmon
and a rich hollandaise sauce and you'll
definitely be set for the day.

River Kitchen
Cafe $$

(☏07-839 2906; www.theriverkitchen.co.nz; 237
Victoria St; mains $10-20; ⊙7am-4pm Mon-Fri,
8am-3pm Sat & Sun; ✍) River Kitchen does
things with simple style: cakes, gourmet
breakfasts and fresh seasonal lunches
(angle for the salmon hash), and a barista
who knows his beans. It's the kind of place
you visit for breakfast, come back to for
lunch, then consider for breakfast the next
day.

 Sanctuary Mountain Maungatautari

Can a landlocked volcano become an
island paradise? Inspired by the success
of pest eradication and native species
reintroduction in the Hauraki Gulf, a
community trust has erected 47km of
pest-proof fencing around the triple
peaks of Maungatautari (797m) to
create **Sanctuary Mountain Maun-
gatautari** (www.sanctuarymountain.co.nz;
adult/child $18/8). This atoll of rainfor-
est dominates the skyline between
Te Awamutu and Karapiro and is now
home to its first kiwi chicks in 100 years.
There is also a 'tuatarium,' where NZ's
iconic reptile the tuatara can be seen.

The main entrance is at the visitor
centre at the sanctuary's southern
side. Guided tours (adult/child $35/15)
leaving from the visitor centre from
Tuesday to Sunday include an afternoon
wetlands tour, and morning and after-
noon departures exploring the bird and
insect life of the sanctuary's Southern
Enclosure. Online or phone bookings for
guided tours must be made at least 24
hours in advance.

Chim Choo Ree
Modern NZ $$$

(☏07-839 4329; www.chimchooree.co.nz; 14
Bridge St; mains $36-37; ⊙11.30am-2pm &
5pm-late Mon-Sat) In an airy heritage building
beside the river, Chim Choo Ree focuses on
small plates like Thai fish and papaya salad,
gin-cured salmon and confit pork belly, plus
larger, equally inventive mains using duck,
lamb, venison and snapper. Local foodies
wash it all down with a great wine list and
flavourful NZ craft beers.

Palate
Modern NZ, Fusion $$$

(☏07-834 2921; www.palaterestaurant.co.nz; 20
Alma St; mains $34-38; ⊙11.30am-2pm Tue-Fri,
5.30pm-late Mon-Sat) Simple, sophisticated
Palate has a well-deserved reputation for
lifting the culinary bar across regional NZ.

Kingitanga King Movement

The concept of a Māori people is a relatively new one. Until the mid-19th century, New Zealand was effectively comprised of many independent tribal nations, operating in tandem with the British from 1840.

In 1856, faced with a flood of Brits, the Kingitanga King Movement formed to unite the tribes to better resist further loss of land and culture. A gathering of leaders elected Waikato chief Potatau Te Wherowhero as the first Māori king, hoping that his increased *mana* (prestige) could achieve the cohesion that the British had under their queen.

Despite the huge losses of the Waikato War and the eventual opening up of the King Country, the Kingitanga survived – although it has no formal constitutional role. A measure of the strength of the movement was the huge outpouring of grief when Te Arikinui Dame Atairangikaahu, Potatau's great-great-great-granddaughter, died in 2006 after 40 years at the helm. Although it's not a hereditary monarchy (leaders of various tribes vote on a successor), Potatau's line continues to the present day with King Tuheitia Paki.

The innovative menu features highlights like red roasted duck with yams, scallops, shiitake and a chilli broth. The wine selection is Hamilton's finest.

DRINKING & NIGHTLIFE

The city has a good craft-beer scene worth exploring. Friday is the big night of the week.

Craft Craft Beer
(☎07-839 4531; www.facebook.com/craft beerhamilton; 15 Hood St; ☺3pm-late Wed-Thu, 11.30am-late Fri-Sun) Fifteen rotating taps of amber goodness flow at Craft, which is plenty to keep the city's craft beer buffs coming back. Brews from around NZ make a regular appearance, with occasional surprising additions from international cult breweries. Quiz night kicks off most Wednesdays at 7.30pm, and decent sliders and wood-fired pizza could well see you making a night of it.

Good George Brewing Brewery
(☎07-847 3223; www.goodgeorge.co.nz; 32a Somerset St, Frankton; tours incl beer & food $19; ☺11am-late, tours from 6pm Tue-Thu) Channelling a cool industrial vibe, the former Church of St George is now a shrine to craft beer. Order a flight of five beers ($16), and partner the hoppy heaven with wood-fired pizzas ($20 to $23) or main meals ($18 to $33). Our favourite brews are the citrusy American Pale Ale and the zingy Drop Hop Cider. Tours must be booked ahead.

Wonderhorse Cocktail Bar, Craft Beer
(☎07-839 2281; www.facebook.com/wonder horsebar; 232 Victoria St; ☺5pm-3am Wed-Sat) Tucked away around 20m off Victoria St, Wonderhorse regularly features craft beers from niche local brewers like Shunters Yard and Brewaucracy. Vintage vinyl is often spinning on the turntable, and sliders and Asian street eats combine with killer cocktails at one of Hamilton's best bars.

SL28 Cafe
(☎07-839 6422; www.facebook.com/sl28. coffee; 298 Victoria St; ☺7.30am-4pm Mon-Fri) Hamilton java-hounds in need of the city's best coffee make tracks to this specialist coffee bar. If you know the difference between your Chemex and your cold brew and you're searching for a shot of Sumatran single origin, here's where to come.

Little George Craft Beer
(☎07-834 4345; www.facebook.com/lit tlegeorgepopupbar; 15 Hood St; ☺4-11pm Tue-Thu, 2pm-1am Fri-Sun) The more compact and central sibling to Good George, Little George is another excellent bar along Hood St's nightlife strip. Beers from Good George are regularly featured, but guest taps often showcase other Kiwi craft breweries. Good

Waikato Museum (p108)

bar snacks – check out $3 Taco Tuesdays – and a concise wine list are other diverting attractions.

Local Taphouse Bar
(☏07-834 4923; www.facebook.com/thelocal taphouse; 346 Victoria St, City Co-Op; ⊙11am-late) Part of Hamilton's new City Co-Op eating and drinking precinct, the Local Taphouse features locally sourced beers from the nearby regions of Waikato, Bay of Plenty and Coromandel. Food is served, including hearty pots of mussels and gourmet burgers.

ℹ INFORMATION

Hamilton i-SITE (☏07-958 5960, 0800 242 645; www.visithamilton.co.nz; cnr Caro & Alexandra Sts; ⊙9am-5pm Mon-Fri, 9.30am-3.30pm Sat & Sun; 🛜) Accommodation, activities and transport bookings, plus free wi-fi right across Garden Pl.

ℹ GETTING THERE & AWAY

Hamilton Airport (HIA; ☏07-848 9027; www.hamiltonairport.co.nz; Airport Rd) is 12km south of the city. **Super Shuttle** (☏0800 748 885, 07-843 7778; www.supershuttle.co.nz; one-way $30) offers a door-to-door service into the city. **Aerolink Shuttles** (☏0800 151 551; www.aerolink.nz; one-way $80) also has airport services, while **Raglan Scenic Tours** (☏021 0274 7014, 07-825 0507; www.raglanscenictours.co.nz) links the airport with Raglan. A taxi costs around $50.

Air New Zealand (☏0800 737 000; www.airnewzealand.co.nz) has regular direct flights from Hamilton to Auckland, Christchurch and Wellington. **Kiwi Regional Airlines** (☏07-444 5020; www.flykiwiair.co.nz) flies between Hamilton and Nelson.

All buses arrive and depart from the Hamilton Transport Centre (☏07-834 3457; www.hamilton.co.nz; cnr Anglesea & Bryce Sts; 🛜).

ℹ GETTING AROUND

Central Hamilton is relatively compact and the CBD can be explored on foot. Victoria St is the city's main shopping area and parking can be difficult to secure. You'll have more luck finding parking a few blocks to the west.

Surfing lesson

MATTHEW MICAH WRIGHT/GETTY IMAGES ©

Raglan

Raglan combines spectacular surf beaches – including views stretching along the North Island's rugged west coast – with arts, crafts and a hip dining scene. Around 40km west of Hamilton, it's well worth a detour.

Great For...

☑ Don't Miss

Eating fish and chips and exploring the craft shops at Raglan Wharf, 1km north of town.

Laid-back Raglan may well be NZ's perfect surfing town. It's small enough to have escaped mass development, but big enough to have good eateries and a cool bar. Along with the famous surf spots to the south, the harbour just begs to be kayaked upon. There's also an excellent arts scene with interesting galleries and shops. For contemporary Māori design check out **Toi Hauāuru Studio** (☑07-825 0244; www.toihauauru.com; 4338 Main Rd; ☺10am-5pm Wed-Sun).

Beaches

South of Raglan, the west coast unfurls with a series of excellent surf beaches.

Ngarunui Beach   Surfing, Swimming
Around 4km southeast of Raglan, Ngarunui Beach is area's best ocean beach for swimming. Lifeguards patrol part of the black-sand beach from late October until April.

Fish & chips

GREG ELMS/GETTY IMAGES ©

ℹ Need to Know

Buses link Raglan and Hamilton (one hour) two to three times a day.

✕ Take a Break

Raglan Roast (📞07-825 8702; www.raglanroast.co.nz; Volcom Lane; coffee $4; ⏱7am-5pm, shorter hours in winter) is a hole-in-the-wall coffee roaster with the best brew in town.

★ Top Tip

There's an interesting display on the local surfing scene at the **Raglan i-SITE** (📞07-825 0556; www.raglan.org.nz; 13 Wainui Rd; ⏱9am-7pm Mon-Fri, 9.30am-6pm Sat & Sun).

Eating & Drinking

Shack   International $$
(www.theshackraglan.com; 19 Bow St; tapas $6-14, mains $12-21; ⏱8am-5pm Sun-Thu, until late Fri & Sat; 🛜🍽) Brunch classics – try the chickpea-and-corn fritters – and interesting shared-plate mains like tempura squid and star-anise chicken feature at the best cafe in town. A longboard strapped to the wall, wobbly old floorboards, uptempo tunes, Kiwi wines and craft beers complete the picture.

Bow St Depot   Bar, Cafe
(📞07-825 0976; www.bowstreetdepot.co.nz; 2 Bow St; ⏱11am-1am) On a warm summer's night, the best place to be in town is at Bow St Depot's spacious garden bar. Kick back with a few craft beers from Hamilton's Good George, relax into the beats of the occasional DJs, or graze on shared plates including prawn and lemongrass dumplings or pulled pork sliders.

Manu Bay   Surfing
About 2.5km from Ngarunui Beach, Manu Bay is a legendary surf spot said to have the longest left-hand break in the world.

Whale Bay   Surfing
Whale Bay is a renowned surf spot 1km west of Manu Bay. It's usually less crowded than Manu Bay, but from the bottom of Calvert Rd you have to clamber 600m over the rocks to get to the break.

Activities

Raglan Watersports   Water Sports
(📞07-825 0507; www.raglanwatersports.co.nz; 5a Bankart St; group/private paddle-boarding lessons per person $45/65) A well-run, one-stop spot for paddle-boarding lessons, hire and guided tours, kayak rental and tours, kiteboarding and surfing lessons, and board and bike hire.

Performers at the Rotorua Māori Arts Festival

ROTORUA

Rotorua at a glance...

Catch a heady whiff of Rotorua's sulphur-rich air for your initial taste of NZ's most dynamic thermal area, home to spurting geysers, steaming hot springs and exploding mud pools. The Māori revered this place; today 35% of the population is Māori, and their cultural performances and traditional hangi are very popular attractions. Beyond the lure of the geothermal landscape and Māori culture, travellers also enjoy adventure activities and extreme sports.

Rotorua in two days

Explore Rotorua's geothermal landscape at **Te Puia** (p121) and **Whakarewarewa Village** (p120) before experiencing a Māori concert and *hangi* in the evening. Kick off the following day with a robust breakfast at **Urbano Bistro** (p131) before continuing for forest walking or mountain biking in the **Redwoods Whakarewarewa Forest** (p122). Excellent options for a relaxed dinner include **Abracadabra Cafe Bar** (p131) or a spicy time at **Sabroso** (p131).

Rotorua in three days

After exploring the Redwoods, challenge yourself even further in the outdoors. Zip-lines, platforms and bridges feature in forest adventures with **Rotorua Canopy Tours** (p128), while **Ogo** (p127) will have you rolling downhill in a giant plastic sphere. Rafting or sledging on the **Kaituna River** (p127) is huge fun before recounting all the action over a few craft beers at **Brew** (p132).

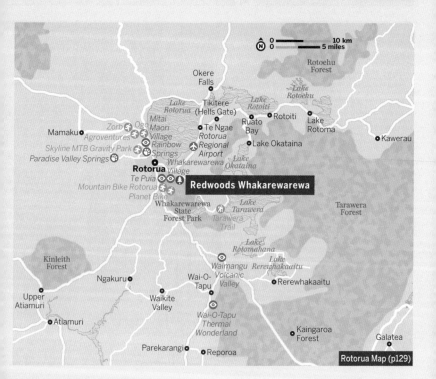

Redwoods Whakarewarewa

Rotorua Map (p129)

Arriving in Rotorua

Rotorua Regional Airport Around 10km northeast of the city on the edge of Lake Rotorua. Regular Air New Zealand flights go to/from Auckland, Wellington and Christchurch.

Rotorua Bus Depot Centrally located in town beside the Rotorua i-SITE with regular departures to destinations across the North Island.

Where to Stay

Rotorua has plenty of holiday parks and an ever-changing backpacker scene. Generic motels crowd Fenton St: better and more interesting rooms are away from the main drag.

Geothermal Rotorua

The fascinating geothermal landscape of the Rotorua area also provides an insight into the culture of local Māori who have lived on this bubbling and steaming terrain for centuries.

Great For...

☑ Don't Miss

A tour with the Māori guides at Whakarewrewa, many descended from the area's first families.

Whakarewarewa Village Village

(☎07-349 3463; www.whakarewarewa.com; 17 Tyron St; tour & cultural performance adult/child $35/15; ☺8.30am-5pm, tours hourly 9am-4pm & cultural performances 11.15am & 2pm) Whakarewarewa Thermal Village is a living village where *tangata whenua* (the locals) still reside, as they have for centuries. The villagers show you around and tell you the stories of their way of life and the significance of the steamy bubbling pools, silica terraces and geysers which, although inaccessible from the village, are easily viewed from vantage points (the view of Pohutu is just as good from here as it is from Te Puia, and considerably cheaper).

The village shops sell authentic arts and crafts, and you can learn about Māori traditions such as flax weaving, carving, and *ta moko* (tattooing). Nearby you can eat tasty,

Pohutu geyser

MUHA/GETTY IMAGES ©

30m skyward. You'll know when it's about to blow because the adjacent **Prince of Wales' Feathers** geyser will start up shortly before. Tours (90 minutes) depart hourly from 9am, and daytime 45-minute cultural performances start at 10.15am, 12.15pm and 3.15pm.

Also here is the National Carving School and the National Weaving School, where you can discover the work and methods of traditional Māori woodcarvers and weavers, plus a carved meeting house, a cafe, galleries, a kiwi reserve and gift shop.

buttery sweetcorn ($2) pulled straight out of the hot mineral pool – the only genuine geothermal *hangi* in town. Other bigger *hangi* meal options range from $18.50 to $21 per person.

Te Puia   Geyser, Cultural Centre

(☏0800 837 842, 07-348 9047; www.tepuia.com; Hemo Rd; adult/child tours $49.50/23, daytime tour & performance combos $58/29, evening tour, performance & hangi combos $140/70; ⊗8am-6pm Oct-Apr, to 5pm May-Sep) This thermal reserve is 3km south of the city centre, and features more than 500 springs. The most famous is **Pohutu** ('Big Splash' or 'Explosion'), a geyser which erupts up to 20 times a day, spurting hot water up to

What's Nearby

Ask at the Rotorua i-SITE about visiting the region's other geothermal attractions, including **Wai-O-Tapu Thermal Wonderland** (☏07-366 6333; www.waiotapu.co.nz; 201 Waiotapu Loop Rd, off SH5; adult/child/family $32.50/11/80; ⊗8.30am-5pm, last admission 3.45pm) and **Waimangu Volcanic Valley** (☏07-366 6137; www.waimangu.co.nz; 587 Waimangu Rd; adult/child walking tours $37/12, boat cruises $42.50/12; ⊗8.30am-5pm, to 6pm Jan, last admission 3pm, 4pm Jan), both south of Rotorua en route to the lakeside town of Taupo.

MATTEO COLOMBO/GETTY IMAGES ©

Redwoods Whakarewarewa Forest

Welcome to a real favourite of Rotorua families. A short drive from central Rotorua, meandering walking trails and mountain-bike tracks course through a verdant labyrinth of towering redwood trees.

Great For...

☑ **Don't Miss**

Traversing the Redwoods Treewalk, an extended and elevated walk between century-old redwood trees.

This forest park is 3km southeast of town on Tarawera Rd. It was originally home to over 170 tree species planted from 1899 to see which could be grown successfully for timber. Mighty Californian redwoods give the park its grandeur today. Walking tracks range from a half-hour wander through the Redwood Grove to a whole-day route to the Blue and Green Lakes.

A new attraction in the forest is the **Redwoods Treewalk** (☎07-350 0110; www. treewalk.co.nz; Redwoods Whakarewarewa Forest; adult/child $25/15; ⊗8.30am-6pm). More than 500m is traversed on this suspended walkway combining 21 wooden bridges between well-established redwood trees. Most of the pathway is around 6m off the forest floor, but it ascends to 12m in some parts. The Treewalk opened in January 2016; plans for

❶ Need to Know

Redwoods Whakarewarewa Forest
(☏07-350 0110; www.redwoods.co.nz; Long
Mile Rd, off Tarawera Rd; ⊗8.30am-5pm)
FREE has excellent online information on
walking and activities.

✕ Take a Break

After mountain biking, head to **Mistress
of Cakes** (☏07-345 6521; www.mistressof
cakes.co.nz; Shop 2, 26 Lynmore Ave; snacks
$4-8; ⊗8.30am-5.30pm Tue-Fri, 9am-3pm
Sat & Sun) in the Lynmore shops for great
baking.

★ Top Tip

Visit on a weekday to have forest's
shaded glens largely to yourself.

stage two of the project include raising the
height to 20m.

Aside from walking, the park is great for
picnics and accessible mountain biking.

What's Nearby

Around 16km from the Redwoods Whakarewarewa Forest – via the pretty Blue
and Green Lakes – Lake Tarawera offers
swimming, fishing, cruises and walks.
Clearwater Cruises (☏027 362 8590, 07-345
6688; www.clearwater.co.nz; per hour cruise
vessels/self-drive runabouts $550/145) runs
scenic cruises and self-drive boat options,
while **Lake Tarawera Water Taxi & Eco
Tours** (☏07-362 8080; www.ecotoursrotorua.
co.nz; 1375 Tarawera Rd; adult/child $65/35;

⊗departs at 2pm) offers boat trips and water
taxi transfers (must be prebooked) to Hot
Water Beach and for the Tarawera Trail
(15km, five to six hours). The **Landing Café**
(☏07-362 8502; mains $15-40; ⊗10am-late)
has fresh fruit ice creams and lake views.

Fifteen kilometres from Rotorua on
Tarawera Rd is the buried village of Te
Wairoa, interred by the 1886 eruption of Mt
Tarawera. Te Wairoa was the staging post
for travellers coming to see the Pink and
White Terraces. Today a museum houses
objects dug from the ruins, and guides in
period costume escort groups through the
excavated sites. There's also a walk to the
30m Te Wairoa Falls.

GRANT DIXON/GETTY IMAGES ©

Mountain Biking Rotorua

NZ is blessed with one of the world's best mountain-biking scenes and Rotorua offers superb forest and downhill tracks.

Great For...

☑ Don't Miss

Catching the gondola up Mt Ngongotaha and zooming down one of 11 downhill tracks.

Welcome to one the southern hemisphere's finest destinations for mountain biking, offering a range of experiences for everyone from families and beginners, through to gung ho two-wheeled adventurers.

On the edge of town is the Redwoods Whakarewarewa Forest (p122), home to some of the best mountain-bike trails in the country. There are close to 100km of tracks to keep bikers of all skill levels happy for days on end. Note that not all tracks in the forest are designated for bikers, so adhere to the signposts. Pick up a trail map at the forest visitor centre. **Mountain Bike Rotorua** (⌀0800 682 768; www.mtbrotorua. co.nz; Waipa State Mill Rd; mountain bikes per 2hr/day from $35/45, guided half-/full-day rides from $130/275; ⊙9am-5pm) hires out bikes at the Waipa Mill car park entrance to the forest, the starting point for the bike trails.

GRANT DIXON/GETTY IMAGES ©

You can also stop by their new central Rotorua **adventure hub** (☏07-348 4290; www.mtbrotorua.co.nz; 1128 Hinemoa St; ⊙9am-5pm) for rentals, mountain-biking information, and a cool cafe. Another option for mountain biking is **Planet Bike** (☏027 280 2817; www.planetbike.co.nz; Waipa Bypass Rd; mountain bikes per 2hr/day from $35/60), which offers bike-hire and guided mountain-bike rides (three hours/half-day $150/199).

Another essential destination for mountain bikers is the new **Skyline MTB Gravity Park** (☏07-347 0027; www.skyline.co.nz/rotorua; Fairy Springs Rd; 1/15 gondola rides with bike $28/55; ⊙9am-5pm) where access up Mt Ngongotaha is provided by a gondola. This new network of 11 MTB tracks courses down the forest-clad mountain, and there are options for riders of all experience. Bike rental (two hours/half day from $60/90) is available on-site from Mountain Bike Rotorua.

For a kick-ass breakfast before heading off mountain biking, combine lake views at the **Third Place Cafe** (☏07-349 4852; www.thirdplacecafe.co.nz; 36 Lake Rd; mains $14-19; ⊙7.30am-4pm Mon-Fri, to 3.30pm Sat & Sun) with their awesome 'mumble jumble,' a massive mashup of crushed kumara (sweet potato), green tomatoes and spicy chorizo topped with bacon, a poached egg and hollandaise sauce. Sorted.

Also nearby is the Te Ara Ahi ride, one of the New Zealand Cycle Trail's 'Great Rides' (www.nzcycletrail.com). It's an intermediate, two-day, 66km ride heading south of town to Wai-O-Tapu Thermal Wonderland and beyond.

For more information, the Rotorua i-SITE (p132) has a special display area dedicated to the growing mountain-biking scene.

Freefall Xtreme

JOHN BORTHWICK/GETTY IMAGES ©

Adrenaline Rotorua

Queenstown definitely gets the international kudos as NZ's adventure capital, but Rotorua is also a fantastic place to scare yourself silly and get the souvenir T-shirt and DVD afterwards.

Great For...

☑ **Don't Miss**

River rafting over the 7m-high Tutea Falls on the Kaituna River.

Extreme Adventures

Agroventures   Adventure Sports
(☎0800 949 888, 07-357 4747; www.agro ventures.co.nz; Western Rd, off Paradise Valley Rd, Ngongotaha; 1/2/4/5 rides $49/79/109/189; ☺9am-5pm) Agroventures is a hive of action, 9km north of Rotorua on SH5 (shuttles available). Start off with the 43m bungy and the Swoop, a 130km/h swing. The Free-fall Xtreme simulates skydiving, and also here is the Shweeb, a monorail velodrome from which you hang in a clear capsule and pedal yourself along at speeds of up to 60km/h.

Zorb   Adventure Sports
(☎07-357 5100, 0800 227 474; www.zorb.com; cnr Western Rd & SH5, Ngongotaha; rides from $39; ☺9am-5pm, to 7pm Dec-Mar) The Zorb is 9km north of Rotorua on SH5 – look for the

Rafting on the Kaituna River

FRANS LEMMENS/GETTY IMAGES ©

River Activities

Raftabout   Rafting

(☎0800 723 822, 07-343 9500; www.raftabout.co.nz) Rafting trips on the Kaituna ($105), Rangitaiki ($139) and Wairoa ($129), plus sledging on the Kaituna ($129). The Kaituna rafting option features the exciting highlight of going over the 7m-high Tutea Falls.

River Rats   Rafting

(☎07-345 6543, 0800 333 900; www.riverrats.co.nz) Takes on the Wairoa ($129), Kaituna ($105) and Rangitaiki ($139), and runs a scenic trip on the lower Rangitaiki (Grade II) that is good for youngsters (adult/child $139/110). Kayaking options include freedom hire (adult/child $59/39) and there's also exciting river sledging on the Kaituna ($129).

Wet 'n' Wild   Rafting

(☎0800 462 7238, 07-348 3191; www.wetnwildrafting.co.nz) Runs trips on the Kaituna ($99), Wairoa ($110) and Mokau ($160), as well as easy-going Rangitaiki trips (adult/child $130/100) and longer trips to remote parts of the Motu and Mohaka (two to five days, $650 to $1095).

grassy hillside with large, clear, people-filled spheres rolling down it. Your eyes do not deceive you! There are three courses: 150m straight, 180m zigzag or 250m 'drop'. Do your zorb strapped in and dry, or freestyle with water thrown in. A recent addition is 'zurfing' where you can ride a boogie board inside one of the giant spheres.

Ogo   Adventure Sports

(☎0800 646 768, 07-343 7676; www.ogo.co.nz; 525 Ngongotaha Rd; rides from $45; ⊗9am-5pm, to 6.30pm Dec-Feb) The Ogo (about 5km north of town) involves careening down a grassy hillside in a big bubble, with water or without. Silly? Fun? Terrifying? All of the above...

Rotorua

Dubbed 'Rotovegas' by domestic NZ tourists who have been flocking to holiday in Rotorua for decades, the city's compelling mix of geothermal activity, Māori culture and family-friendly activities is also perfect for international travellers.

◎ SIGHTS

Rotorua Museum   Museum, Gallery

(☏07-350 1814; www.rotoruamuseum.co.nz; Queens Dr, Government Gardens; adult/child $20/8; ◷9am-5pm Mar-Nov, to 6pm Dec-Feb, tours hourly 10am-4pm, plus 5pm Dec-Feb) This outstanding museum occupies a grand Tudor-style edifice. A 20-minute film on the history of Rotorua, including the Tarawera eruption, runs every 20 minutes from 9am. The Don Stafford Wing, dedicated to Rotorua's Te Arawa people, features woodcarving, flax weaving, jade and the stories of the revered WWII 28th Māori Battalion. Also here are two art galleries and a cool cafe with garden views (although the best view in town is from the viewing platform on the roof).

Ohinemutu   Historic Site

FREE Ohinemutu is a lakeside Māori village (access via Kiharoa, Haukotuku or Korokai Sts off Lake Rd, north of Rotorua Hospital) that traces the fusing of European and Māori cultures. Highlights include the sacred 1905 Tama-te-kapua Meeting House (not open to visitors), many steaming volcanic vents, and the historic timber **St Faith's Anglican Church** (☏07-348 2393; cnr Mataiawhea & Korokai Sts, Ohinemutu; admission by donation; ◷8am-6pm, services 9am Sun & 10am Wed), which features intricate Māori carvings, *tukutuku* (woven panels) and a stained-glass window of Christ wearing a Māori cloak as he walks on the waters of Lake Rotorua.

Be respectful if you're visiting the village: this is private land, and locals don't appreciate loud, nosy tourists wandering around taking photos.

Paradise Valley Springs   Wildlife Reserve

(☏07-348 9667; www.paradisevalleysprings. co.nz; 467 Paradise Valley Rd; adult/child $30/15; ◷8am-dusk, last entry 5pm) In Paradise Valley at the foot of Mt Ngongotaha, 8km from Rotorua, is Paradise Valley Springs, a six-hectare park with trout springs, big slippery eels and various land-dwelling animals such as deer, alpacas, possums and a pride of lions (fed at 2.30pm). There's also a coffee shop and an elevated treetop walkway.

Rainbow Springs   Wildlife Reserve

(☏0800 724 626; www.rainbowsprings.co.nz; 192 Fairy Springs Rd; 24hr passes adult/child/ family $40/20/99; ◷8.30am-late) The natural springs here are home to wild trout and eels, which you can peer at through an underwater viewer. There are interpretive walkways, a new 'Big Splash' water ride, and plenty of animals, including tuatara (a native lizard) and native birds (kea, kaka and pukeko). A highlight is the Kiwi Encounter, offering a rare peek into the lives of these endangered birds: excellent 30-minute tours (an extra $10 per person) have you tiptoeing through incubator and hatchery areas.

Rainbow Springs is around 3km north of central Rotorua.

◎ ACTIVITIES

Rotorua Canopy Tours   Adventure Sports

(☏07-343 1001, 0800 226 679; www.canopy tours.co.nz; 173 Old Taupo Rd; 3hr tours per adult/child/family $139/95/419; ◷8am-8pm Oct-Apr, to 6pm May-Sep) Explore a 1.2km web of bridges, flying foxes, zip-lines and platforms, 22m high in a lush native forest canopy 10 minutes out of town (...they say that rimu tree is 1000 years old!). Plenty of native birds to keep you company. Free pickups available.

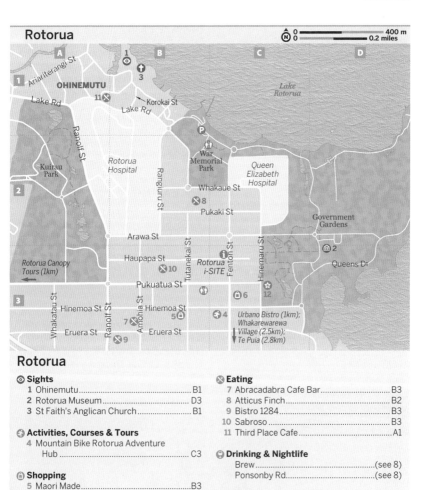

Rotorua

Rotorua

◎ Sights
1 Ohinemutu...B1
2 Rotorua Museum.......................................D3
3 St Faith's Anglican Church......................B1

⊕ Activities, Courses & Tours
4 Mountain Bike Rotorua Adventure
   Hub..C3

⊞ Shopping
5 Māori Made..B3
6 Rākai Jade...C3

⊗ Eating
7 Abracadabra Cafe Bar..............................B3
8 Atticus Finch..B2
9 Bistro 1284...B3
10 Sabroso..B3
11 Third Place Cafe......................................A1

◉ Drinking & Nightlife
Brew...(see 8)
Ponsonby Rd..(see 8)

✪ Entertainment
12 Tamaki Maori Village..............................C3

⊕ TOURS

Mt Tarawera Volcanic
Experience   Hiking
(Katikati Adventures; ☑0800 338 736; www.
mt-tarawera.com; per person $149) Get up close
and personal with the massive volcanic
landscapes of nearby Mt Tarawera on this
guided adventure combining an exciting
4WD drive with a walk around the crater's
edge. There's even the opportunity to make

a run down the volcanic scree into the
crater. Combo deals feature a helicopter
ride above the mountain and nearby lakes.

Geyser Link Shuttle   Tour
(☑03-477 9083, 0800 304 333; www.travel
headfirst.com/local-legends/geyser-link-shuttle)
Tours of some of the major sights, including
Wai-O-Tapu (half-day adult/child $75/35),
Waimangu (half-day $75/35), or both (full

day $125/65). Trips incorporating Hobbiton and Whakarewarewa are also available.

Happy Ewe Tours · Cycling

(☏022 622 9252; www.happyewetours.com; adult/child $55/35; ☺10am & 2pm) Saddle-up for a three-hour, small-group bike tour of Rotorua, wheeling past 20 sights around the city. It's all flat and slow-paced, so you don't need to be at your physical peak (you're on holiday after all).

🅰 SHOPPING

Maori Made · Clothing, Crafts

(☏022 047 5327, 021 065 9611; maorimade. rotorua@gmail.com; 1180 Hinemoa St; ☺10am-5pm Mon-Fri, to 2pm Sat) Traditional and contemporary Māori design merge at this excellent shop showcasing work from several local designers. Apparel, homewares, weaving and jewellery are all represented, and much of the work is uniquely available at this shop. Check out the quirky Kiwiana T-shirts from Paua Frita, stylish women's fashion from Mereana Ngatai, or Mahi Toi's vibrant paintings.

Rākai Jade · Crafts

(☏027 443 9295; www.rakaijade.co.nz; 1234 Fenton St) In addition to purchasing off-the-shelf *pounamu* (jade) pieces, you can work with Rākai's on-site team of local Māori carvers to design and carve your own pendant or jewellery. A day's notice for 'Carve Your Own' experiences ($150 to $180) is preferred if possible. Look forward to spending a full day creating your personal memento of Rotorua.

❌ EATING

The lake end of Tutanekai St – known as 'Eat Streat' – has a strip of eateries beneath a roof. Indian, Thai and Italian flavours all feature.

Gold Star Bakery · Bakery $

(☏07-349 1959; 89 Old Taupo Rd; pies $4-5; ☺6am-3pm Mon-Sat) As you head into Rotorua from the north, it's essential that you stop at this award-winning bakery with a stellar reputation for turning out some of NZ's best pies. Great-value savoury treats to devour include chicken and mushroom,

Rotorua Museum (p128)

or the classic steak 'n' cheese. Good luck choosing from the huge selection.

Abracadabra Cafe Bar
Middle Eastern **$$**

(07-348 3883; www.abracadabracafe.
com; 1363 Amohia St; mains $15-30, tapas
$10-15; 10.30am-11pm Tue-Sat, to 3pm Sun)
Channelling Spain, Mexico and Morocco,
Abracadabra is a magical cave of spicy
delights, from beef-and-apricot tagine to
king-prawn fajitas and Tijuana pork chilli.
There's a great beer terrace out the back –
perfect for combining a few local craft
brews and shared tapas. We can highly
recommend the breakfast burrito and a
revitalising bottle of kombucha for the
morning after.

Sabroso
Latin American **$$**

(07-349 0591; www.sabroso.co.nz; 1184 Hau-
papa St; mains $19-30; 5-9pm Wed-Sun) This
modest Latin American cantina – adorned
with sombreros, guitars and salt-and-
pepper shakers made from Corona
bottles – serves zingy south-of-the-bor-
der fare. The black-bean chilli and the
calamari tacos are excellent, as are the
zesty margaritas. Booking ahead is highly
recommended as Sabroso is *muy popular*.
Buy a bottle of the owners' hot sauce to
enliven your next Kiwi barbecue.

Urbano Bistro
Modern NZ **$$**

(07-349 3770; www.urbanobistro.co.nz; cnr
Fenton & Grey Sts; mains breakfast & lunch
$14-21, dinner $24-43; 9am-11pm Mon-Sat,
to 3pm Sun) This hip suburban diner, with
mega-checkerboard carpet and curvy
wallpaper, is a bold move by reputable local
restaurateurs. Try the beef, pineapple and
kumara curry – rich in flavour and well
executed. Fine wines and five-star service
to boot. During the day it's a more casual
and good-value cafe.

Atticus Finch
Bistro **$$**

(07-460 0400; www.atticusfinch.co.nz; 1106
Tutanekai St, Eat Street; shared plates $15-32;
noon-3pm & 5pm-late) With a Harper Lee
cocktail, the iconic novel *To Kill a Mocking-
bird* certainly features at this relaxed spot

 Experiencing Māori Culture

Māori culture is a big-ticket item in
Rotorua and, although it is commercial-
ised, it's a great opportunity to learn
about the indigenous culture of NZ.
The two big activities are concerts and
hangi feasts, often packaged together
in an evening's entertainment featuring
the famous *hongi* (Māori greeting; the
pressing of foreheads and noses, and
sharing of life breath) and *haka* and *poi*
dances.

Tamaki Maori Village (0508 826
254, 07-349 2999; www.tamakimaorivillage.
co.nz; booking office 1220 Hinemaru St; adult/
family $115/310, child $25-65; tours depart
5pm, 6.15pm & 7.30pm Nov-Apr, 6.15pm May-
Oct) and family-run **Mitai Maori Village**
(07-343 9132; www.mitai.co.nz; 196 Fairy
Springs Rd; adult/family $116/315, child $23-
58; 6.30pm) are established favourites.
Te Puia (p121) and **Whakarewarewa
Village** (p120) also put on shows, and
many of the big hotels offer mainstream
Māori concerts and *hangi*.

Wood carving at Te Puia (p121)
HOLGER LEUE/GETTY IMAGES ©

along Eat Streat. Beyond the literary refer-
ences, the menu of shared plates channels
Asian and Mediterranean flavours – try the
chilli and ginger prawns or the mozzarella
balls – and a concise menu of NZ beer and
wine imparts a local flavour.

The cheese or charcuterie platters
($17 to $34) are good value for snacking
couples or grazing groups.

The Legend of Hinemoa & Tutanekai

Hinemoa was a young woman of a *hapu* (subtribe) that lived on the western shore of Lake Rotorua, while Tutanekai was a young man of a Mokoia Island *hapu*. The pair met and fell in love during a regular tribal meeting. While both were of high birth, Tutanekai was illegitimate, so their marriage was forbidden.

Home on Mokoia, the lovesick Tutanekai played his flute for his love, the wind carrying the melody across the water. Hinemoa heard his declaration, but her people took to tying up the canoes at night to ensure she wouldn't go to him.

Finally, Tutanekai's music won her over. Hinemoa undressed and swam the long distance from the shore to the island. When she arrived on Mokoia, Hinemoa found herself in a quandary. Having shed her clothing in order to swim, she could hardly walk into the island's settlement naked. She hopped into a hot pool to think about her next move.

Eventually a man came to fetch water from a cold spring beside the hot pool. In a deep man's voice, Hinemoa called out, 'Who is it?' The man replied that he was Tutanekai's slave on a water run. Hinemoa grabbed the slave's calabash and smashed it to pieces. More slaves came, but she smashed their calabashes too, until finally Tutanekai came to the pool and demanded that the interloper identify himself. Astonished when it turned out to be Hinemoa, he smuggled her into his hut.

Next morning, after a suspiciously long lie-in, a slave reported that someone was in Tutanekai's bed. The two lovers were rumbled, and when Hinemoa's superhuman efforts to reach Tutanekai had been revealed, their union was celebrated.

Descendants of Hinemoa and Tutanekai still live around Rotorua today.

Bistro 1284   Modern NZ $$$

(☑07-346 1284; www.bistro1284.co.nz; 1284 Eruera St; mains $36-42; ◷6pm-late) A fine-dining hot spot on an unremarkable stretch of Eruera St, this intimate place (all chocolate and mushroom colours) serves stylish NZ cuisine with Asian and European influences. Try the pecan-crusted lamb, and definitely leave room for a dessert of the peach and mango crumble.

🍸 DRINKING & NIGHTLIFE

Brew   Craft Beer

(☑07-346 0976; www.brewpub.co.nz; 1103 Tutanekai St, Eat Street; ◷11am-late Mon-Fri, 9am-late Sat & Sun) Run by the lads from Croucher Brewing Co, Rotorua's best microbrewers, Brew sits in a sunny spot on Rotorua's 'Eat Streat'. Thirteen taps showcase the best of Croucher's brews as well as guest beers from NZ and overseas. Try the hoppy Croucher Pilsner with the pulled pork and prawn pizza. Good coffee too, plus occasional Friday night bands and DJs.

Ponsonby Rd   Cocktail Bar

(☑021 640 292; www.ponsonbyrd.co.nz; 1109 Tutanekai St, Eat Street; ◷5pm-late) Former TV weatherman Tamati Coffey has introduced flash big-city style to Rotorua – the bar is named after Auckland's pre-eminent eating and drinking strip. Drenched in red light and trimmed with velvet, the decor is certainly vibrant, and cosy booths are perfect for sipping on cocktails named after local Māori legends. Look forward to live music from 9pm most weekends.

INFORMATION

Rotorua i-SITE (☑0800 768 678, 07-348 5179; www.rotoruanz.com; 1167 Fenton St; ◷7.30am-6pm) The hub for travel information and bookings, including Department of Conservation (DOC) walks. Also has a cafe, showers and lockers, and plenty of information on Rotorua's world class mountain-biking scene.

Inferno Crater, Waimangu Volcanic Valley (p121)

GETTING THERE & AWAY

Rotorua Regional Airport (ROT; ☎07-345 8800; www.rotorua-airport.co.nz; SH30) is 10km northeast of town. **Super Shuttle** (☎09-522 5100, 0800 748 885; www.supershuttle.co.nz; 1st passenger/each additional passenger $21/5) offers a door-to-door airport service for $21 for the first person then $5 per additional passenger. **Baybus** (☎0800 422 928; www. baybus.co.nz) runs an airport bus service (route 10, $2.30). A taxi to/from the city centre costs about $30. **Air New Zealand** (☎0800 737 000;

www.airnewzealand.co.nz) flies to/from Auckland, Wellington and Christchurch.

All the major bus companies stop outside the Rotorua i-SITE, where you can arrange bookings to destinations around the North Island,

GETTING AROUND

The big-name car-hire companies vie for your attention at the Rotorua airport.

TAUPO & AROUND

Taupo & Around at a glance...

From river deep to mountain high, NZ's geology takes centre stage in this diverse region. Much of the drama happens along the Taupo Volcanic Zone – a line of geothermal activity that stretches via Rotorua to Whakaari (White Island) in the Bay of Plenty. This commotion below the surface has gifted the region with some of the North Island's star attractions, including the country's largest lake and the three volcanic peaks of Tongariro National Park.

Taupo in two days

Take a boat trip to the **Māori rock carvings** (p144) on **Lake Taupo** before checking out the excellent **Taupo Museum** (p144) in the afternoon. Have a local Lakeman beer at the **Lakehouse** (p148) – with views of the peaks of Tongariro National Park – before exploring the **Wairakei** (p140) area the following day. Geothermal energy and masses of water reinforce the region's rugged landscapes.

Taupo in four days

Continue south along **Lake Taupo** to **Turangi** (p142), a world-renowned mecca for trout-fishing, before continuing to **Ohakune** (p149) or **National Park Village**. Both are excellent bases for tackling the one-day adventure of the **Tongariro Alpine Crossing** (p138), and if you're feeling really energetic, consider a two-wheeled discovery of the excellent **Ohakune Old Coach Road** (p149) mountain-bike track on day four.

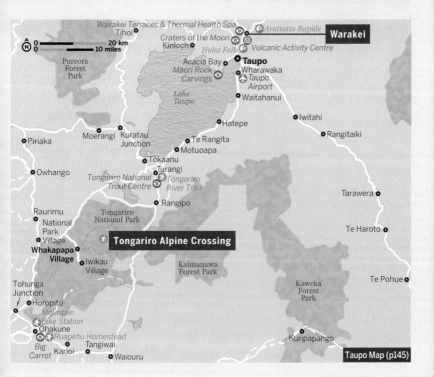

Arriving in Taupo & Ohakune

Taupo Airport Located around 8km south of town with flights to/from Auckland and Wellington.

Taupo i-SITE Buses terminate here from destinations including Auckland, Rotorua and Hamilton. Shuttles and buses continue to National Park Village and Ohakune for the Tongariro Alpine Crossing.

Ohakune Railway Station The *Northern Explorer* train linking Auckland and Wellington stops here and at nearby National Park Village.

Where to Stay

Taupo has plenty of accommodation, all of which is in hot demand during late December, January and during major sporting events. Book ahead at these times. Ohakune has a decent selection of motels and hostels. Expect to pay around 50% more in winter during the ski season, and book well ahead. An alternative accommodation base for undertaking the Tongariro Alpine Crossing hike or the Old Coach Road mountain bike trail is National Park Village, 36km north of Ohakune.

Mt Ngauruhoe

Tongariro Alpine Crossing

This popular crossing is lauded as NZ's finest one-day hike, and amid the thrilling scenery are steaming vents and springs, crazy rock formations and peculiar moonscape basins, and vast views.

Great For...

☑ Don't Miss

Descending carefully down scoria slopes from Red Crater to the turquoise shimmer of Blue Lake.

Around 10,000 trampers complete the Tongariro Alpine Crossing each year, negotiating diverse vegetation zones ranging from alpine scrub and tussock to higher zones with no plant life at all.

The Crossing starts at Mangatepopo Rd car park, off SH47, and finishes at Ketetahi Rd, off SH46. It takes seven to eight hours to make the 19.4km journey, although this will vary significantly if you decide to take side trips up to the summits of Ngauruhoe or Tongariro – both are worthy and take around two and three hours respectively. A word of warning: if you summit Ngauruhoe, keep an eagle-eye out for dislodged boulders careering down.

When to Go

The most crowded times on the track are the first good weather days after Christmas

❶ Need to Know

Both www.tongarirocrossing.org.nz and www.doc.govt.nz are invaluable for pre-trip planning.

✘ Take a Break

Celebrate completing the Crossing at the **Station Cafe** (☏07-892 2881; www.stationcafe.co.nz; cnr Findlay St & Station Rd; mains lunch $15-20, dinner $28-34; ⊗9am-4pm Mon-Tue, to 9pm Wed-Sun) in National Park Village.

★ Top Tip

National Park Village and Ohakune both make good accommodation bases for the Tongariro Alpine Crossing.

---

and Easter, when there can easily be more than 1000 people strung out between the two road ends. The upside of this popularity is excellent shuttle connections, with plenty of operators offering round-trip transport. Be sure to book your ride in advance, and keep an eye on your progress so you don't miss your ride.

Safety Considerations

This is a fair-weather tramp. In poor conditions it is little more than an arduous up-and-down, with only orange-tipped poles to mark the passing of the day. Should strong winds be blowing on top, you'll be practically crawling along the ridge of Red Crater, the high point of the trek.

This is an alpine crossing, and it needs to be treated with respect. You need a reasonable level of fitness and you should be pre-

pared for all types of weather. Shockingly ill-equipped trampers are legendary on this route – stupid shoes, no rain jackets, blue jeans soaked to the skin – we've seen it all. As well as proper gear, you'll need plenty of water, as there is none available between Mangatepopo and Ketetahi.

Transport

Shuttles operate from Whakapapa Village, National Park, Ohakune and Taumarunui, making them all possible overnight bases.

Guided Tramps

If you're keen to undertake a guided tramp, contact **Adrift Guided Outdoor Adventures** (☏07-892 2751; www.adriftnz.co.nz; 3 Waimarino–Tokaanu Rd) or **Adventure Outdoors** (☏0800 386 925, 027 242 7209; www.adventureoutdoors.co.nz), both in National Park Village.

Huka Falls

Geothermal Wairakei

A short drive north of Taupo, the Wairakei region is a powerful reminder of the natural forces that have shaped the rugged and spectacular landscapes of the central North Island.

Great For...

☑ Don't Miss

The thundering and roiling roar of either Huka Falls or the Aratiatia Rapids.

Wairakei Terraces & Thermal Health Spa · Hot Spring

(☏07-378 0913; www.wairakeiterraces.co.nz; Wairakei Rd; thermal walk adult/child $18/9, pools $25, massage from $85; ⊙8.30am-8.30pm Fri-Wed, to 7pm Thu) ✈ Mineral-laden waters from the Wairakei geothermal steamfield cascade over silica terraces into pools (open to those 14 years and older) nestled in native gardens. Take a therapeutic soak and a self-guided tour on the Terraces Walkway, featuring a re-created Māori village, carvings depicting the history of NZ, Māori and local *iwi* Ngati Tuwahretoa, and artificially made geysers and silica terraces echoing – on a smaller scale – the famous Pink and White Terraces that were destroyed by the Tarawera eruption in 1886.

Craters of the Moon

PAWEL TOCZYNSKI/GETTY IMAGES ©

as a result of the hydroelectric tinkering that created the power station. When underground water levels fell and pressure shifted, new steam vents and bubbling mud pools sprang up. The perimeter loop walk takes about 45 minutes and affords great views down to the lake and mountains beyond. There's a kiosk at the entrance, staffed by volunteers who keep an eye on the car park. The area is signposted from SH1 about 5km north of Taupo.

Aratiatia Rapids   Waterfall

Two kilometres off SH5, this was a spectacular part of the Waikato River until the government plonked a hydroelectric dam across the waterway, shutting off the flow. The spectacle hasn't disappeared completely, with the floodgates opening from October to March at 10am, noon, 2pm and 4pm and April to September at 10am, noon and 2pm. Watch the water surge through the dam from two good vantage points. The rapids are 13km northeast of Taupo.

Craters of the Moon   Thermal Area

(✆027 6564 684; www.cratersofthemoon.co.nz; Karapiti Rd; adult/child $8/4; ☺8.30am-5pm) This geothermal area sprang to life

Huka Falls   Waterfall

(Huka Falls Rd) Clearly signposted and with a car park and kiosk, these falls mark where NZ's longest river, the Waikato, is slammed into a narrow chasm, making a dramatic 10m drop into a surging pool. From the footbridge you can see the full force of this torrent that the Māori called Hukanui (Great Body of Spray). Take one of the short walks around the area, or walk the Huka Falls Walkway back to town or the Aratiatia Rapids Walking/Cycling Track to the rapids.

On sunny days the water is crystal clear, and great photographs can be taken from the lookout on the other side of the footbridge.

Fly fishing on the Tongariro River

JOHAN_KOK/GETTY IMAGES ©

Trout Fishing

Famed around the world, the stellar trout fishing scene around Turangi is also a very scenic opportunity for some relaxed holiday downtime amid the mountain-fed rivers of Tongariro National Park.

Great For...

☑ Don't Miss

Walking or cycling part of the 18km Tongariro River Trail (www.tongariroriver trail.co.nz).

Early European settlers, wishing to improve New Zealand's hunting and fishing opportunities, were responsible for the release of brown and rainbow trout into NZ rivers in the second half of the 19th century. The Tongariro River is now the largest and most important spawning river in the Taupo district, and renowned internationally for its fish. More than 28,000 legal trout are bagged annually by domestic and international fishing enthusiasts. At the southern tip of Lake Taupo, Turangi is the major hub for trout fishing in the area, but guides and gear can also be arranged in Taupo itself.

Trout fishing is highly regulated, with plenty of rules regarding where and how to fish, and licences are most certainly required. Read more at Fish & Game New Zealand (www.fishandgame.org.nz), but our best advice is to seek out a guide. Most

Angler with brown trout

PETER G KNOTT/GETTY IMAGES ©

⊙8.30am-5.30pm Mon-Sat, 9.15am-5pm Sun) Sports store laden with fishing paraphernalia. Its website details the latest fishing conditions.

Ian & Andrew Jenkins (📞07-386 0840; www.tui-lodge.co.nz) Father and son fly-fishing guides.

Central Plateau Fishing (📞027 681 4134, 07-378 8192; www.cpf.net.nz) Turangi-based guide Brett Cameron.

Even if you don't have the fishing bug, a visit to the **Tongariro National Trout Centre** (📞07-386 8085; www.troutcentre. com; SH1; adult/child $12/free; ⊙10am-4pm Dec-Apr, 10am-3pm May-Nov) is definitely worthwhile. Around 4km south of Turangi, this DOC-managed trout hatchery has polished educational displays, a collection of rods and reels dating back to the 1880s, and freshwater aquariums displaying river life, both nasty and nice. A gentle stroll along the landscaped walkway leads to the hatchery, keeping ponds, an underwater viewing chamber, the Tongariro River and a picnic area.

offer flexible trips, with $250 for a half-day a ballpark figure.

Recommended Turangi operators include the following:

Creel Tackle House & Cafe (📞07-386 7929; www.creeltackle.com; 183 Taupahi Rd; ⊙cafe 8am-4pm, tackle shop 7.30am-5pm) Fishing equipment, tips, guiding and damn fine coffee.

Greig's Sporting World (📞07-386 6911; www. greigsports.co.nz; 59 Town Centre; ⊙7.30am-5pm Mon-Sat) Hires and sells gear and handles bookings for guides and charters.

Sporting Life (📞07-386 8996; www.sporting life-turangi.co.nz; The Mall, Town Centre;

Taupo

With a postcard-perfect setting on the northeastern shores of the lake, Taupo now rivals Rotorua as the North Island's premier resort town. There's an abundance of adrenaline-pumping activities on offer but for those with no appetite for white knuckles and churned stomachs, there's plenty of enjoyment to be had simply strolling by the lake and enjoying the views, which on clear days encompass the snowy peaks of Tongariro National Park.

◉ SIGHTS

Taupo's main attraction is the lake and all the things you can do in, on and around it.

Taupo Museum　　　Museum
(☏07-376 0414; www.taupodc.govt.nz; Story Pl; adult/child $5/free; ☺10am-4.30pm) With an excellent Māori gallery and quirky displays, which include a 1960s caravan set up as if the occupants have just popped down to the lake, this little museum makes an interesting rainy-day diversion. The centrepiece is an elaborately carved Māori meeting house, Te Aroha o Rongoheikume. Historical displays cover local industries, a mock-up of a 19th-century shop and a moa skeleton, and there's also a gallery devoted to local and visiting exhibitions. Don't miss the rose garden alongside.

Māori Rock Carvings　　　Carvings
Accessible only by boat, these 10m-high carvings were etched into the cliffs near Mine Bay in the late 1970s by master carver Matahi Whakataka-Brightwell. They depict Ngatoro-i-rangi, the visionary Māori navigator who guided the Tuwharetoa and Te Arawa tribes to the Taupo area a thousand years ago.

✪ ACTIVITIES

Adrenaline addicts should look out for special deals that combine several activities for a reduced price.

Taupo Bungy　　　Adventure Sports
(☏0800 888 408, 07-377 1135; www.taupobungy. co.nz; 202 Spa Rd; solo/tandem jump $169/338; ☺9am-5pm, extended hours summer) On a cliff high above the Waikato River, this picturesque bungy site is the North Island's most popular, with plenty of vantage points for the chickens. The courageous can throw themselves off the edge of a platform, jutting 20m out over the cliff, for a heart-stopping 47m plunge. Tandem leaps are available, as they are for the Cliffhanger giant swing (solo/tandem $119/238).

Craters of the Moon
MTB Park　　　Mountain Biking
(www.biketaupo.org.nz; Craters Rd) For a good selection of exciting off-road mountain-biking options, head to the Craters of the Moon MTB Park, around 10 minutes' drive north of Taupo in the Wairakei Forest. Don't forget to arrange a temporary membership with Bike Taupo before heading up there. See **Bike Barn** (☏07-377 6060; www. bikebarn.co.nz; cnr Horomatangi & Ruapehu Sts; half-/full day $35/50; ☺8.30am-5pm Mon-Fri, 9am-4.30pm Sat & Sun) for bike rental and temporary membership.

Canoe & Kayak　　　Canoeing, Kayaking
(☏0800 529 256, 07-378 1003; www.canoeand kayak.co.nz/taupo; 54 Spa Rd) Instruction and boat hire, as well as guided tours, including a two-hour trip on the Waikato River ($59) or a half-day to the Māori rock carvings for $95.

Rafting NZ Adventure
Centre　　　Adventure Sports
(☏0800 238 3688; www.raftingnewzealand.com; 47 Ruapehu St; ☺8.30am-5pm) With a handy location in central Taupo, this well-run operation can hook you up with everything from rafting on the Tongariro River through to skydiving, jetboating and bungy jumping, and more leisurely pursuits like lake cruises and fishing.

Taupo DeBretts Hot
Springs　　　Hot Spring
(☏07-378 8559; www.taupodebretts.co.nz; 76 Napier Taupo Rd; adult/child $22/11; ☺8.30am-

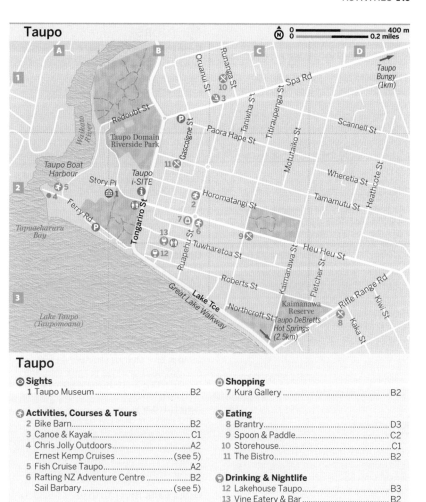

Taupo

◉ Sights
1 Taupo Museum B2

◎ Activities, Courses & Tours
2 Bike Barn.. B2
3 Canoe & Kayak... C1
4 Chris Jolly Outdoors.................................. A2
   Ernest Kemp Cruises .... (see 5)
5 Fish Cruise Taupo...................................... A2
6 Rafting NZ Adventure Centre B2
   Sail Barbary .... (see 5)

⊜ Shopping
7 Kura Gallery B2

⊗ Eating
8 Brantry... D3
9 Spoon & Paddle.. C2
10 Storehouse.. C1
11 The Bistro... B2

⊜ Drinking & Nightlife
12 Lakehouse Taupo....................................... B3
13 Vine Eatery & Bar....................................... B2

9.30pm) ✦ A variety of therapeutic mineral-rich indoor and outdoor thermal pools and freshwater chlorinated pools are on offer. The kids will love the heated dragon slide, two curved racing hydroslides and the interactive 'Warm Water Playground' with a tipping bucket, while the adults can enjoy a great selection of treatments, such as relaxation massages and body treatments.

Hukafalls Jet   Jetboating
(⌨0800 485 253, 07-374 8572; www.hukafallsjet. com; 200 Karetoto Rd; adult/child $115/69) ✦ This 30-minute thrill ride takes you up the river to the spray-filled foot of the Huka Falls and down to the Aratiatia Dam, all the while dodging daringly and doing acrobatic 360-degree turns. Trips run all day (prices include shuttle transport from Taupo).

Resounding Taupo

When Māori chief Tamatea-arikinui first visited this area, his footsteps reverberated, making him think the ground was hollow; he therefore dubbed the area Tapuaeharuru (Resounding Footsteps). The modern name, however, originates from the story of Tia. After Tia discovered the lake and slept beside it draped in his cloak, the area became known as Taupo Nui a Tia (Great Cloak of Tia).

Europeans settled here in force during the East Coast Land War (1868–72), when it was a strategic military base. A redoubt was built in 1869 and a garrison of mounted police remained until the defeat of Te Kooti later that year.

In the 20th century the mass ownership of motorcars saw Taupo grow from a lakeside village of about 750 people to a large resort town, easily accessible from most points on the North Island. Today the population increases considerably at peak holiday times, when New Zealanders and international visitors alike flock to the 'Great Lake'.

Rapids Jet Jetboating
(☑0800 727 437, 07-374 8066; www.rapidsjet. com; Nga Awa Purua Rd; adult/child $105/60; ◷9am-5pm summer, 10am-4pm winter) This sensational 35-minute ride shoots along the lower part of the Aratiatia Rapids – rivalling boat trips to Huka Falls for thrills. The boat departs from the end of the access road to the Aratiatia lookouts. Go down Rapids Rd and then turn into Nga Awa Purua Rd.

Heli Adventure Flights Scenic Flights
(☑0508 435 474, 07-374 8680; www.helicopter tours.co.nz; 415 Huka Falls Rd; flights $99-740) Offers a variety of scenic helicopter flights, from 10 minutes to 1½ hours. Combine a flight with the Hukafalls Jet (p145) in the Helijet combo ($189). Heli-biking and hunting adventures also available.

 TOURS

Ernest Kemp Cruises Boating
(☑07-378 3444; www.ernestkemp.co.nz; Taupo Boat Harbour, Redoubt St; adult/child $40/10; ◷10.30am & 2pm year-round, additional 5pm departure Oct-Apr) Board the *Ernest Kemp* replica steamboat for a two-hour cruise to view the Māori rock carvings, Hot Water Beach, lakefront and Acacia Bay. Lively commentary and complimentary tea and coffee. Book at **Fish Cruise Taupo** (Launch Office; ☑07-378 3444; www.fishcruisetaupo. co.nz; Taupo Boat Harbour, Redoubt St; ◷9am-5pm Oct-Mar, 9.30am-3pm Apr-Sep). A special 90-minute cruise sometimes departs at 12.30pm.

Chris Jolly Outdoors Boating, Fishing
(☑07-378 0623, 0800 252 628; www.chrisjolly. co.nz; Taupo Boat Harbour, Ferry Rd; ◷adult/ child $44/16) Operates the *Cruise Cat,* a large, modern launch that offers fishing trips and daily cruises to the Māori rock carvings (10.30am, 1.30pm and 5pm). Sunday brunch trips (adult/child $62/34) are also worthwhile, as are charters, and guided hiking and mountain-biking trips.

Sail Barbary Boating
(☑07-378 5879; www.sailbarbary.com; Taupo Boat Harbour, Redoubt St; adult/child $44/25; ◷10.30am & 2pm year-round, plus 5pm Dec-Feb) A classic 1926 yacht offering 2½-hour cruises to the Māori rock carvings daily.

Huka Falls River Cruise Boating
(☑0800 278 336; www.hukafallscruise.co.nz; Aratiatia Dam; adult/child $37/15; ◷10.30am, 12.30pm & 2.30pm year-round, plus 4.30pm Dec-Feb) ✱ For a photo-friendly ride, this boat offers a relaxed jaunt (80 minutes) from Aratiatia Dam to Huka Falls.

SHOPPING

Lava Glass Crafts
(☑07-374 8400; www.lavaglass.co.nz; 165 SH5; ◷10am-5pm) More than 500 unique glass sculptures fill the garden and surroundings of this gallery around 10km north of

Taupo on SH5. Glass-blowing displays and an excellent cafe provide great reasons to linger while you're considering what to purchase in the Lava Glass shop. All items can be (very carefully) shipped anywhere in the world.

Kura Gallery   Arts

(☑07-377 4068; www.kura.co.nz; 47a Heu Heu St; ☺10am-4pm) This compact gallery represents more than 70 artists from around New Zealand. Works for sale include weaving, carving, painting and jewellery, and many items are imbued with a Māori or Pasikifa influence.

✖ EATING

L'Arté   Cafe $

(☑07-378 2962; www.larte.co.nz; 255 Mapara Rd, Acacia Bay; snacks $4-9, mains $10-19; ☺8am-4pm Wed-Sun, daily Jan) Lots of mouth-watering treats are made from scratch at this fantastically artful cafe on the hill that backs Acacia Bay. Brunch in the sunshine, then check out the sculpture garden and gallery.

Spoon & Paddle   Cafe $$

(☑07-378 9664; www.facebook.com/spoon andpaddle; 101 Heu Heu St; mains $12-19; ☺8am-4pm) Filling a spacious and airy 1950s house with colourful decor, Spoon & Paddle is more evidence you'll find great cafes pretty well anywhere in NZ. Excellent coffee partners with a concise beer and wine list, and the energetic and youthful owners focus on delivering dishes like tasty lamb shoulder tortillas, and just maybe the country's best eggs Benedict.

Storehouse   Cafe $$

(☑07-378 8820; www.facebook.com/store housenz; 14 Runanga St; shared plates $7-14; ☺7am-4pm Mon-Wed, 7am-10pm Thu-Fri, 8am-10pm Sat, 8am-3.30pm Sun) Hands-down Taupo's coolest eatery, Storehouse does tasty double duty as a cool daytime cafe serving a hipsters' holy trinity of bagels, sliders and coffee, before morphing into a night-time bar with craft beer on tap, cocktails, wine, and shared plates including tacos, empanadas, and garlic and chilli prawns. Leave room for dessert of the

Bungy jumping over the Waikato River (p144)

CHAMP FONSEFF/SHUTTERSTOCK ©

salted caramel and macadamia ice-cream sundae.

The Bistro — Modern NZ $$

(☏07-377 3111; www.thebistro.co.nz; 17 Tamamutu St; mains $24-36; ☻5pm-late) Popular with locals – bookings are recommended – The Bistro focuses on doing the basics very, very well. That means harnessing local seasonal produce for dishes like confit duck with truffle potatoes or crab and pork belly tortellini, and channelling an intimate but unpretentious ambience. A small but perfectly formed beer and wine list makes it a very reliable choice.

Brantry — Modern NZ $$$

(☏07-378 0484; www.thebrantry.co.nz; 45 Rifle Range Rd; 2-/3-course set menu $45/55; ☻from 5.30pm Tue-Sat) Operating out of an unobtrusive 1950s house, the Brantry continues its reign as one of the best in the region for its well-executed, good-value offerings centred on meaty mains turned out in classical style. Book-ending with entrée and dessert is highly recommended.

🍷 DRINKING & NIGHTLIFE

Lakehouse Taupo — Craft Beer

(☏07-377 1545; www.lakehousetaupo.co.nz; 10 Roberts St; ☻7.30am-midnight) Craft beer central is the Lakehouse with a fridge full of interesting bottled offerings and five taps serving a rotating selection of brews from around New Zealand. Order a tasting box of four beers ($15), partner them with a pizza or stone-grilled steak, and sit outside for lake views – and, if the clouds lift – glimpses of the mountains.

Vine Eatery & Bar — Wine Bar

(☏07-378 5704; www.vineeatery.co.nz; 37 Tuwharetoa St; ☻11am-late) The clue's in the name at this wine bar sharing its barn-like home with the Scenic Cellars wine store. Share traditional tapas ($9 to $18) alongside larger divisible dishes (mains $32 to $35), accompanied by your choice of an expansive array of wines at keen prices. This is Taupo's best bet for a sophisticated nibble and natter among the town's well-heeled.

Skiing at Mt Ruapehu

ℹ️ INFORMATION

Taupo i-SITE (☎07-376 0027, 0800 525 382; www.greatlaketaupo.com; Tongariro St; ⏰8.30am-5pm) Handles bookings for accommodation, transport and activities; dispenses cheerful advice; and stocks Department of Conservation (DOC) maps and town maps.

ℹ️ GETTING THERE & AWAY

Taupo Airport (☎07-378 7771; www.taupoair port.co.nz; Anzac Memorial Dr) is 8km south of town. **Air New Zealand** (☎0800 737 000; www.airnz.co.nz) links Taupo to Auckland and **Sounds Air** (☎0800 505 005; www.soundsair. com) flies to/from Wellington.

InterCity (☎07-348 0366; www.intercity coach.co.nz), **Mana Bus** (www.manabus.com) and **Naked Bus** (www.nakedbus.com) services stop outside the Taupo i-SITE, where bookings can also be made. Destinations include Auckland, Hamilton and Rotorua.

Shuttle services operate year-round to Tongariro National Park. Ask at the Taupo i-SITE.

ℹ️ GETTING AROUND

Local Connector buses are run by **Busit!** (☎0800 4287 5463; www.busit.co.nz); the Taupo North service runs as far as Huka Falls and Wairakei.

Ohakune

A pretty retreat in summer, Ohakune offers many outdoor adventures, including the excellent Old Coach Road mountain-bike trail and easy access to the Whanganui National Park to the south. Ohakune gets even busier in winter when the snow drifts down on Turoa Ski Area and the snow bunnies invade.

 Mountain Biking the Old Coach Road

The **Ohakune Old Coach Road** (www. ohakunecoachroad.co.nz) is a fantastic adventure for moderately fit cyclists, with local operators offering everything to make things easy.

One of NZ's most enjoyable half-day (three to four hours) cycle rides, the gently graded route passes a number of unique engineering features, including the historic Hapuawhenua and Toanui viaducts – the only two remaining curved viaducts in the southern hemisphere. It also passes through ancient forest of giant rimu and totara that survived the massive Taupo volcanic blast of AD 180, being in the lea of Ruapehu. Views extend over the odd-shaped hillocks and mesa around the foot of the volcano.

Cyclists are best to start at Horopito (where you can check out the car-graveyard known as 'Smash Palace'), as this gives you more downhill, overall. The odd push uphill may well be required, but you'll get sufficient in-the-saddle time to justify the effort – especially on some of the sweeping downhills underlaid with historic cobblestones. This is wobbly, freewheeling fun for the whole family.

For bike hire and shuttles, visit **TCB** (☎06-385 8433; www.tcbskiandboard.co.nz; 29 Ayr St) and **Mountain Bike Station** (p150) in Ohakune, or **Kiwi Mountain Bikes** (☎0800 562 4537, 07-892 2911; www. kiwimountainbikes.com; Macrocarpa Cafe, 3 Waimarino–Tokaanu Rd) and **My Kiwi Adventure** (☎021 784 202, 0800 784 202; www.mykiwiadventure.co.nz; 15 Findlay St; paddle boarding $50, mountain biking $45-95) in National Park Village.

Carrot Capital

Expect to see carrots crop up all over Ohakune, for this is indisputably the country's carrot capital. Carrots were first grown in the area during the 1920s by Chinese settlers, who cleared the land by hand and explosives. Today the venerable vegetable is celebrated during the annual **Carrot Carnival** (www.carrotcarnival.org.nz; ⊙early Jun), and immortalised in a roadside tribute – the impossible-to-miss Big Carrot. Erected in 1984, it quickly became one of NZ's most hugged 'Big Things'.

 ACTIVITIES

Mountain Bike Station
Mountain Biking
(☑06-385 8797; www.mountainbikestation. co.nz; 60 Thames St) Rents mountain bikes (half-/full day from $35/50) and provides transfers to biking routes, including the Ohakune Old Coach Road for $20; bike and transport packages are available. It can also arrange transfers and rentals for the Bridge to Nowhere and Mangapurua tracks on the Whanganui River, and the 17km Turoa Downhill Madness ride down the Mt Ruapehu ski-field access road.

Ruapehu Homestead
Horse Riding
(☑027 267 7057; www.ruapehuhomestead.co.nz; cnr Piwara St & SH49, Rangataua; 30min-3hr adult $30-120, child $15-90) Four kilometres east of Ohakune (near Rangataua), Ruapehu Homestead offers guided treks around its paddocks, as well as longer rides along the river and on backcountry trails with views of the mountain.

Waitonga Falls Track
Hiking
The path to Waitonga Falls (1½ hours return, 4km), Tongariro's highest waterfall (39m), offers magnificent views of Mt Ruapehu. The track starts from Ohakune Mountain Rd.

 EATING

Eat
Cafe $
(☑027 443 1426; 49 Clyde St; snacks & mains $9-14; ⊙9am-4pm) Bagels, innovative salads, and tasty American and Tex Mex–influenced dishes combine with the best coffee in town at this modern spot on Ohakune's main drag. There's a strong focus on organic ingredients and sustainable practices, and dishes like the breakfast burrito or the chicken tacos with carrot and cumin slaw really hit the spot after a busy day's adventuring.

Cyprus Tree
Italian $$
(☑06-385 8857; www.cyprustree.co.nz; cnr Clyde & Miro Sts; mains $16-34; ⊙9am-late) Open year-round, this restaurant and bar serves up Italian and Kiwi-influenced dishes; think pizza, pasta, risotto and sumac-spiced lamb. The high-season chaos is tempered by a friendly team, and we're pleased to see Ohakune's best range of NZ craft beers join the comprehensive drinks menu, which also features cocktails and wine. Bar snacks are served from 3pm to 5pm.

OCR
Cafe $$
(☑06-385 8322; www.ocrcafe.co.nz; 2 Tyne St; mains $10-29; ⊙9am-late Fri & Sat, 9am-3pm Sun, daily in ski season) Housed in an old bungalow, this groovy cafe has limited opening hours but remains a favourite among locals and visitors. Burgers, sandwiches, salads and breakfasts are made with care, as are the home-baked cakes and slices. A rootsy soundtrack and wood burner lend a rustic vibe. Ask if they have Scoria Red IPA craft beer from Ohakune-based Little Thief Brewing.

Powderkeg
Bar, Restaurant $$
(☑06-385 8888; www.powderhorn.co.nz; cnr Thames St & Mangawhero Tce; bar menu $11-22, mains $22-42; ⊙4pm-late) The Powderkeg is the party bar of the Powderhorn Chateau, with DJs in winter and occasional dancing on the tables. Food-wise, it's also no slouch year-round with top-notch burgers and pizza, meaty mains such as lamb rump,

Wairakei Terraces & Thermal Health Spa (p140)

and another good selection of NZ craft beers that are just the thing after negotiating the Old Coach Road on two wheels.

🛈 INFORMATION

Ruapehu i-SITE (☏06-385 8427; www.visit ruapehu.com; 54 Clyde St; ⊗8am-5.30pm) Can make bookings for activities, transport and accommodation; DOC officers are usually on hand from 10am to 4.30pm most days.

🛈 GETTING THERE & AWAY

BUS

Passing through Ohakune are buses linking to Auckland and Wellington.

TRAIN

Travelling between Auckland and Wellington, the *Northern Explorer* train run by **KiwiRail Scenic** (☏04-495 0775, 0800 872 467; www.kiwirail scenic.co.nz) stops at both Ohakune and nearby National Park Village.

🛈 GETTING AROUND

Based in Ohakune, **Ruapehu Connexions** (☏021 045 6665, 06-385 3122; www.ruapehuconnex ions.co.nz) provides shuttle services around the Ruapehu region, including to biking and walking tracks and the Tongariro Alpine Crossing.

WELLINGTON

Wellington at a glance...

A small city with a big reputation, Wellington is famous for being NZ's constitutional and cultural capital: it is infamous for its weather, particularly the gale-force winds that barrel through. Gorgeous Victorian architecture laces the hillsides above the harbour. There are hill-top lookouts, waterfront promenades and craggy shorelines to the south. Downtown, the compact CBD vibrates with museums, theatres and boutiques, all fuelled by kickin' caffeine and craft beer scenes.

Wellington in two days

After breakfast at **Nikau Cafe** (p167), wander along to **Te Papa** (p156). A day exploring NZ's national museum will be a day well spent. Kick on for a hoppy discovery of Wellington's brilliant **craft beer scene** (p158). The following day, take the **Wellington Cable Car** (p162) for harbour views before shopping along bohemian Cuba St and dinner at the **Ortega Fish Shack** (p167).

Wellington in four days

Start with brunch at **Loretta** (p167) then head to Miramar to experience the movie-making magic of blockbusters like *The Hobbit* and *Avatar* at the **Weta Cave** (p164). Return to the city to fast-track your knowledge of Kiwi cinema and culture at **Ngā Taonga Sound & Vision** (p164). Finish with live theatre at **BATS** (p169) or the **Circa Theatre** (p169) before late-night cocktails at the **Hawthorn Lounge** (p168).

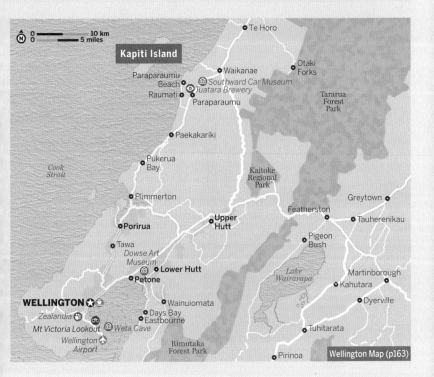

Arriving in Wellington

Wellington International Airport
Located 8km southeast of the city with
regular flights to/from Auckland, Taupo,
Nelson, Christchurch and Queenstown.
Also to/from Australia including Sydney
and Melbourne.

Waterloo Quay & Aotea Quay Regular
ferries across Cook Strait to Picton.

Wellington Railway Station Terminus
for the *Northern Explorer* service linking
Auckland and Wellington via Tongariro
National Park. InterCity buses also
depart from here.

Where to Stay

Accommodation in Wellington is more
expensive than in regional areas, but
there are plenty of options close to
the city centre. Parking spots are a
rarity – ask in advance about options.
Self-contained apartments are popular,
and often offer bargain weekend rates.
Book your bed well in advance in peak
season (December to February) and
during major events.

JIRI FOLTYN/SHUTTERSTOCK ©

Te Papa

With a harbourfront location and a spectacular architectural profile, New Zealand's national museum is an essential destination to understand the past, present and future of this diverse and ever-evolving country.

Great For...

☑ Don't Miss

The hyper realistic – and massive – figures of Gallipoli soldiers crafted by Weta Workshop.

Wellington's 'must-see' attraction is Te Papa for reasons well beyond the fact that it's NZ's national museum. It's highly interactive, fun and full of surprises: aptly, 'Te Papa Tongarewa' loosely translates as 'treasure box.' The riches inside include an amazing collection of Māori artefacts and the museum's own colourful marae; natural history and environment exhibitions; Pacific and NZ history galleries; the National Art Collection; and themed hands-on 'discovery centres' for children. Big-name temporary exhibitions incur an admission fee, though general admission is free.

You could spend a day exploring Te Papa's six floors and still not see it all. To cut to the chase, head to the information desk on level two and collect a map. For exhibition highlights and to get your bear-

ℹ Need to Know

📞 04-381 7000; www.tepapa.govt.nz; 55 Cable St; ⊙10am-6pm; 👶 ♿ **FREE**

✕ Take a Break

Gelato and sorbet, often laced with NZ fruit, stars at **Gelissimo Gelato** (📞04-385 9313; www.gelissimo.co.nz; 11 Cable St, Taranaki Wharf; gelato 1/2/3 flavours $4.50/6/7.50; ⊙8am-5.30pm Mon-Fri, 10.30am-5.30pm Sat & Sun).

★ Top Tip

Check the Te Papa website for special events, including curator presentations and one-off shows and events.

ings, the one-hour 'Introducing Te Papa' tour (adult/child $15/7) is a good idea; tours leave from the info desk at 10.15am, noon and 2pm daily, plus 7pm on Thursday. The 'Māori Highlights' tours ($20/10) run at 2pm daily. Two cafes and two gift shops complete the Te Papa experience, which could well consume a couple of rainy-day visits. The museum's current star attraction is the state-of-the-art exhibition 'Gallipoli: The Scale of Our War', charting the country's involvement in WWI's Gallipoli campaign through the experiences of eight ordinary New Zealanders. It runs until 2018.

What's Nearby

From Te Papa, there's a pleasant waterfront walkway passing the Te Raukura whare waka, housing a spectacular Māori canoe, and public art including the graceful Albatross Fountain. As you're walking, keep an eye out for Wellington Writers Walk (www.wellingtonwriterswalk.co.nz) plaques and typographical sculptures commemorating NZ authors including Katherine Mansfield, performance poet Sam Hunt and James K Baxter.

Wellington Museum Museum

(📞04-472 8904; www.museumswellington.org.nz; Bond Store, Queens Wharf; ⊙10am-5pm; 👶) **FREE**. Occupying an 1892 Bond Store, the museum offers an imaginative and interactive showcase of the city's social and maritime history. Highlights include a moving documentary on the *Wahine*, the interisland ferry that sank in the harbour in 1968 with the loss of 51 lives. Māori legends are dramatically told using tiny holographic actors and special effects. The new 'Attic' exhibition space opened in 2015.

Interior of Garage Project

MICHAEL VALLI/GARAGE PROJECT ©

Wellington Craft Beer

Fuelled by a mix of musos, web developers and filmmakers, Wellington features the best beer scene in the southern hemisphere. It's also a compact scene, best explored on foot.

Great For...

☑ Don't Miss

Garage Project's Death from Above Pale Ale – brewed with Vietnamese mint, mango and chilli.

Bars

Little Beer Quarter   Craft Beer

(LBQ; ☎04-803 3304; www.littlebeerquarter. co.nz; 6 Edward St; ⊙3.30pm-late Mon, noon-late Tue-Sat, 3pm-late Sun) Buried in a back lane, lovely LBQ is warm, inviting and moodily lit in all the right places. Well-curated taps and a broad selection of bottled beer pack a hop-ish punch. Good cocktails, wines, and whiskies, too, plus zesty bar food. Pizza-and-a-pint for $20 on Monday nights; Mark Knopfler on the stereo (never a bad thing).

Golding's Free Dive   Craft Beer

(☎04-381 3616; www.goldingsfreedive.co.nz; 14 Leeds St; ⊙noon-11pm; 🛜) Hidden down a busy little back alley near Cuba St, gloriously garish Golding's is a bijou craft-beer bar with far too many merits to mention. We'll single out ex-casino swivel chairs, a

Garage Project beers on tap

MICHAEL VALLY/GARAGE PROJECT ©

Microbreweries

Fork & Brewer
Craft Beer

(F&B; ☏04-472 0033; www.forkandbrewer.co.nz; 14 Bond St; ⊙11.30am-late Mon-Sat) Aiming to improve on the 'kebab at 2am' experience, F&B offers excellent burgers, pizzas, pies, share plates and meaty mains to go along with their crafty brews (of which there are dozens – the Low Blow IPA comes highly recommended). Oh, and dark-beer dough-nuts for dessert!

Garage Project
Brewery

(☏04-384 3076; www.garageproject.co.nz; 68 Aro St, Aro Valley; ⊙noon-6pm Mon, noon-8pm Tue-Thu, 10am-9pm Fri & Sat, 10am-7pm Sun) Put yourself in the pitcher at Garage Project microbrewery in bohemian Aro Valley, where you can buy craft beer by the litre, petrol-pump style. Try the Vesuvian Pale Ale or chance your arm on the Pernicious Weed. Free tastings. They've also opened a great GP bar across the road at 91 Aro St (closed Mondays).

Festivals

Beervana
Beer

(www.beervana.co.nz; ⊙Aug) A barrel-load of craft-beer aficionados roll into town for a weekend of supping and beard-stroking. Join them at Westpac Stadium on the path to enlightened Beervana.

nice wine list, a ravishing Reuben sandwich, and pizza from Pomodoro next door. Blues, Zappa and Bowie conspire across the airways.

Hashigo Zake
Craft Beer

(☏04-384 7300; www.hashigozake.co.nz; 25 Taranaki St; ⊙noon-late; 🛜) This bricky bunker is the HQ for a zealous beer-im-port business, splicing big-flavoured international brews into a smartly selected NZ range. Hop-heads stand elbow-to-elbow around the bar, ogling the oft-changing taps and brimming fridges, and squeeze into the sweet little side-lounge on live-mu-sic nights (Saturdays from 9.30pm). Neil Young rules.

New Zealand bellbird feeding on flax flowers

NICOLA M MORA/DESIGN PICS/GETTY IMAGES ©

Kapiti Island

An easy day trip from Wellington, Kapiti Island is a fascinating sanctuary for bird life, and if you're into craft beer or cars (or both), nearby Paraparaumu is also a worthy destination.

Great For...

☑ **Don't Miss**

Spying bird species, including red-fronted parakeets, the North Island robin and bellbirds.

A 10km by 2km slice that has been a protected reserve since 1897, Kapiti Island is the dominant feature of the North Island's west coast north of Wellington. Largely predator-free, it's now home to a remarkable range of birds, including many species that are endangered or extinct on the mainland.

To visit the island, you must make your arrangements in advance with one of three licensed operators. All boats depart from Paraparaumu, 59km north of Wellington, and reached by train from the city.

The island is open to day walkers, limited daily to 100 at Rangatira, where you can hike up to the 521m high point, Tuteremo-ana; and 60 visitors at the northern end, which has short, gentle walks to viewpoints and around a lagoon.

Unless you've booked an overnight tour and accommodation the island is for

Transport to and from Kapiti Island; fares include DOC landing permit.

day-trippers only.

More information can be found in DOC's *Kapiti Island Nature Reserve* brochure (downloadable from www.doc.govt.nz),

Tours

Kapiti Island Nature Tours Tour

(☑06-362 6606, 021 126 7525; www.kapitiisland naturetours.co.nz; transport per person $75, day tours $165) Tours look at the island's birds (incredible in range and number), seal colony, history and Māori traditions. Overnight stays include an after-dark walk in the bush to spot the cutest-ever bird, the rare little spotted kiwi (tour plus meals and camping/cabins $335/405).

Kapiti Marine Charter Boating

(☑027 655 4739, 0800 433 779; www.kapiti marinecharter.co.nz; adult/child from $75/40)

Kapiti Tours Boating

(☑04-237 7965, 0800 527 484; www.kapititours. co.nz; adult/child $75/40, with guided tour $95/50) Transport to and from Kapiti Island; fares include DOC landing permit. Guided tours available.

What's Nearby

The hangar-like **Southward Car Museum** (☑04-297 1221; www.southwardcarmuseum. co.nz; off Otaihanga Rd; adult/child $17/3; ☺9am-4.30pm; 🖼) has one of Australasia's largest collections of antique and unusual cars. It's a few kilometres north of the main Paraparaumu shops. While you're in the area, pop in to the **Tuatara Brewery** (☑04-296 1953; www.tuatarabrewing.co.nz; 7 Sheffield St; ☺3-7pm Wed & Thu, noon-7pm Fri-Sun, tours 1.15pm & 3.15pm Sat), one of the pioneers of Wellington's craft beer scene. Our favourite beer is the zingy Sauvinova Pale Ale.

Wellington

With a compact CBD, Wellington is easily explored by walking, and it's easy to spend a few days perusing the city's excellent museums and galleries, shopping at hip and interesting boutiques, and then joining the locals in their love of eating and drinking in the evening.

⊙ SIGHTS

Wellington is an arty kinda town – expect quality gallery experiences and some fab museums. There are also some great wilderness-in-the city experiences to be had here, some interesting old buildings and a couple of awesome lookouts from which to look out.

Wellington Cable Car   Cable Car

(☑04-472 2199; www.wellingtoncablecar.co.nz; Cable Car Lane, rear 280 Lambton Quay; adult/child one way $4/2, return $7.50/3.50; ⊙departs every 10min, 7am-10pm Mon-Fri, 8.30am-10pm Sat, 9am-9pm Sun; ⊛) One of Wellington's big-ticket attractions is the little red cable car that clanks up the steep slope from Lambton Quay to Kelburn. At the top are the Wellington Botanic Gardens (p164), the **Carter Observatory** (Space Place; ☑04-910 3140; www.carterobservatory.org; 40 Salamanca Rd, Kelburn; adult/child/family $12.50/8/39; ⊙4-11pm Tue & Thu, 10am-11pm Sat, 10am-5.30pm Sun) and the small-but-nifty **Cable Car Museum** (☑04-475 3578; www.museumswellington.org.nz; Upland St, Kelburn; ⊙9.30am-5pm) **FREE**. The latter evocatively depicts the cable car's story since it was built in 1902 to open up hilly Kelburn for settlement. Ride the cable car back down the hill, or wander down through the gardens.

City Gallery Wellington   Gallery

(☑04-913 9032; www.citygallery.org.nz; Civic Sq, Wakefield St; ⊙10am-5pm) **FREE** Housed in the monumental old library in Civic Sq, Wellington's much-loved City Gallery does a cracking job of securing acclaimed contemporary international exhibitions, as well

as unearthing up-and-comers and supporting those at the forefront of the NZ scene. Charges may apply for major exhibits; the Nikau Cafe (p167) compensates.

Dowse Art Museum   Gallery

(☑04-570 6500; www.dowse.org.nz; 45 Laings Rd, Lower Hutt; ⊙10am-5pm; ⊛) **FREE** A beacon of culture and delight, the excellent Dowse is worth visiting for its jaunty architecture alone. It's a family-friendly, accessible art museum showcasing NZ art, craft and design, with a nice cafe to boot (and a winter ice rink!). It's a 15-minute drive or a short ride on bus 83 from central Wellington.

Mt Victoria Lookout   Viewpoint

(Lookout Rd) The city's most accessible view point is atop 196m-high Mt Victoria, east of the city centre. You can take the No 20 bus most of the way up, but the rite of passage is to sweat it out on the walk (ask a local for directions or just follow your nose). If you've got wheels, take Oriental Pde along the waterfront and then scoot up Carlton Gore Rd. Awesome views and actually rather interesting info panels.

Beehive   Architecture

(☑04-817 9503; www.parliament.nz; Molesworth St; ⊙10am-4pm) **FREE** Office workers swarm around the distinctive modernist Beehive (1980), which is exactly what it looks like, and which forms part of NZ's parliamentary complex. It was designed by British architect Sir Basil Spence. Controversy dogged its construction and, love it or loathe it, it's the architectural symbol of the country. Tours – (including the adjacent **Parliament House** (☑04-817 9503; www.parliament.nz; Molesworth St; ⊙10am-4pm) **FREE**) – depart from the foyer on the hour from 10am to 4pm – arrive 15 minutes early.

Zealandia   Wildlife Reserve

(☑04 920 9213; www.visitzealandia.com; 53 Waiapu Rd, Karori; adult/child/family exhibition only $9/5/21, exhibition & admission $18.50/10/46; ⊙9am-5pm, last entry 4pm) This groundbreaking eco-sanctuary is hidden in the hills about 2km west of town: the Karori

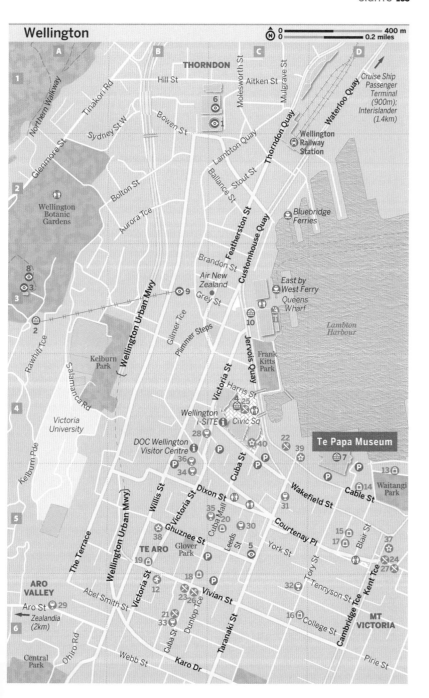

Wellington

0 — 400 m
0 — 0.2 miles

THORNDON

Hill St
Aitken St
Molesworth St
Mulgrave St

Waterloo Quay

Cruise Ship
Passenger
Terminal
(900m);
Interislander
(1.4km)

Tinakori Rd
Northern Walkway
Sydney St W
Bowen St
Lambton Quay
Glenmore St

6
1

Thorndon Quay

**Wellington
Railway
Station**

Bolton St
Ballance St
Stout St
Featherston St
Aurora Tce

**Wellington
Botanic
Gardens**

Bluebridge
Ferries

8
3

Brandon St
Air New
Zealand
Grey St
Customhouse Quay

East by
West Ferry
Queens
Wharf

9

*Lambton
Harbour*

2

Wellington Urban Mwy
Gilmer Tce
Plimmer Steps

10

Kelburn
Park

Jervois Quay

Harris St
Frank
Kitts
Park

Rawhiti Tce
Salamanca Rd

Victoria St

4 25

**Wellington
i-SITE** Civic Sq

**Victoria
University**

Kelburn Pde

**DOC Wellington
Visitor Centre**

28

**22
39**

Te Papa Museum

40

**36
34**

7

Cuba St

13

14   Waitangi
Park

Dixon St
Willis St
Victoria St

35
20
30

Wakefield St

Cable St

The Terrace

Cuba Mall
Leeds St

Courtenay Pl

31

**15
17**   Blair St

37

38

Ghuznee St
TE ARO
Glover
Park

5

York St

19

Wellington Urban Mwy
Victoria St

18

12

Vivian St

23 26

Tory St
Tennyson St

**24
27**

32

Cambridge Tce
Kent Tce

**ARO
VALLEY**

Abel Smith St

**21
33**

Dunlop Tce

Taranaki St

16   College St

**MT
VICTORIA**

Aro St **29**
*Zealandia
(2km)*

Cuba St

Ohiro Rd

Webb St

*Central
Park*

Karo Dr

Pirie St

Wellington

Sights

1 Beehive ... C1
2 Cable Car Museum ... A3
3 Carter Observatory ... A3
4 City Gallery Wellington ... C4
5 Ngā Taonga Sound & Vision ... C5
6 Parliament House ... C1
7 Te Papa ... D4
8 Wellington Botanic Gardens ... A3
9 Wellington Cable Car ... B3
10 Wellington Museum ... C3

Activities, Courses & Tours

11 Ferg's Kayaks ... C3
12 On Yer Bike ... B6

Shopping

13 City Market ... D5
14 Harbourside Market ... D5
15 Kura ... D5
16 Moore Wilson Fresh ... C6
17 Ora Gallery ... D5
18 Slow Boat Records ... B6
19 Victoria Street Farmers Market ... B5
20 Wellington Night Market ... C5

Eating

21 Fidel's ... B6
22 Gelissimo Gelato ... C4
23 Logan Brown ... B6
Loretta ... (see 18)
24 Mt Vic Chippery ... D5
25 Nikau Cafe ... C4
26 Ombra ... B6
27 Ortega Fish Shack ... D5

Drinking & Nightlife

28 Fork & Brewer ... B4
29 Garage Project ... A6
30 Golding's Free Dive ... C5
31 Hashigo Zake ... C5
32 Hawthorn Lounge ... C6
33 Laundry ... B6
34 Little Beer Quarter ... B5
35 Matterhorn ... C5
36 Thief ... B4

Entertainment

37 BATS ... D5
38 Bodega ... B5
39 Circa Theatre ... C4
40 Michael Fowler Centre ... C4
San Fran ... (see 18)

bus (No 3) passes nearby, or see the website for info on the free shuttle. Living wild within the fenced valley are more than 30 native bird species, including rare takahe, saddleback, hihi and kaka, as well as tuatara and little spotted kiwi. An excellent exhibition relays NZ's natural history and world-renowned conservation story.

More than 30km of tracks can be explored independently, or on regular guided tours. The night tour provides an opportunity to spot nocturnal creatures including kiwi, frogs and glowworms (adult/child $75/36). Cafe and shop on-site.

Wellington Botanic Gardens — Gardens

(☎04-499 4444; www.wellington.govt.nz; 101 Glenmore St, Thorndon; ⏲daylight hours) FREE These hilly, 25-hectare botanic gardens can be *almost* effortlessly visited via the Wellington Cable Car (p162; nice bit of planning, eh?), although there are several other entrances hidden in the hillsides. The gardens boast a tract of original native forest, the beaut Lady Norwood Rose Garden, 25,000 spring tulips and various international plant collections. Add in fountains, a playground, sculptures, a duck pond, a cafe and city skyline views, and you've got a grand day out indeed.

Ngā Taonga Sound & Vision — Cinema

(☎04-384 7647; www.ngataonga.org.nz; cnr Taranaki & Ghuznee Sts; screenings from $8; ⏲library noon-5pm Tue-Fri) FREE Ngā Taonga is a vortex of NZ moving images, into which you could get sucked for days. Its library holds more than 30,000 titles: feature films, documentaries, short films, home movies, newsreels, TV programs, advertisements... There are regular screenings in the cinema (check the website for the schedule), and a viewing library (free) where you can watch films until you're square-eyed.

Weta Cave — Museum

(☎04-909 4100; www.wetanz.com; cnr Camperdown Rd & Weka St, Miramar; admission & tour adult/child $25/12, with return transport $65/40; ☺9am-5.30pm) **FREE** Film buffs will dig the Weta Cave, a mind-blowing mini-museum of the Academy Award–winning special-effects company that brought *The Lord of the Rings, King Kong, The Adventures of Tintin* and *The Hobbit* to life. Learn how they do it on 45-minute guided tours, starting every half-hour. Weta Cave is 9km east of the city centre: drive, ride your bike, catch the Miramar bus (No 2) or book transport with your admission. Book online.

🜚 ACTIVITIES

Ferg's
Kayaks   Kayaking, Bicycle Rental
(🖉04-499 8898; www.fergskayaks.co.nz; Shed 6, Queens Wharf; ☺10am-8pm Mon-Fri, 9am-6pm Sat & Sun) Stretch your tendons with indoor rock climbing (adult/child $15/10), cruise the waterfront wearing in-line skates ($20 for two hours) or go for a paddle in a kayak or on a stand-up paddle board (from $20 for one hour). There's also bike hire (one hour from $20) and guided kayaking trips.

Te Wharewaka o Pōneke
Waka Tours   Boating
(🖉04-901 3333; www.wharewakaoponeke. co.nz; tours per person from $45) Get set for (and maybe a little bit wet on) a two-hour paddle tour in a Māori *waka* (canoe) around Wellington's waterfront, with lots of cultural insights along the way. Call for the latest tour times and bookings – minimum numbers apply. Walking tours also available ($35 per person).

🜚 TOURS

Kiwi Coastal Tours   Driving
(🖉027 252 0099, 021 464 957; www.kiwi coastaltours.co.nz; 3/5hr tours $150/250) Excellent 4WD exploration of the rugged south coast in the company of a local Māori guide with plenty of stories to tell.

Flat Earth   Tour
(🖉04-472 9635, 0800 775 805; www.flatearth. co.nz; half-/full-day tours $175/385) An array

of themed small-group guided tours: city highlights, Māori treasures, arts, wilderness and Middle-earth filming locations. Martinborough wine tours also available.

Walk Wellington   Walking
(🖉04-473 3145; www.walkwellington.org. nz; adult/child $20/10) Informative and great-value two-hour walking tours focusing on the city and waterfront, departing from the i-SITE. Book online, by phone or just turn up. Tours 10am daily, plus 5.30pm Monday, Wednesday and Friday December to February.

Wellington Movie Tours   Tour
(🖉027 419 3077; www.adventuresafari.co.nz; adult/child tours from $45/30) Half- and full-day tours with more props, clips, and Middle-earth film locations than you can shake a staff at.

Zest Food Tours   Food
(🖉04-801 9198; www.zestfoodtours.co.nz; tours from $179) Runs three- to 5½-hour small-group foodie tours around the city, plus day tours over the hills into Wairarapa Wine Country.

🜚 SHOPPING

Kura   Arts
(🖉04-802 4934; www.kuragallery.co.nz; 19 Allen St; ☺10am-6pm Mon-Fri, 11am-4pm Sat & Sun) Contemporary indigenous art: painting, ceramics, jewellery and sculpture. A gorgeous gallery – come for a look even if you're not buying.

Ora Gallery   Arts
(🖉04-384 4157; 23 Allen St; ☺9am-6pm Mon-Fri, to 5pm Sat, 10am-4pm Sun) Fresh, bold, bright contemporary art including sculpture, weaving, glass and jewellery: gifts for someone who's waiting for you back home. You can get a coffee here too.

Slow Boat Records   Music
(🖉04-385 1330; www.slowboatrecords.co.nz; 183 Cuba St; ☺9.30am-5.30pm Mon-Thu, to 7.30pm Fri, 10am-5pm Sat & Sun) Country, folk, pop, indie, metal, blues, soul, rock,

Hawaiian nose-flute music – it's all here at Slow Boat, Wellington's long-running music shop and Cuba St mainstay. Time to stock up on some NZ sounds maybe.

Moore Wilson Fresh   Food & Drink
(☑04-384 9906; www.moorewilsons.co.nz; 93 Tory St; ☺7.30am-7pm Mon-Fri, to 6pm Sat, 9am-6pm Sun) A call-out to self-caterers: this positively swoon-inducing grocer is one of NZ's most committed supporters of independently produced and artisanal produce. If you want to chew on the best of Wellington and NZ, here's your chance. Wine, beer and cooking demonstrations too.

✖ EATING

Three excellent inner-city food markets run from dawn till around 2pm on Sunday: the seriously fruit-and-veg **farmers market** (cnr Victoria & Vivian Sts; ☺6.30am-2.30pm Sun) and, next to Te Papa, the varied **Harbourside Market** (☑04-495 7895; www. harboursidemarket.co.nz; cnr Cable & Barnett Sts; ☺7.30am-2pm Sun) and artisanal **City**

Market (☑04-801 8158; www.citymarket.co.nz; Chaffers Dock Bldg, 1 Herd St; ☺8.30am-12.30pm Sun).

Fidel's   Cafe $
(☑04-801 6868; www.fidelscafe.com; 234 Cuba St; mains $10-24; ☺7.30am-late Mon-Fri, 8am-late Sat, 9am-late Sun; ☑) A Cuba St institution for caffeine-craving alternative types. Eggs any which way, pizza and super salads are cranked out of the itsy kitchen, along with Welly's best milkshakes. Revolutionary memorabilia adorns the walls of the deeply funky interior; there are chipper outdoor areas, too. A superbusy crew copes with the chaos admirably. Street-facing booth for takeaway coffees.

Mt Vic Chippery   Fish & Chips $
(☑04-382 8713; www.mtvicchippery.co.nz; 5 Majoribanks St; meals $8-16; ☺noon-8.45pm; ☑) At this backwater fish shack it's fish and chips by numbers: 1. Choose your fish (from at least three varieties). 2. Select your coating (beer batter, panko crumb, tempura...). 3. Choose your chips (five varieties!). 4. Add

One of Wellington's historic buildings – Wellington Harbour Board office aioli, coleslaw, salad or sauce, and a quality soft drink. 5. Chow down inside or takeaway. Burgers and battered sausages will placate the pescaphobes.

Loretta   Modern NZ $$

(☑04-384 2213; www.loretta.net.nz; 181 Cuba St; mains $10-28; ☺7am-10pm Tue-Fri, 8am-10pm Sat, 8am-9pm Sun) From breakfast (waffles, crumpets, granola) through lunch (sandwiches, fritters, soup) and into dinner (pizzas, pastas, big salads), Loretta has been winning leagues of fans with her classy, well-proportioned offerings. Is this Wellington's ultimate risotto? Bright, airy and good-humoured. Bookings for lunch only.

Nikau Cafe   Cafe $$

(☑04-801 4168; www.nikaucafe.co.nz; City Gallery, Civic Sq; mains $15-27; ☺7am-4pm Mon-Fri, 8am-4pm Sat; ☑) An airy affair at the sophisticated end of Wellington's cafe spectrum, Nikau consistently dishes up simple but sublime stuff (pan-fried halloumi, sage eggs, legendary kedgeree). Refreshing aperitifs, divine sweets and a sunny courtyard complete the package. The organic, seasonal menu changes daily. Good one!

Ombra   Italian $$

(☑04-385 3229; www.ombra.co.nz; 199 Cuba St; snacks $5-14, mains $12-19; ☺10am-late Mon-Fri, 8am-late Sat & Sun; ☑) This Venetian-style *bacaro* (taverna) dishes up mouth-watering Italian fare in warm, uptempo surrounds. Assess the on-trend distressed interior while sipping an aperitif, then share tasty morsels like *arancino* (fried risotto ball), *pizzette* (mini-pizza) and vegetarian gnocchi. Round things off with a sumptuous tiramisu or a basil and blueberry panna cotta. *Delizioso!*

Ortega Fish Shack   Seafood $$$

(☑04-382 9559; www.ortega.co.nz; 16 Majoribanks St; mains $34-39; ☺5.30pm-late Tue-Sat) Mounted trout, salty portraits, marine-blue walls and Egyptian floor tiles

Welcome to Wellywood

In recent years Wellington has stamped its name firmly on the world map as the home of New Zealand's dynamic film industry, earning itself the nickname 'Wellywood'. Acclaimed director Peter Jackson still calls Wellington home; the success of his *The Lord of the Rings* films and subsequent productions such as *King Kong, The Adventures of Tintin* and *The Hobbit* have made him a powerful Hollywood player, and have bolstered Wellington's reputation.

Canadian director James Cameron is also in on the action; preproduction is under way for his three *Avatar* sequels to be shot in NZ. Cameron and his family are NZ residents, with landholding in rural Wairarapa.

Movie buffs can experience some local movie magic by visiting the **Weta Cave** (p164) or one of many film locations around the region – a speciality of local guided-tour companies.

cast a Mediterranean spell over Ortega – a magical spot for a seafood dinner. Fish comes many ways (roasted with laksa sauce; with mango chutney and raita), while desserts continue the Med vibes with Catalan orange crêpes and one of Welly's best cheeseboards. Excellent stuff.

Logan Brown   Modern NZ $$$

(☑04-801 5114; www.loganbrown.co.nz; 192 Cuba St; mains $37-42; ☺noon-2pm Tue-Sat, 5pm-late daily; ☑) Deservedly touted as Wellington's best restaurant, Logan Brown oozes class without being overly formal. Its 1920s banking-chamber dining room is a stunner, as is the menu, which features such treats as Fiordland venison with black pudding, parsnip and sour cherries. The three-course bistro menu ($45) won't hurt your wallet too badly (but the epic wine list might force a blowout

Days Bay & Matui-Somes Island

The sweet little **East by West Ferry** (📞04-499 1282; www.eastbywest.co.nz; Queens Wharf) plies the waters between Queens Wharf and Days Bay in Eastbourne, via Matiu-Somes Island, and on fine weekends via Petone and Seatoun as well.

Locals have been jumping on a boat to Days Bay for decades. At the bay there's a beach, a park and a cafe, and a boatshed with kayaks and bikes for hire. A 10-minute walk from Days Bay leads to Eastbourne, a beachy township with cafes, a cute pub, a summer swimming pool and a playground.

Some ferries also stop at Matiu-Somes Island in the middle of the harbour, a DOC-managed reserve where you might see weta, tuatara, kakariki and little blue penguins, among other critters. The island is rich in history, having once been a prisoner-of-war camp and quarantine station. Take a picnic lunch, or even stay overnight.

It's a 20- to 30-minute chug across the harbour. There are 16 sailings on weekdays, eight on Saturday and Sunday (return fare adult/child $22/12).

DRINKING & NIGHTLIFE

Wellingtonians love a late night. The inner city is riddled with bars, especially around Courtenay Pl, Cuba St and the waterfront.

Hawthorn Lounge   Cocktail Bar
(📞04-890 3724; www.hawthornlounge.co.nz; L1, 2 Tory St; ☺5pm-late) This uppercut cocktail bar has a 1920s speakeasy feel, suited-up in waistcoats and wide-brimmed fedoras. Sip a whisky sour and play poker, or watch the behind-the-bar theatrics from the Hawthorn's mixologists, twisting and turning classics into modern-day masterpieces. Open 'til the wee small hours.

Laundry   Bar
(📞04-384 4280; www.laundry.net.nz; 240 Cuba St; ☺4.30pm-late Mon-Fri, 9am-late Sat & Sun) Tumble into this lurid-green, junk-shop juke joint any time of the day or night for a tipple and a plate of jerk chicken, then hang with the hipsters in a wrinkle-free zone. Regular live music and DJs offset Southern-style bar food and carnivalesque decor pasted up with a very rough brush. Trailer-trash backyard complete with a caravan.

Thief   Wine Bar
(📞04-384 6400; www.thiefbar.co.nz; 19 Edward St; ☺3pm-late) If your idea of a good time is fine wine, cocktails and conversation, steal away to Thief. It's a brick-lined, timbered, cellar-like space. Twinkly lighting plays across the faces of good-looking after-workers, and there's a rack of *Encyclopaedia Britannicas* behind the bar if you need to check any facts from 1986. One of the city's hidden gems.

Matterhorn   Bar
(📞04-384 3359; www.matterhorn.co.nz; 106b Cuba St; ☺3pm-late Mon-Sat, 1pm-late Sun) An early riser in Welly's 21st-century bar scene, the 'Horn peaks with its reputable food (tapas and dinner), snappy service and regular live music. The sultry, designerly interiors still hold up, the wine list is as long as your leg, and it's still the best place for a drink on Cuba Mall.

☺ ENTERTAINMENT

Peruse listings at www.eventfinder.co.nz. Many events are ticketed via Ticketek (box office at the **Michael Fowler Centre**; 📞0800 842 538, 04-801 4231; www.ticketek.co.nz; 111 Wakefield St; ☺box office 9am-5pm Mon-Fri, 10am-4pm Sat & Sun) or TicketDirect (www.ticketdirect.co.nz).

Bodega   Live Music
(📞04-384 8212; www.bodega.co.nz; 101 Ghuznee St; ☺4pm-late) Proudly displaying its 'since 1991' credentials, the good-old 'Bodge' remains at the fore of Wellington's live-music scene. Expect a varied program of gigs –

including frequent international acts – in a rock-vibed space with solid acoustics.

San Fran
Live Music

(☏04-801 6797; www.sanfran.co.nz; 171 Cuba St; ◷3pm-late Tue-Sat) This much-loved, mid-size music venue is moving to a new beat; it's boarded the craft-beer bandwagon and rocks out smoky, meaty food along the way. Gigs still rule, dancing is de rigueur, and the balcony still gets good afternoon sun.

BATS
Theatre

(☏04-802 4175; www.bats.co.nz; 1 Kent Tce; tickets from $10; ◷box office 5pm-late Tue-Sat) Wildly alternative but accessible BATS presents cutting-edge and experimental NZ theatre – varied, cheap and intimate – in its freshly revamped theatre.

Circa Theatre
Theatre

(☏04-801 7992; www.circa.co.nz; 1 Taranaki St; ◷box office 10am-2pm Mon, to 6.30pm Tue, to 4pm Wed, to 8pm Thu-Sat, 1-7pm Sun) Waterfront Circa houses two auditoriums in which it shows everything from edgy new works to Christmas panto. Standby tickets available an hour before the show. Dinner-and-show packages available.

ℹ INFORMATION

Wellington i-SITE (☏04-802 4860; www.wellingtonnz.com; Civic Sq, cnr Wakefield & Victoria Sts; ◷8.30am-5pm Mon-Fri, 9am-5pm Sat & Sun) Staff book almost everything here, and cheerfully distribute Wellington's *Official Visitor Guide*, and other maps and info.

ℹ GETTING THERE & AWAY

AIR

Wellington Airport (p306) lies 5½km southeast of the city, in the suburb of Rongotai.

Air New Zealand (☏04-474 8950; www.airnewzealand.co.nz; 154 Fetherston St; ◷9am-5pm Mon-Fri, 10am-1pm Sat) Flights between Wellington and most New Zealand domestic centres, including Auckland, Nelson, Christchurch and Queenstown. It also flies direct to/from key Australian cities.

Jetstar (www.jetstar.com) Offers economical flights from Wellington to Auckland and Christchurch, and also flies direct to the Gold Coast and Melbourne across the ditch.

Soundsair (www.soundsair.com) Flies between Wellington across to Picton and Nelson in the South Island.

Qantas (www.qantas.com.au) Flies direct between Wellington and Auckland, and Wellington and Christchurch. Also has direct connections with Sydney, Melbourne and the Gold Coast in Australia.

BOAT

To cross from Wellington on the North Island to Picton in the South Island, there are two ferry options.

Bluebridge Ferries (☏04-471 6188, 0800 844 844; www.bluebridge.co.nz; 50 Waterloo Quay) Crossing takes 3½ hours; up to four sailings daily in each direction. Cars and campervans from $120; motorbikes $51; bicycles $10. Passenger fares from adult/child $53/27.

Interislander (☏04-498 3302, 0800 802 802; www.interislander.co.nz; Aotea Quay) Crossings take three hours 10 minutes; up to five sailings daily in each direction. Cars are priced from $119; campervans from $153; motorbikes from $56; bicycles $15. Passenger fares from adult/child $55/28.

Bluebridge is based at Waterloo Quay, opposite Wellington train station. Interislander is about 2km northeast of the city centre at Aotea Quay; a shuttle bus ($2) runs to/from platform 9 at Wellington train station (from where InterCity buses also depart).

BUS

North Island destinations from Wellington include Auckland, Rotorua and Taupo.

ℹ GETTING AROUND

Largely flat and compact, central Wellington is easily explored by walking or biking. For bike hire, see **On Yer Bike** (☏04-384 8480; www.onyerbikeavantiplus.co.nz; 181 Vivian St; city/mountain bike per day $30/40; ◷8.30am-5.30pm Mon-Fri, 9am-5pm Sat) near Cuba St.

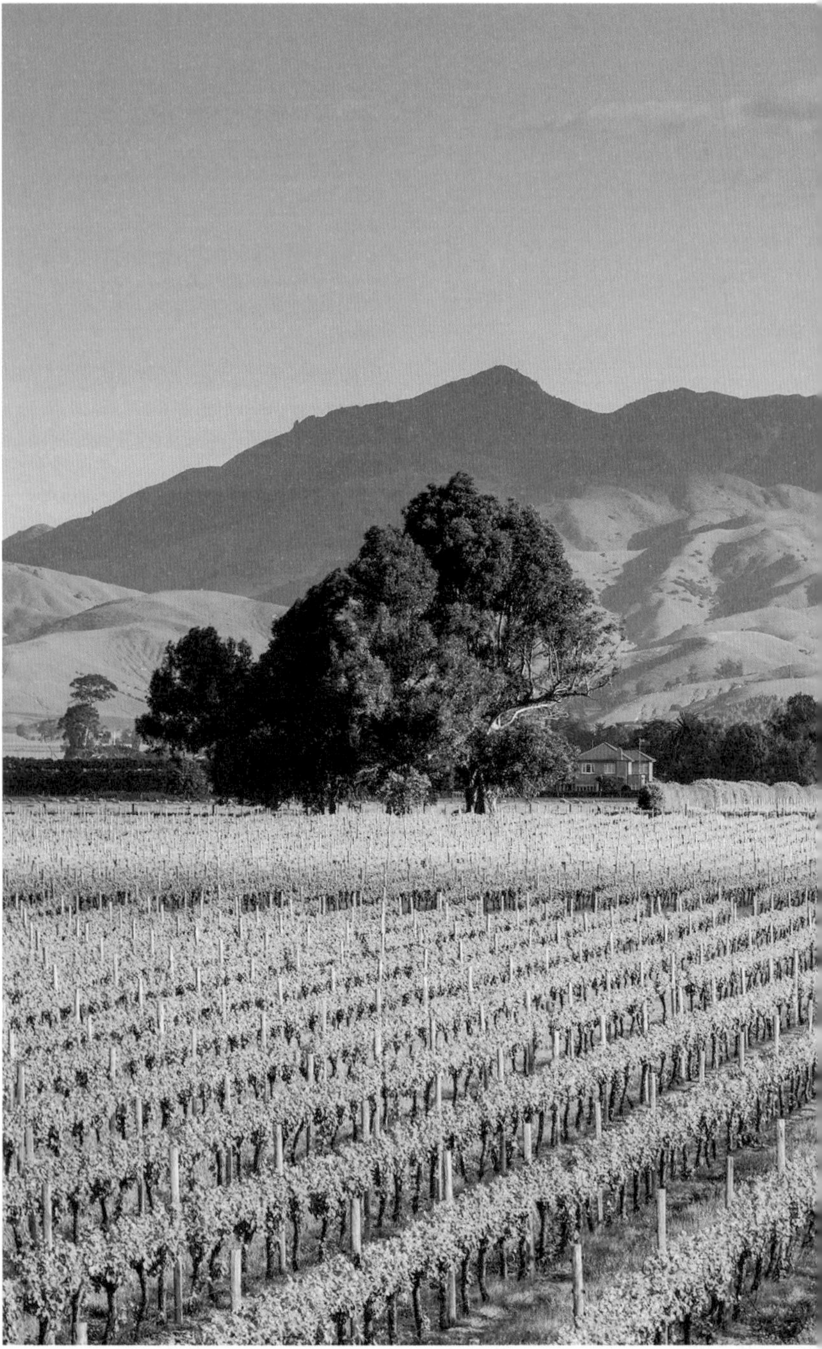

Vineyards near Blenheim (p174)

MARLBOROUGH

Marlborough at a glance...

Marlborough and Nelson have much in common: both boast renowned coastal holiday spots, particularly the Marlborough Sounds and Abel Tasman National Park. Both regions also offer abundant produce, from game and seafood to summer fruits, and most famously the grapes that fill the wine glasses of the world's finest restaurants. Most of NZ's zesty hops also grow here, fuelling a great craft beer scene.

Marlborough in two days

On day one explore the sunny sweet spot of **Nelson** (p180) soaking up the craft galleries, luscious food and beachy vibe. End the day with dinner at the classy **Hopgood's** (p183).

On day two chill out and enjoy the **Marlborough wine country** – standout vineyards include **Saint Clair Estate** (p174) and **Framingham** (p174), while **Rock Ferry** (p175) is a seamless blend of relaxed Kiwi informality and culinary sophistication.

Marlborough in four days

For days three and four rev up the energy levels by exploring the spectacular **Abel Tasman National Park** (p176), either on a boat trip, tramping, in a kayak, or all three. Great water taxi services mean it's a breeze to walk one section of the track, then switch to a kayak for a relaxed paddle exploring tiny hidden coves and perfect beaches, then rendezvous with your ride back to base at the end of a few days' adventures.

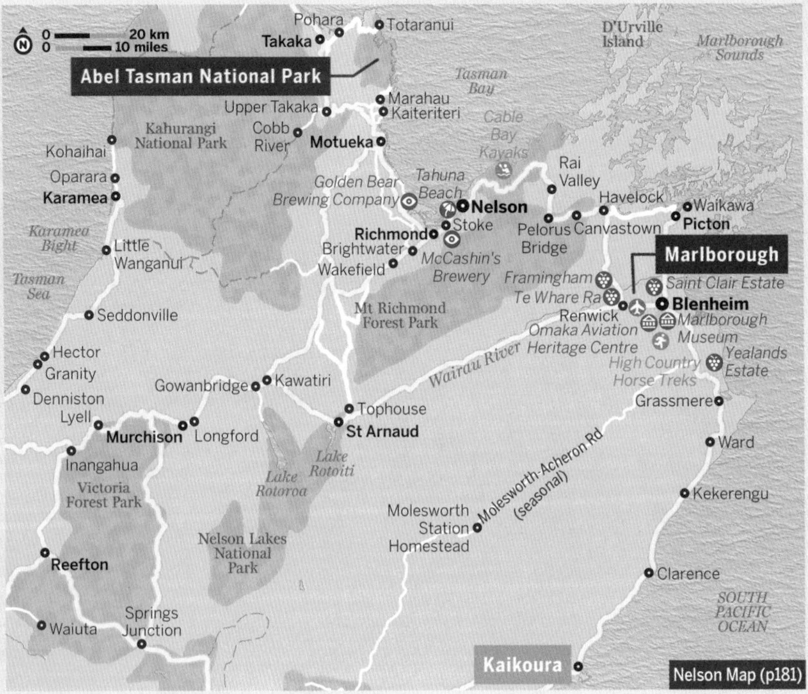

Ô N
0 ——— 20 km
0 ——— 10 miles

Pohara ○ Totaranui
Takaka ○

Abel Tasman National Park

Upper Takaka ○   ○ Marahau
Cobb   ○ Kaiteriteri
Kahurangi   River **Motueka** ○
National Park

*Tasman
Bay*

*Marlborough
Sounds*

D'Urville
Island

*Cable
Bay
Kayaks*

Kohaihai ○
Oparara ○
Karamea ○

*Golden Bear
Brewing Company* ○

*Tahuna
Beach*

Nelson ○
Stoke ○

Rai
Valley

Havelock ○   ○ Waikawa
Pelorus Canvastown   **Picton**
Bridge

Marlborough

*Karamea
Bight*

○ Little
Wanganui

Richmond ○
Brightwater ○
Wakefield ○

*McCashin's
Brewery*

Framingham ○
Te Whare Ra ○

○ Saint Clair Estate
Blenheim ○
*Marlborough
Museum*

*Tasman
Sea*

○ Seddonville

*Mt Richmond
Forest Park*

Renwick
Omaka Aviation
Heritage Centre

*High Country
Horse Treks*

Yealands
Estate

○ Hector
Granity ○
Denniston ○
Lyell ○

Gowanbridge ○ ○ Kawatiri

○ Tophouse
St Arnaud ○

Wairau River

Grassmere ○

Murchison ○ ○ Longford
Inangahua ○

*Victoria
Forest Park*

*Lake
Rotoiti*

*Lake
Rotoroa*

*Molesworth-Acheron Rd
(seasonal)*

○ Ward

○ Kekerengu

*Nelson Lakes
National Park*

Molesworth
Station ○
Homestead

Reefton ○

○ Clarence

*SOUTH
PACIFIC
OCEAN*

○ Waiuta

Springs
Junction

Kaikoura ○

Nelson Map (p181)

Arriving in Marlborough

Picton Ferry Terminal Terminus for vehicle ferries crossing Cook Strait from Wellington. Buses and shuttles depart from here or the nearby i-SITE for Christchurch, Kaikoura and Nelson.

Picton Train Station The Coastal Pacific train service links Picton and Christchurch.

Nelson Flights to/from Auckland, Hamilton, Wellington, Christchurch and Dunedin. Buses from Queenstown, Christchurch, Picton, Greymouth and Kaikoura.

Where to Stay

The region is well set up for visitors with a full range of accommodation options from hiking huts, hostels and holiday parks to chi-chi B&Bs and holiday homes.

ROB BLAKERS/GETTY IMAGES ©

Marlborough Wine

Languidly exploring the wineries of the Marlborough Wine Region is a quintessential NZ experience, and dining among the vines on a sunny southern hemisphere afternoon is also an absolute highlight.

Great For...

☑ Don't Miss

Being surprised that Marlborough's wine excellence stretches well beyond zesty sauvignon blanc.

Marlborough produces around three-quarters of New Zealand's wine, and sunny days and cool nights create the perfect conditions for cool-climate grapes. Standouts are world-famous sauvignon blanc, top-notch pinot noir, and notable chardonnay, riesling, gewürztraminer, pinot gris and bubbly.

Top Tastings

Around 35 wineries are open to the public. Our picks of the bunch provide a range of high-quality cellar-door experiences. Pick up a copy of the *Marlborough Wine Trail* map from the Blenheim i-SITE (p187), the main town at the heart of wine country.

Saint Clair Estate (www.saintclair.co.nz; 13 Selmes Rd, Rapaura; ⊙9am-5pm)

Framingham (www.framingham.co.nz; 19 Conders Bend Rd, Renwick; ⊙10.30am-4.30pm)

DANITA DELIMONT/GETTY IMAGES ©

❶ Need to Know

Wine Marlborough (www.wine-marlborough.co.nz) incorporates all the region's wineries and has an interactive map.

✖ Take a Break

In the heart of Renwick wine country, **Arbour** (☑03-572 7989; www.arbour. co.nz; 36 Godfrey Rd, Renwick; mains $31-38; ☺3pm-late Tue-Sat year-round, 6pm-late Mon Jan-Mar; ☑) ✿ showcases local produce and a mesmerising wine list.

★ Top Tip

Time your visit for the annual **Marlborough Wine Festival** (www.wine-marlborough-festival.co.nz; tickets $57) in February.

Yealands Estate (☑03-575 7618; www.yealandsestate.co.nz; cnr Seaview & Reserve Rds, Seddon; ☺10am-4.30pm)

Te Whare Ra (www.twrwines.co.nz; 56 Anglesea St, Renwick; ☺11am-4.30pm Mon-Fri, noon-4pm Sat & Sun Nov-Mar)

Best Wining & Dining

Opening hours are for summer, when bookings are recommended.

Rock Ferry   Cafe $$
(☑03-579 6431; www.rockferry.co.nz; 80 Hammerichs Rd, Blenheim; mains $23-27; ☺11.30am-3pm) ✿ Pleasant environment inside and out, with a slightly groovy edge. The compact summery menu – think roasted salmon and peppers or organic open steak sandwich – is accompanied by wines from Marlborough and Otago.

Wither Hills   Modern NZ $$
(☑03-520 8284; www.witherhills.co.nz; 211 New Renwick Rd, Blenheim; mains $24-33, platters $38-68; ☺11am-4pm) Simple, well-executed food in a stylish space. Pull up a beanbag on the Hockneyesque lawns and enjoy smoked lamb, Asian pork belly or a platter, before climbing the ziggurat for impressive views across the Wairau.

Wine Tours

Highlight Wine Tours   Wine
(☑03-577 9046, 027 434 6451; www.highlightwinetours.co.nz) Visit a chocolate factory, too. Custom tours available.

Bubbly Grape Wine Tours   Wine
(☑027 672 2195, 0800 228 2253; www.bubblygrape.co.nz) Three different tours including a gourmet lunch option.

Bike2Wine   Wine
(☑03-572 8458, 0800 653 262; www.bike2wine.co.nz; 9 Wilson St, Renwick; standard/tandem per day $30/60, pick ups from $10) An alternative to a minibus tour – get around the grapes on two wheels. This operator offers self-guided, fully geared and supported tours.

Waiharakeke Beach, Abel Tasman National Park

Abel Tasman National Park

Sea kayaking, boating and tramping are the best ways to experience the beautiful beaches and forested coves of this national park on the South Island's northwestern tip.

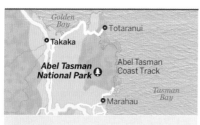

Great For...

ⓘ Need to Know

See www.doc.govt.nz/abeltasmantrack for detailed planning information on the Abel Tasman Coast Track.

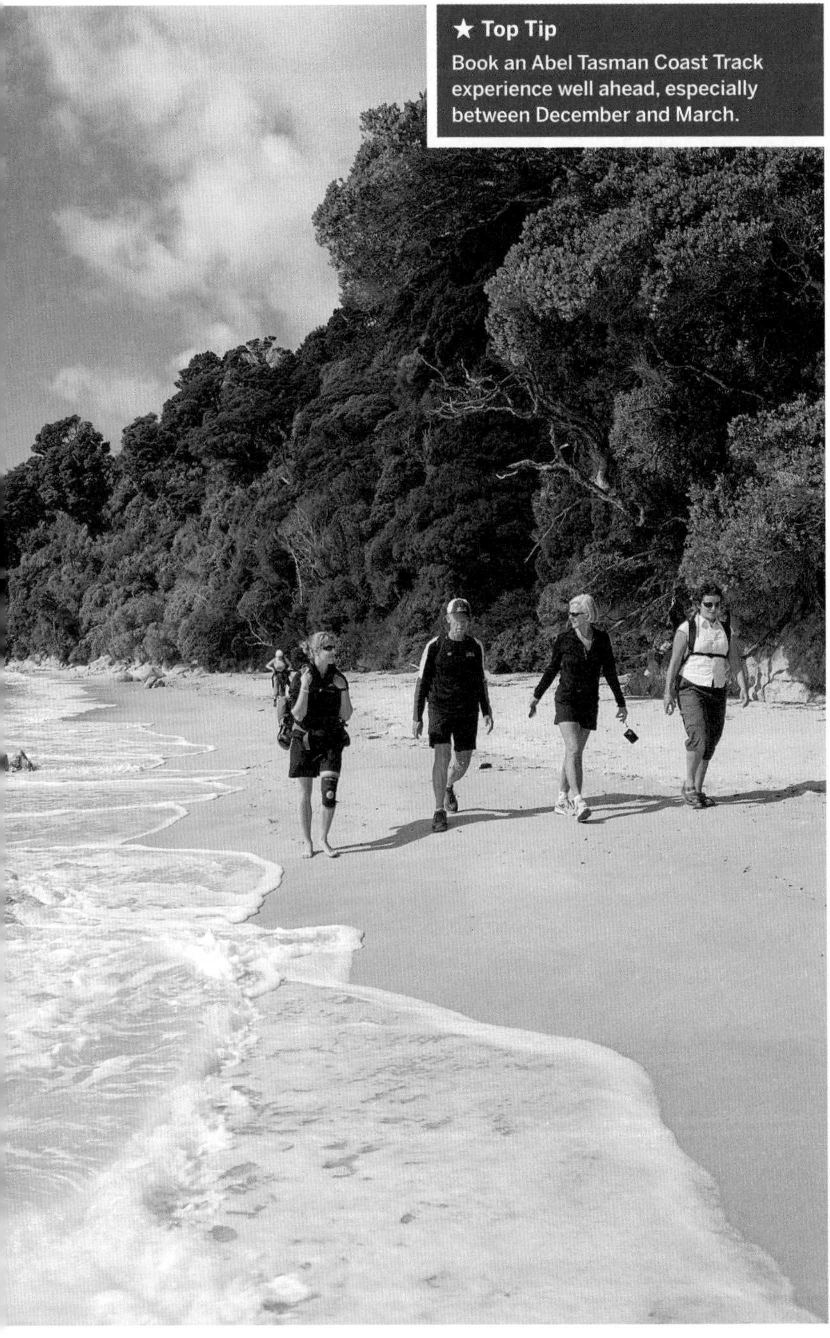

★ **Top Tip**

Book an Abel Tasman Coast Track experience well ahead, especially between December and March.

HAUKE DRESSLER/GETTY IMAGES ©

The closest big town to Abel Tasman is Motueka, with nearby Marahau the southern gateway. All gateways are serviced by either **Abel Tasman Coachlines** (☏03-548 0285; www.abeltasmantravel.co.nz) and **Golden Bay Coachlines** (☏03-525 8352; www.gbcoachlines.co.nz).

Abel Tasman Coast Track

This is arguably NZ's most beautiful Great Walk – 60km of sparkling seas, golden sand and coastal forest. It is also well-graded and well-marked.

The entire tramp takes only three to five days, although with water taxi transport you can convert it into an almost endless array of options, particularly if you combine it with a kayak leg. A rewarding two-day option is a loop around the park's northern end, hiking from Totaranui, passing Anapai

Bay and Mutton Cove, overnighting at Whariwharangi Hut, then returning to Totaranui via the Gibbs Hill Track. This showcases the park's best features (beaches, seals, coastal scenery) while being far less crowded than other segments.

The track operates on DOC's Great Walks Pass. Children are free but bookings are still required. Book online (www.doc. govt.nz), contact the **Nelson Marlborough Bookings Helpdesk** (☏03-546 8210), or book in person at the Nelson, Motueka or Takaka i-SITES or DOC offices, where staff can offer suggestions to tailor the track to your needs and organise transport at each end.

Paddling the Abel Tasman

The Abel Tasman Coast Track has long been tramping territory, but its coastal

Kayaking near Kaiteriteri

beauty makes it an equally seductive spot for sea kayaking, which can easily be combined with walking and camping. Options include either guided tours or freedom trips.

Kahu Kayaks (☑0800 300 101, ☑03-527 8300; www.kahukayaks.co.nz; 11 Marahau Valley Rd) Based in Marahau.

Kaiteriteri Kayaks (☑0800 252 925, ☑03-527 8383; www.seakayak.co.nz) Based in Kaiteriteri Beach.

Sea Kayak Company (☑0508 252 925, ☑03-528 7251; www.seakayaknz.co.nz; 506 High St, Motueka) Based in Motueka.

> **ⓘ Need to Know**
>
> Typical water taxi one-way prices from either Marahau or Kaiteriteri: Anchorage and Torrent Bay ($35), Bark Bay ($40), Awaroa ($45) and Totaranui ($47).

DOUGLAS PEEBLES/GETTY IMAGES ©

Other Activities

Abel Tasman Canyons
Adventure Sports
(☑0800 863 472, ☑03-528 9800; www.abeltasmancanyons.co.nz; full-day trips $259) Few Abel Tasman visitors see the Torrent River; here's your chance to journey down its staggeringly beautiful granite-lined canyon, via a fun-filled combination of swimming, sliding, abseiling and big leaps into jewel-like pools.

Abel Tasman Sailing Adventures
Boating
(☑0800 467 245, ☑03-527 8375; www.sailingadventures.co.nz; Kaiteriteri; day trips $185) Scheduled and on-demand catamaran trips, with sail/walk/kayak combos available. The popular day trip includes lunch on Anchorage Beach.

Wilsons Abel Tasman
Tour
(☑03-528 2027, ☑0800 223 582; www.abeltasman.co.nz; 409 High St, Motueka) This long-standing, family-owned operator offers an impressive array of cruises, walking, kayaking and combo tours, including a $36 day-walk special. Overnight stays are available at Wilsons' lodges in pretty Awaroa and Torrent Bay.

Abel Tasman Tours & Guided Walks
Walking
(☑03-528 9602; www.abeltasmantours.co.nz; tours from $245) Small-group, day-long walking tours (minimum two people) that include a packed lunch and water taxis.

Abel Tasman Sea Shuttle
Tour
(☑0800 732 748, ☑03-527 8688; www.abeltasmanseashuttles. co.nz; Kaiteriteri) Scheduled transport and cruises plus a raft of tour options and combos featuring tramping, kayaking and wildlife spotting.

> **✗ Take a Break**
>
> Food is available at Marahau and Kaiteriteri. In the park itself it's self-catering all the way, except for cafe lunches at Awaroa Lodge.

Nelson

Dishing up a winning combination of beautiful surroundings, sophisticated art and culinary scenes, plus lashings of sunshine, Nelson is hailed as one of New Zealand's most 'liveable' cities. In summer it fills up with local and international visitors, who lap up its diverse offerings.

◉ SIGHTS

Nelson has an inordinate number of galleries, most of which are listed in the *Art & Crafts Nelson City* brochure (with walking-trail map) available from the i-SITE (p184). A fruitful wander can be had by starting at the woolly **Fibre Spectrum** (☑03-548 1939; www.fibrespectrum.co.nz; 280 Trafalgar St), before moving on to *Lord of the Ring* jeweller **Jens Hansen** (☑03-548 0640; www.jenshansen.com; 320 Trafalgar Sq), glass-blower **Flamedaisy** (☑03-548 4475; www.flamedaisy.co.nz; 324 Trafalgar Sq), then around the corner to the home of Nelson pottery, **South Street Gallery** (☑03-548 8117; www.nelsonpottery.co.nz; 10 Nile St W). More interesting local creations can be found at the Nelson Market (p182) on Saturday.

Tahuna Beach   Beach
Nelson's primo playground takes the form of an epic sandy beach (with lifeguards in summer) backed by dunes, and a large grassy parkland with a playground, an espresso cart, a hydroslide, bumper boats, a roller-skating rink, a model railway, and an adjacent restaurant strip. Weekends can get veerrrrry busy!

Nelson Provincial
Museum   Museum
(☑03-548 9588; www.nelsonmuseum.co.nz; cnr Trafalgar St and Hardy St; adult/child $5/3; ☺10am-5pm Mon-Fri, to 4.30pm Sat & Sun) This modern museum space is filled with cultural heritage and natural history exhibits which have a regional bias, as well as regular touring exhibitions (for which admission

fees vary). It also features a great rooftop garden.

Christ Church Cathedral   Church
(www.nelsoncathedral.org; Trafalgar Sq; ☺9am-6pm) **FREE** The enduring symbol of Nelson, the art-deco Christ Church Cathedral lords it over the city from the top of Trafalgar St. The best time to visit is during the 10am and 7pm Sunday services when you can hear the organist and choir on song.

Botanical Reserve   Park
(Milton St) Walking tracks ascend Botanical Hill, where a spire proclaims the **Centre of New Zealand**. NZ's first-ever rugby match was played at the foot of the hill on 14 May 1870: Nelson Rugby Football Club trounced the lily-livered players from Nelson College 2-0.

Founders Heritage Park   Museum
(☑03-548 2649; www.founderspark.co.nz; 87 Atawhai Dr; adult/child/family $7/5/15; ☺10am-4.30pm) Two kilometres from the city centre, this park comprises a replica historic village with a museum, gallery displays, and artisan products such as chocolate and clothing. It makes for a fascinating wander, which you can augment with a visit to the on-site **Founders Brewery & Café** (☑03-548 4638; www.foundersbrewery.co.nz; 87 Atawhai Dr; ☺9am-4.30pm, later in summer).

McCashin's Brewery   Brewery
(☑03-547 5357; www.mccashins.co.nz; 660 Main Rd, Stoke; ☺7am-6pm Mon & Tue, 7am-9.30pm Wed-Sat, 9am-6pm Sun) A groundbreaker in the new era of craft brewing in NZ, which started way back in the 1980s. Visit the historic cider factory for a tasting, cafe meal or tour.

Queens Gardens   Gardens
(Bridge St) Immerse yourself in around 125 years of botanical history in this ornamental garden, which commemorates the 50th jubilee of Queen Victoria's coronation. Great for a picnic or lawny lie-down.

Nelson

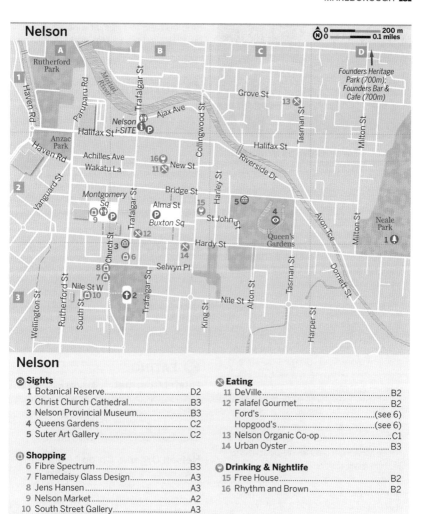

Nelson

◎ Sights
1 Botanical Reserve	D2
2 Christ Church Cathedral	B3
3 Nelson Provincial Museum	B3
4 Queens Gardens	C2
5 Suter Art Gallery	C2

🛍 Shopping
6 Fibre Spectrum	B3
7 Flamedaisy Glass Design	A3
8 Jens Hansen	A3
9 Nelson Market	A2
10 South Street Gallery	A3

⊗ Eating
11 DeVille	B2
12 Falafel Gourmet	B2
Ford's	(see 6)
Hopgood's	(see 6)
13 Nelson Organic Co-op	C1
14 Urban Oyster	B3

◉ Drinking & Nightlife
15 Free House	B2
16 Rhythm and Brown	B2

Suter Art Gallery   Gallery
(www.thesuter.org.nz; 208 Bridge St; ⊘9.30am-
4.30pm) **FREE** Adjacent to Queen's Gardens,
Nelson's public art gallery presents
changing exhibitions, floor talks, musical
and theatrical performances, and films.
The Suter's long-awaited reopening after
a fabulous redevelopment is scheduled for
late 2016. Check the website to confirm it's
open, and to find out what's on.

🌀 TOURS
Bay Tours   Tour
(☑0800 229 868, 03-540 3873; www.baytours
nelson.co.nz; half-/full-day tours from $85/145)
Nelson city, region, wine, beer, food and art
tours. One full-day scenic tour includes an
Abel Tasman National Park cruise as well as
winery visits and a stop at Mapua.

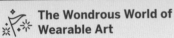

The Wondrous World of Wearable Art

Nelson is the birthplace of New Zealand's most inspiring fashion show, the annual World of WearableArt Awards Show. You can see 70 or so current and past entries in the galleries of the **World of WearableArt & Classic Cars Museum** (03-547 4573; www.wowcars.co.nz; 1 Cadillac Way; adult/child $24/10; 10am-5pm) several sensory-overloading galleries, including a glow-in-the-dark room. Look out for the 'Bizarre Bras'.

More car than bra? Under the same roof are more than 100 mint-condition classic cars and motorbikes. Exhibits change, but may include a 1959 pink Cadillac or a yellow 1950 Bullet Nose Studebaker convertible.

The World of WearableArt Awards Show began humbly in 1987 when Suzie Moncrieff held an off-beat event featuring art that could be worn and modelled. Folks quickly cottoned on and now you name it, they've shown that a garment can be made from it; wood, metal, shells, cable ties, dried leaves, ping-pong balls... The festival now has a new home in Wellington.

Between the galleries, cafe and art shop, allow a couple of hours if you can.

World of WearableArt Fashion Show
DOUGLAS PEEBLES/GETTY IMAGES ©

Gentle Cycling Company
Cycling

(0800 932 453, 03-929 5652; www.gentlecycling.co.nz; day tours $95-105) Self-guided cycle tours along the Great Taste Trail, with drop-ins (and tastings) at wineries, breweries, cafes and occasional galleries. Bike hire (per day $45) and shuttles also available.

ACTIVITIES

Cable Bay Kayaks
Kayaking

(03-545 0332; www.cablebaykayaks.co.nz; Cable Bay Rd, Hira; half-/full day guided trips $85/145) Fifteen-minutes' drive from Nelson city, Nick and Jenny offer richly rewarding guided sea-kayaking trips exploring the local coastline where you'll likely meet local marine life (snorkelling gear on board helps) and may even enter a cave.

SHOPPING

Nelson Market
Market

(03-546 6454; www.nelsonmarket.co.nz; Montgomery Sq; 8am-1pm Sat) Don't miss Nelson Market, a big, busy weekly market featuring fresh produce, food stalls, fashion, local arts, crafts and buskers.

EATING

Falafel Gourmet
Middle Eastern $

(03-545 6220; 195 Hardy St; meals $11-19; 9.30am-5.30pm Mon-Sat, to 8pm Fri;) A cranking joint dishing out the best kebabs for miles around. They're healthy, too!

Nelson Organic Co-op
Organic $

(www.nelsonorganiccoop.nz; 40 Tasman St; 10am-5.30pm Mon-Fri, to 4.30pm Sat;) Community-owned and operated, feel-good business stocking foods and produce, organic tipples and natural body care. Food to go, plus good coffee and cafe fare on offer.

DeVille
Cafe $$

(03-545 6911; www.devillecafe.co.nz; 22 New St; meals $12-21; 8am-4pm Mon-Sat, 8.30am-2.30pm Sun;) Most of DeVille's tables lie in its sweet walled courtyard, a hidden boho oasis in the inner city and the perfect place for a meal or morning tea. The food's good and local – from fresh baking to a chorizo-burrito brunch, Caesar salad and proper burgers, washed down with regional wines and beers. Open late for live music on Fridays in summer.

Ford's Modern NZ $$

(☑03-546 9400; www.fordsnelson.co.nz; 276 Trafalgar St; lunch $17-22; ☺8am-late Mon-Fri, 9am-late Sat & Sun) Sunny pavement tables at the top of Trafalgar St make this a popular lunchtime spot, as does a menu of modern classics such as the excellent seafood chowder, steak sandwich, and house-smoked salmon niçoise. Pop in for coffee and a scone, or linger over dinner, for which prices leap up a tenner or so.

Urban Oyster Modern NZ $$

(☑03-546 7861; www.urbaneatery.co.nz; 278 Hardy St; dishes $13-27; ☺4pm-late Mon, 11am-late Tue-Sat) Slurp oysters from the shell, or revitalise with sashimi and ceviche, then sate your cravings with street-food dishes such as Korean fried chicken, or popcorn prawn tacos and a side of devilish poutine chips. Black butchery tiles, edgy artwork and fine drinks bolster this metropolitan experience.

Hopgood's Modern NZ $$$

(☑03-545 7191; www.hopgoods.co.nz; 284 Trafalgar St; mains $27-40; ☺5.30pm-late Mon-Sat) Tongue-and-groove-lined Hopgood's is perfect for a romantic dinner or holiday treat. The food is decadent and skilfully prepared but unfussy, allowing quality local ingredients to shine. Try confit duck with sour cherries, or pork belly and pine nut butter. Desirable, predominantly Kiwi wine list. Bookings advisable.

🍷 DRINKING & NIGHTLIFE

Free House Craft Beer

(☑03-548 9391; www.freehouse.co.nz; 95 Collingwood St; ☺3pm-late Mon-Fri, noon-late Sat, 10.30am-late Sun) Come rejoice at this church of ales. Tastefully converted from its original, more reverent purpose, it's now home to an excellent, oft-changing selection of NZ craft beers. You can imbibe inside, out, or even in a yurt, where there's regular entertainment. Hallelujah.

Christ Church Cathedral (p180)

Rhythm and Brown — Bar

(☎03-546 56319; www.facebook.com/rhythm
andbrown; 19 New St; ☺4pm-late Tue-Sat)
Nelson's slinkiest late-night drinking den,
where classy cocktails, fine wines and
craft beer flow from behind the bar and
sweet vinyl tunes drift from the speakers.
Regular Saturday-night microgigs in a
compact, groovy space.

ℹ INFORMATION

Nelson i-SITE (☎03-548 2304; www.nelson
nz.com; cnr Trafalgar & Halifax Sts; ☺8.30am-
5pm Mon-Fri, 9am-4pm Sat & Sun) A slick centre
complete with DOC information desk for the
low-down on national parks and walks (including
Abel Tasman and Heaphy tracks). Pick up a copy
of the *Nelson Tasman Visitor Guide*.

ℹ GETTING THERE & AWAY

AIR

Nelson Airport is 5km southwest of town, near
Tahunanui Beach. **Air New Zealand** (☎0800

737 000; www.airnewzealand.co.nz) has direct
flights to/from Auckland, Wellington and
Christchurch; **Jetstar** (☎09-975 9426, 0800
800 995; www.jetstar.com) flies to/from Auckland and Wellington.

BUS

Buses and shuttles to key South Island destinations including Picton (30 minutes) – for
ferries across Cook Strait to Wellington – and
Christchurch, Greymouth and Queenstown.
InterCity runs buses daily to Blenheim (1¾
hours) for the best of the Marlborough wine
region, and to Kaikoura (3¾ hours) for marine
wildlife-watching.

ℹ GETTING AROUND

Bikes are available for hire from **Nelson Cycle
Hire & Tours** (☎03-539 4193; www.nelsoncycle
hire.co.nz; Nelson Airport; bike hire per day $45).
There's plenty of cycling to be enjoyed in and
around the town. The i-SITE has maps.

Nelson town centre

Blenheim

Blenheim is an agricultural town 29km south of Picton on the pretty Wairau Plains between the Wither Hills and the Richmond Ranges. The last decade or so has seen town beautification projects, the maturation of the wine industry and the addition of a landmark museum significantly increase the town's appeal to visitors.

◉ SIGHTS

Omaka Aviation Heritage Centre   Museum

(☑03-579 1305; www.omaka.org.nz; 79 Aerodrome Rd; adult/child $30/12, family from $45; ☻9am-5pm Dec-Mar, 10am-4pm Apr-Nov) This exceptionally brilliant museum houses film-director Peter Jackson's collection of original and replica Great War aircraft, brought to life in a series of dioramas that depict dramatic wartime scenes, such as the death of the Red Baron. A new wing houses Dangerous Skies, a WWII collection. Vintage biplane flights are available (20 minutes, $390 for two people). A cafe and shop are on-site.

Marlborough Museum   Museum

(☑03-578 1712; www.marlboroughmuseum. org.nz; 26 Arthur Baker Pl, off New Renwick Rd; adult/child $10/5; ☻10am-4pm) Besides a replica street-scene, vintage mechanicals and well-presented historical displays, there's the *Wine Exhibition*, for those looking to cap off their vineyard experiences.

Omaka Classic Cars   Museum

(☑03-577 9419; www.omakaclassiccars.co.nz; adult/child $10/free; ☻10am-4pm) Houses more than 100 vehicles dating from the '50s to the '80s. It's right next door to Omaka Aviation Heritage Centre.

 In Pursuit of Hoppiness

The Nelson region lays claim to the title of craft-brewing capital of New Zealand. World-class hops have been grown here since the 1840s, and a dozen breweries are spread between Nelson and .

Pick up a copy of the *Nelson Craft Beer Trail* map (available from the i-SITE and other outlets, and online at www. craftbrewingcapital.co.nz) and wind your way between brewers and pubs. Top picks for a tipple include the **Free House** (p183), **McCashin's** (p180), the **Moutere Inn** (☑03-543 2759; www. moutereinn.co.nz; 1406 Moutere Hwy, Upper Moutere), **Golden Bear** (www.goldenbear brewing.com; Mapua Wharf, Mapua; meals $10-16), and the **Mussel Inn** (☑03-525 9241; www.musselinn.co.nz; 1259 SH60, Onekaka; all-day snacks $5-17, dinner $13-30; ☻11am-late, closed Jul-Aug).

Hop fields
STIRLING ADAMS/GETTY IMAGES ©

✪ ACTIVITIES

Driftwood Eco-Tours   Kayaking, Ecotour

(☑03-577 7651; www.driftwoodecotours.co.nz; 749 Dillons Point Rd; kayak tours $70-180, 4WD tours for 2/3 people from $440/550) Go on a kayak or 4WD tour with passionate locals Will and Rose for fascinating tours on and around the ecologically and historically significant Wairau Lagoon, just a 10-minute drive from Blenheim. Rare birds and the

¡O¡ The Great Taste Trail

In a stroke of genius inspired by great weather and easy topography, the Tasman region has developed one of NZ's most popular cycle trails. Why is it so popular? Because no other is so frequently punctuated by stops for food, wine, craft beer and art, as it passes through a range of landscapes from bucolic countryside to estuary boardwalk.

The 174km Great Taste Trail (www. heartofbiking.org.nz) stretches from Nelson to Kaiteriteri, with plans afoot to propel it further inland. While it can certainly be ridden in full in a few days, stopping at accommodation en route, it is even more easily ridden as day trips of various lengths. Mapua is a great place to set off from, with bike hire from **Wheelie Fantastic** (☑03-543 2245; www. wheeliefantastic.co.nz; self-guided tours from $95, bike hire per day from $30) and **Trail Journeys** (☑03-540 3095; www. trailjourneysnelson.co.nz; full-day tours from $89) at the wharf, and a ferry ride over to the trails of Rabbit Island. The trail also passes through thrilling Kaiteriteri Mountain Bike Park.

Nelson's many other cycle-tour and bike-hire companies can get you out on the trail, with bike drops and pick-ups.

muppetty Royal Spoonbill may well be spotted. The self-contained 'retreat' offers accommodation for up to four people (double/quad $190/310; breakfast extra $15 per person) next to the Opawa River.

High Country Horse Treks
Horse Riding

(☑03-577 9424; www.high-horse.co.nz; 961 Taylor Pass Rd; 1-2hr treks $60-100) These animal-mad folks run horse treks for all abilities from their base 11km southwest of town (call for directions).

🛍 SHOPPING

Wino's
Wine

(www.winos.co.nz; 49 Grove Rd; ⊘10am-7pm Sun-Thu, to 8pm Fri & Sat) If your time is limited, pop into Wino's, a sterling one-stop shop for some of Marlborough's finer and less common drops.

🍴 EATING

Burleigh
Deli $

(☑03-579 2531; 72 New Renwick Rd; pies $6; ⊘7.30am-3pm Mon-Fri, 9am-1pm Sat) The humble pie rises to stratospheric heights at this fabulous deli; try the sweet pork-belly or savoury steak and blue cheese, or perhaps both. Fresh-filled baguettes, local sausage, French cheeses and great coffee also make tempting appearances. Avoid the lunchtime rush.

Gramado's
Brazilian $$

(☑03-579 1192; www.gramadosrestaurant.com; 74 Main St; mains $26-38; ⊘4pm-late Tue-Sat) Injecting a little Latin American flair into the Blenheim dining scene, Gramado's is a fun place to tuck into unashamedly hearty meals such as lamb *assado*, *feijoada* (smoky pork and bean stew) and Brazilian-spiced fish. Kick things off with a caipirinha, of course.

Wairau River Restaurant
Modern NZ $$

(☑03-572 9800; www.wairauriverwines.com; cnr Rapaura Rd & SH6, Renwick; mains $21-27; ⊘noon-3pm) 🍴 Modish mud-brick bistro with wide veranda and beautiful gardens with plenty of shade. Order the mussel chowder, or the double-baked blue-cheese soufflé. Relaxing and thoroughly enjoyable.

🍷 DRINKING & NIGHTLIFE

Dodson Street
Craft Beer

(☑03-577 8348; www.dodsonstreet.co.nz; 1 Dodson St; ⊘11am-11pm) Pub and garden with a beer-hall ambience and suitably Teutonic menu (mains $17 to $27) featuring pork knuckle, bratwurst and schnitzel. The stars of the show are the 24 taps pouring quality, ever-changing craft beer, including award-winning brewer and neighbour, Renaissance.

ℹ INFORMATION

Blenheim i-SITE (☏03-577 8080; www.marlboroughnz.com; 8 Sinclair St, Railway Station; ⊙9am-5pm Mon-Fri, 9am-3pm Sat, 10am-3pm Sun) Information on Marlborough and beyond. Wine-trail maps and bookings for everything under the sun.

ℹ GETTING THERE & AWAY

AIR

Marlborough Airport (www.marlboroughairport. co.nz; Tancred Cres, Woodbourne) is 6km west of town on Middle Renwick Rd. **Air New Zealand** (☏0800 747 000; www.airnewzealand.co.nz) has direct flights to/from Wellington, Auckland and Christchurch with onward connections. **Soundsair** (☏0800 505 005, 03-520 3080; www.soundsair.co.nz; 3 Auckland St) connects Blenheim with Wellington, Paraparaumu and Napier.

BUS

InterCity (☏03-365 1113; www.intercity.co.nz) Buses run daily from the Blenheim i-SITE to Picton (30 minutes) and Nelson (1¾ hours). Buses also head down south to Christchurch (two daily) via Kaikoura. **Naked Bus** (☏0900 625 33; www.nakedbus.com) sells bargain seats on some of the same services, and on its own buses on major routes.

TRAIN

KiwiRail Scenic (☏0800 872 467; www.kiwirailscenic.co.nz) runs the daily Coastal Pacific service (October to May), stopping at Blenheim en route to Picton (from $29) heading north, and Christchurch (from $79) via Kaikoura (from $59) heading south.

ℹ GETTING AROUND

Shuttles around Blenheim and the wider Marlborough region are offered by **Blenheim Shuttles** (☏03-577 5277, 0800 577 527; www.blenheimshuttles.co.nz).

Dusky dolphins

Wildlife-Watching in Kaikoura

Wildlife tours are Kaikoura's specialty, especially those involving whales, dolphins and NZ fur seals. Tucked on the coast between Marlborough and Christchurch it's a great place to break your journey.

Great For...

☑ Don't Miss

Snorkelling with curious NZ fur seal pups as they swoop and dive around you.

Travel for 243km via Blenheim from Nelson – or 180km north from Christchurch – and you'll encounter Kaikoura, a peninsula town backed by the snowcapped Seaward Kaikoura Range. Marine mammals in the area include whales, dolphins and NZ fur seals; penguins, shearwaters, petrels and albatross are also seen.

The abundance of marine animals is due to the area's unique ocean-current and continental-shelf conditions, creating an upwelling of nutrients from the ocean floor into the feeding zone. This also produces superb seafood, especially Kaikoura's legendary crayfish.

Whale Watch Kaikoura   Ecotour

(☑0800 655 121, 03-319 6767; www.whalewatch.co.nz; Railway Station; 3½hr tours adult/child $150/60) ✎ With knowledgeable guides and fascinating 'world of whales' on-board

Yellow-eyed penguin

NATALIA KHALAMAN/SHUTTERSTOCK ©

animation, Kaikoura's biggest operator heads out on boat trips to introduce you to some of the big fellas. It'll refund 80% of your fare if no whales are sighted (success rate: 95%).

Wings over Whales   Scenic Flights

(☑03-319 6580, 0800 226 629; www.whales. co.nz; 30min flights adult/child $180/75) Light-plane flights departing from Kaikoura Airport, 8km south of town on SH1. Spotting success rate: 95%.

Kaikoura Helicopters   Scenic Flights

(☑03-319 6609; www.worldofwhales.co.nz; Whaleway Station Rd; 15-60min flights $100-490) Reliable whale-spotting flights (standard tour 30 minutes, $220 each for three or more people), plus jaunts around the peninsula, Mt Fyffe and peaks beyond.

Dolphin Encounter   Ecotour

(☑03-319 6777, 0800 733 365; 96 Esplanade; www.encounterkaikoura.co.nz; swim adult/child $175/160, observation $95/50; ⊗tours 8.30am & 12.30pm year-round, plus 5.30am Nov-Apr) ✔ Claiming NZ's highest success rate (90%) for both locating and swimming with dolphins, this operator runs feel-good three-hour tours, which often encounter sizeable pods of sociable duskies – the classic Kaikoura treat.

Seal Swim Kaikoura   Ecotour

(☑0800 732 579, 03-319 6182; www.sealswim kaikoura.co.nz; 58 West End; tours $70-110, viewing adult/child $55/35; ⊗Oct-May) Take a (warmly wet-suited) swim with Kaikoura's healthy population of playful seals – including very cute pups – on two-hour guided snorkelling tours (by boat).

Albatross Encounter   Birdwatching

(☑0800 733 365, 03-319 6777; 96 Esplanade; www.encounterkaikoura.co.nz; adult/child $125/60; ⊗tours 9am & 1pm year-round, plus 6am Nov-Apr) ✔ Even if you don't consider yourself a bird-nerd, you'll love this close encounter with pelagic species such as shearwaters, shags, mollymawks and petrels. It's the various albatross species, however, that steal the show. Just awesome.

Christchurch at a glance...

Nowhere in New Zealand is developing as fast as post-earthquake Christchurch. Visiting the country's second-largest city as it's being rebuilt and reborn is both interesting and inspiring. A short drive from Christchurch's dynamic re-emergence, Banks Peninsula conceals hidden bays and beaches, and is a stunning backdrop for wildlife cruises promising a sunset return to the attractions of Akaroa, a spectacular harbour town with an interesting French colonial heritage.

Christchurch in two days

Spend a few dyas exploring the different ways the city is being re-energised following the 2011 earthquake. Take a **Red Bus Rebuild Tour** (p195), visit **Quake City** (p194) and the **Transitional Cathedral** (p195). **Addington Coffee Co-op** (p204) or **Caffeine Laboratory** (p204) will keep you fuelled up during the days, then cruise into the evenings with drinks at the quirky **Smash Palace** (p205) or dinner at **Twenty Seven Steps** (p204).

Christchurch in three days

On day three head out of town to the charming **Banks Peninsula** (p196), including the oh-so-chic harbour town of **Akaroa** (p206) for French colonial history and wildlife-watching. Take time to get out on the water and try to spot the rare Hector's dolphins.

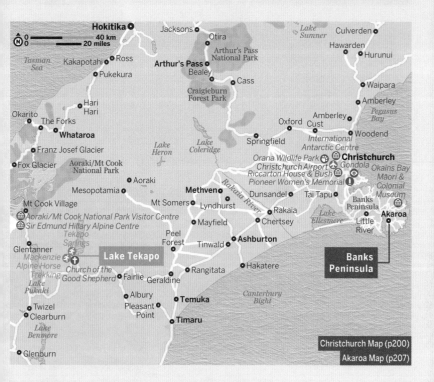

Arriving in Christchurch

Christchurch International Airport
Located 10km from the city with flights
to/from Auckland, Wellington, Hamilton,
Nelson, Queenstown, Australia, Singapore and China.

Rolleston Ave Buses and shuttles to
Akaroa and Lake Tekapo depart from
outside the Canterbury Museum.

Christchurch Bus Interchange
Shuttles to Greymouth.

Christchurch Railway Station The
terminus for the *Coastal Pacific* to/from
Picton, and the TranzAlpine heading
west across the Southern Alps to
Greymouth.

Where to Stay

As the rebuild progresses, more
beds are becoming available in
Christchurch city centre and its inner
fringes. Merivale, Riccarton and around
Colombo St offer good motels, while
the heritage suburb of Fendalton has
good boutique B&Bs. A good range of
B&Bs, motels and holiday homes line
Akaroa's pretty streets and decorate the
surrounding hills.

Re:START Mall

Post-Earthquake Renaissance

Resilience and creativity have defined the people of Christchurch since the 2011 earthquake, and while the planned rebuild slowly progresses, quirky initiatives are also inspiring NZ's second biggest city.

Great For...

☑ **Don't Miss**

Admiring the innovative use of shipping containers as bars and shops.

Following the Christchurch earthquake of 22 February 2011, diverse creativity and DIY entrepreneurship has emerged as the city works through the painstaking process of a 20-year rebuild that's been estimated to cost up to $50 billion. While a compact, low-rise city centre, green spaces, and parks and cycleways along the Avon River slowly take shape, Christchurch locals are just getting on with making the city a more interesting and rewarding place to live. Here are our top picks to experience a fascinating city in transition.

Sights

Quake City   Museum

(www.quakecity.co.nz; 99 Cashel St; adult/child $20/free; ☉10am-5pm) A must-visit for anyone interested in the Canterbury earthquakes and conveniently located in the

ⓘ Need to Know

See www.rebuildchristchurch.co.nz for an independent point of view on the progress of the city's rebuild.

✕ Take a Break

Revival (☏03-379 9559; www.revivalbar. co.nz; 92-96 Victoria St; ◷3pm-late Mon-Thu, noon-late Fri-Sun) is the hippest of Christchurch's shipping container bars.

★ Top Tip

See www.neatplaces.co.nz to find out about newly opened shops, bars and restaurants in ever-changing Christchurch.

Tours

Red Bus Rebuild Tour   Bus

(☏0800 500 929; www.redbus.co.nz; adult/child $35/17) Commentaries focus on the past, present and future of earthquake-damaged sites in the city centre. Tours include video footage of the old street-scapes.

Shopping

Re:START Mall   Mall

(www.restart.org.nz; Cashel St; ◷10am-5pm; 🛜) This labyrinth of shipping containers was the first retail 'mall' to reopen in the CBD postquakes. With cafes, food trucks, shops and people-watching opportunities, it remains a pleasant place to hang out, particularly on a sunny day.

Watch This Space...Gap Filler

Starting from the ground up after the earthquakes, the Gap Filler (www.gapfiller. org.nz) folks fill the city's empty spaces with creativity and colour. Projects range from temporary art installations, performance spaces and gardens, to a minigolf course scattered through empty building sites and the 'Grandstandium' – a mobile grandstand that's a total fun-magnet. Gaps open up and get filled, so check out the Gap Map on the website.

Re:START Mall, this compact museum tells stories through photography, video footage and various artefacts, including bits that have fallen off the cathedral. Most affecting of all is the film featuring locals recounting their own experiences.

Transitional Cathedral   Church

(www.cardboardcathedral.org.nz; 234 Hereford St; entry by donation; ◷9am-5pm, to 7pm summer) Universally known as the Cardboard Cathedral due to the 98 cardboard tubes used in its construction, this interesting structure serves as both the city's temporary Anglican cathedral and as a concert venue. Designed by Japanese 'disaster architect' Shigeru Ban, the entire building was built in 11 months.

Akaroa Harbour

FRANK KRAHMER/GETTY IMAGES ©

Banks Peninsula

Gorgeous Banks Peninsula (Horomaka) was formed by two giant volcanic eruptions about eight million years ago. Harbours and bays radiate out from the peninsula's centre, giving it an unusual cogwheel shape.

Great For...

☑ Don't Miss

Driving along stunning Summit Rd around the edge of one of Banks Peninsula's original volcanic craters.

The historic town of Akaroa, 80km from Christchurch, is a highlight of the peninsula, as is the absurdly beautiful drive along Summit Rd around the rim of one of the original craters. It's also worth exploring the little bays that dot the peninsula's perimeter.

The waters around the surrounding Banks Peninsula are home to the smallest and one of the rarest dolphin species, the Hector's dolphin, found only in NZ waters. A range of tours depart from Akaroa to spot these and other critters, including white-flippered penguins, orcas and seals.

Sights

Okains Bay Māori & Colonial Museum   Museum

(www.okainsbaymuseum.co.nz; 1146 Okains Bay Rd; adult/child $10/2; ☺10am-5pm) Northeast

❶ Need to Know

Visit **Akaroa i-SITE & Adventure Centre** (p209) for bookings, information and activities.

✖ Take a Break Akaroa's **Little Bistro** (p209) serves local seafood, South Island wines and Canterbury craft beers.

★ Top Tip

Stay overnight and enjoy Akaroa after the daytrippers – and cruise ships in summer – have left.

of Akaroa, this museum has a respectable array of European pioneer artefacts, but it is the nationally significant Māori collection, featuring a replica *wharenui* (meeting house), *waka* (canoes), stone tools and personal adornments, that makes this a must-see.

Activities

Black Cat Cruises   Boating

(☎03-304 7641; www.blackcat.co.nz; Main Wharf; nature cruises adult/child $74/30, dolphin swims adult/child $155/120) As well as a two-hour nature cruise, Black Cat offers a three-hour 'swimming with dolphins' experience. Wet suits and snorkelling gear are provided, plus hot showers back on dry land. Observers can tag along (adult/child $80/40) but only 12 people can swim per trip, so book ahead.

Cruises have a 98% success rate in seeing dolphins, and an 81% success rate in actually swimming with them (there's a $50 refund if there's no swim).

Akaroa Dolphins   Boating

(☎03-304 7866; www.akaroadolphins.co.nz; 65 Beach Rd; adult/child $75/35; ⊙12.45pm year-round, plus 10.15am & 3.15pm Oct-Apr) Two-hour wildlife cruises on a comfortable 50ft catamaran, complete with a complimentary drink, home baking and Sydney, wildlife-spotting dog extraordinaire.

Akaroa Guided Sea Kayaking Safari   Kayaking

(☎021 156 4591; www.akaroakayaks.com; 3hr/ half-day $125/159) Paddle out at 7.30am on a three-hour guided Sunrise Nature Safari, or if early starts aren't your thing, try the 11.30am Bays & Nature Paddle. The half-day Try Sea Kayaking Experience is a more challenging option.

Christchurch

Welcome to a vibrant city in transition, coping creatively with the aftermath of NZ's second-worst natural disaster. Traditionally the most English of NZ cities, Christchurch's heritage heart was all but hollowed out following the 2010 and 2011 earthquakes that left 185 people dead. Today Christchurch boasts more road cones and repurposed shipping containers than anywhere else in the world, waypoints in an epic rebuild that sees construction sites throughout the CBD. The city centre is graced by numerous notable arts institutions, the stunning Botanic Gardens and Hagley Park. Inner-city streets conceal art projects and pocket gardens.

◎ SIGHTS

Cathedral Square   Square
Christchurch's city square stands largely flattened and forlorn amid the surrounding rebuild, with the remains of Christ Church Cathedral emblematic of the loss. The February 2011 earthquake brought down

the 63m-high spire, while subsequent earthquakes in June 2011 and December 2011 destroyed the prized stained-glass rose window. Other heritage buildings around the square were also badly damaged, but one modern landmark left unscathed is the 18m-high metal sculpture *Chalice*, designed by Neil Dawson. It was erected in 2001 to commemorate the new millennium.

The much-loved Gothic Christ Church Cathedral lies at the centre of a battle between those who seek to preserve what remains of Christchurch's heritage, the fiscal pragmatists, and those ideologically inclined to things new. Despite the nave remaining largely intact, the deconstruction and demolition of the cathedral was announced in March 2012 by the Anglican Diocese. Heritage advocates launched court proceedings to prevent the demolition, and an independent consultant was brought in to negotiate between opposing parties. Their report concluded that 'replacing the cathedral presents no particular challenges from an engineering perspective'. In effect this has just muddied the waters, and at

Hagley Park

the time of writing no concrete decisions had been made regarding the cathedral's rebuild, demolition, replacement or 'adaptation'. A plethora of opposing views means the wrangling could go on for years.

Christchurch Art Gallery   Gallery

(☑03-941 7300; www.christchurchartgallery.org.nz; cnr Montreal St & Worcester Blvd; ⊙10am-5pm Thu-Tue, to 9pm Wed) **FREE** Damaged in the earthquakes, Christchurch's fantastic art gallery has reopened brighter and bolder, presenting a stimulating mix of primarily New Zealand exhibitions.

Botanic Gardens   Gardens

(www.ccc.govt.nz; Rolleston Ave; ⊙7am-8.30pm Oct-Mar, to 6.30pm Apr-Sep) **FREE** Strolling through these blissful 30 riverside hectares of arboreal and floral splendour is a consummate Christchurch experience. Gorgeous at any time of the year, the gardens are particularly impressive in spring when the rhododendrons, azaleas and daffodil woodland are in riotous bloom. There are thematic gardens to explore, lawns to sprawl on, and a playground adjacent to the **Botanic Gardens Information Centre** (☑03-941 8999; ⊙9am-4pm Mon-Fri, 10.15am-4pm Sat & Sun).

Guided walks ($10) depart at 1.30pm (mid-September to mid-May) from the Canterbury Museum, or you can chug around the gardens on the Caterpillar train (p203).

Hagley Park   Park

(Riccarton Ave) Wrapping itself around the Botanic Gardens, Hagley Park is Christchurch's biggest green space, stretching for 165 hectares. Riccarton Ave splits it in two and the Avon River snakes through the north half. It's a great place to stroll, whether on a foggy autumn morning, or a warm spring day when the cherry trees lining Harper Ave are in flower. Joggers make the most of the tree-lined avenues-year-round.

Canterbury Museum   Museum

(☑03-366 5000; www.canterburymuseum.com; Rolleston Ave; ⊙9am-5pm) **FREE** Yes, there's

 The Canterbury Earthquakes

Christchurch's seismic nightmare began at 4.35am on 4 September 2010. Centred 40km west of the city, a 40-second, 7.1-magnitude earthquake caused widespread damage to older buildings in the central city. Close to the quake's epicentre in rural Darfield, huge gashes erupted amid grassy pastures, and the South Island's main railway line was bent and buckled.

Fast forward to 12.51pm on 22 February 2011, when central Christchurch was busy with shoppers and workers enjoying their lunch break. This time the 6.3-magnitude quake was much closer, centred just 10km southeast of the city and only 5km deep. The tremor was significantly greater, and many locals report being flung violently and almost vertically into the air. The peak ground acceleration exceeded 1.8, almost twice the acceleration of gravity.

When the dust settled after 24 traumatic seconds the towering spire of the iconic Christ Church Cathedral lay in ruins; walls and verandas had cascaded down on shopping strips; and two multistorey buildings had pancaked. Elsewhere, the historic port town of Lyttelton was badly damaged; roads and bridges were crumpled; and residential suburbs in the east were inundated as a process of rapid liquefaction saw tons of oozy silt rise from the ground.

The earthquakes resulted in 185 deaths across 20 nationalities.

a mummy and dinosaur bones, but the highlights of this museum are more local and more recent. The Māori galleries contain some beautiful *pounamu* (greenstone) pieces, while Christchurch Street is an atmospheric walk through the colonial past. The reproduction of Fred & Myrtle's gloriously kitsch Paua Shell House embraces Kiwiana at its best, and kids

Christchurch

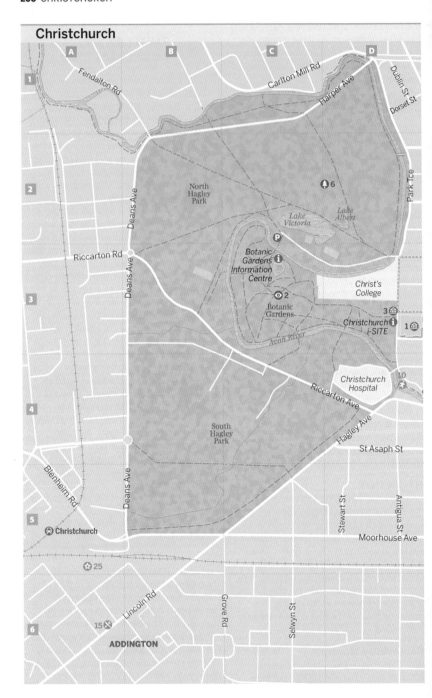

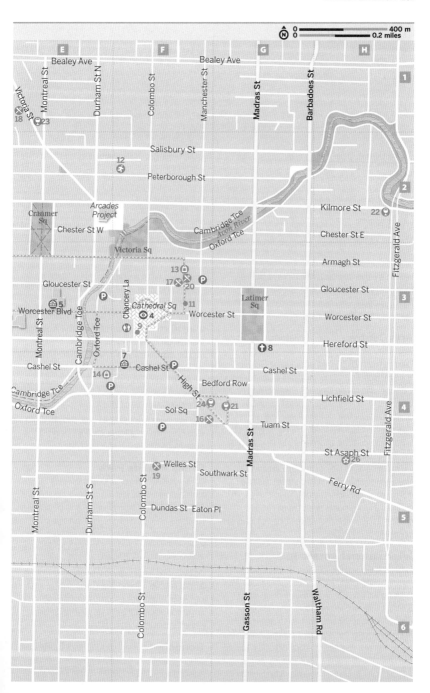

Christchurch

will enjoy the interactive displays in the Discovery Centre (admission $2). Hour-long guided tours commence at 3.30pm on Tuesday and Thursday.

Arts Centre — Historic Building

(www.artscentre.org.nz; 2 Worcester Blvd) Dating from 1877, this enclave of Gothic Revival buildings was originally Canterbury College, the forerunner of Canterbury University. The college's most famous alumnus was the father of nuclear physics Lord Ernest Rutherford, the NZ physicist who first split the atom in 1917 (that's him on the $100 bill).

You'll have to be content to admire the architecture from the street, as the complex was badly damaged in the earthquakes. Some parts are due to reopen during 2016, with the whole project due for completion in 2019.

International Antarctic Centre — Museum

(☏0508 736 4846; www.iceberg.co.nz; 38 Orchard Rd, Christchurch Airport; adult/child $39/19; ☺9am-5.30pm) Part of a huge complex built for the administration of the NZ, US and Italian Antarctic programs, this centre gives visitors the opportunity to see penguins and learn about the icy continent. Attractions include the Antarctic Storm chamber, where you can get a taste of -18°C wind chill.

A free shuttle departs from outside the Canterbury Museum (p199) on the hour from 10am to 4pm, and from the Antarctic Centre on the half-hour.

The 'Xtreme Pass' (adult/child $59/29) includes the '4D theatre' (a 3D film with moving seats and a water spray) and rides on a Hägglund all-terrain amphibious Antarctic vehicle. An optional extra is the Penguin Backstage Pass (adult/child $25/15), which allows visitors behind the scenes of the Penguin Encounter.

Orana Wildlife Park — Zoo

(☏03-359 7109; www.oranawildlifepark.co.nz; McLeans Island Rd, McLeans Island; adult/child $34.50/9.50; ☺10am-5pm) Orana describes itself as an 'open range zoo' and you'll know what they mean if you opt to jump in the cage for the lion encounter (an additional $45). There's an excellent, walk-through native-bird aviary, a nocturnal kiwi house, and a reptile exhibit featuring tuatara. Most of the 80-hectare grounds are devoted to Africana, including rhino, giraffe, zebras, cheetahs and even gorillas.

Gondola — Cable Car

(www.gondola.co.nz; 10 Bridle Path Rd; return adult/child $28/12; ☺10am-5pm) Take a ride to the top of Mt Cavendish (500m) on this 945m cable car for wonderful views over the city, Lyttelton, Banks Peninsula and the Canterbury Plains. At the top there's a cafe and the child-focused *Time Tunnel* ride through historical scenes. You can also walk to Cavendish Bluff Lookout (30 minutes return) or the Pioneer Women's Memorial (one hour return).

🎯 ACTIVITIES

Tram Tram
(📞03-377 4790; www.tram.co.nz; adult/child $20/free; ⊘9am-6pm Oct-Mar, 10am-5pm Apr-Sep) Excellent driver commentary makes this so much more than a tram ride. The beautifully restored old dears trundle around a 17-stop loop, leaving every 15 minutes, taking in a host of city highlights including Cathedral Sq and New Regent St. The full circuit takes just under an hour, and you can hop-on and hop-off all day.

Punting on the Avon Boating
(www.punting.co.nz; 2 Cambridge Tce; adult/child $28/20; ⊘9am-6pm Oct-Mar, 10am-4pm Apr-Sep) ✔ The Antigua Boat Sheds are the starting point for half-hour punting trips through the Botanic Gardens. Relax in a flat-bottomed boat while a strapping lad in Edwardian clobber with a long pole does all the work. An alternative trip departs from the Worcester St Bridge and punts through the city's regenerating centre.

Caterpillar Train Tour
(📞0800 88 22 23; www.welcomeaboard.co.nz; adult/child $20/9; ⊘11am-3pm) Chug around Christchurch's Botanic Gardens on the Caterpillar train.

🎯 TOURS

Christchurch Free Tours Walking
(www.freetours.co.nz; Cathedral Sq; ⊘11am)
FREE Yes, a free tour. Just turn up at the *Chalice* sculpture in Cathedral Sq and look for the red-T-shirted person. If you enjoy your two-hour amble, tip your guide. Nice!

Garden City Helicopters Scenic Flights
(📞03-358 4360; www.helicopters.net.nz; 515 Memorial Ave; 20min $199) Flights above the city and Lyttelton let you observe the impact of the earthquake and the rebuilding efforts.

🛍 SHOPPING

New Regent St Mall
(www.newregentstreet.co.nz) A forerunner to the modern mall, this pretty little stretch of pastel Spanish Mission–style shops was described as NZ's most beautiful street when it was completed in 1932. Fully restored postearthquake, it's once again a delightful place to stroll and peruse the tiny galleries, gift shops and cafes.

Tannery Shopping Centre
(www.thetannery.co.nz; 3 Garlands Rd, Woolston; ⊘10am-5pm Mon-Wed, Fri & Sat, to 8pm Thu)
In a city mourning the loss of its heritage, this postearthquake conversion of a 19th-century tannery couldn't be more welcome. The Victorian buildings have been zhooshed up in period style, and filled with boutique shops selling everything from books to fashion to surfboards. Don't miss the woolly hats. Nonshoppers can slink off to The Brewery (p206) or catch a movie in the brand new cinemas.

🍴 EATING

Supreme Supreme Cafe $
(📞03-365 0445; www.supremesupreme.co.nz; 10 Welles St; breakfast $7-18, lunch $10-20; ⊘7am-4pm Mon-Fri, 8am-4pm Sat & Sun; ☕)
With so much to love, where to start? Perhaps with a kimchi Bloody Mary, a chocolate-fish milkshake, or maybe just an exceptional espresso alongside ancient-grain muesli or pulled corned-beef hash. One of New Zealand's original and best coffee roasters comes to the party with a right-now cafe of splendid style, form and function.

Christchurch's Early Days

The first people to live in what is now Christchurch were moa hunters, who arrived around 1250. Immediately prior to colonisation, the Ngāi Tahu tribe had a small seasonal village on the banks of the Avon called Otautahi.

When British settlers arrived in 1880 it was an ordered Church of England project; the passengers on the 'First Four Ships' were dubbed 'the Canterbury Pilgrims' by the British press. Christchurch was meant to be a model of class-structured England in the South Pacific, not just another scruffy colonial outpost. Churches were built rather than pubs, the fertile farming land was deliberately placed in the hands of the gentry, and wool made the elite of Christchurch wealthy.

In 1856 Christchurch officially became NZ's first city, and a very English one at that. Town planning and architecture assumed a close affinity with the 'Mother Country' and English-style gardens were planted, earning it the nickname, the 'Garden City'. To this day, Christchurch in spring is a glorious place to be.

Addington Coffee Co-op   Cafe $

(☎03-943 1662; www.addingtoncoffee.org.nz; 297 Lincoln Rd; meals $8-21; ◷7.30am-4pm Mon-Fri, 9am-4pm Sat & Sun; 🛜🍴) You will find one of Christchurch's biggest and best cafes packed to the rafters most days. A compact shop selling fair-trade gifts jostles for attention with delicious cakes, gourmet pies and the legendary house breakfasts (until 2pm). An on-site launderette completes the deal for busy travellers.

Christchurch Farmers Market   Market $

(www.christchurchfarmersmarket.co.nz; 16 Kahu Rd, Riccarton; ◷9am-1pm Sat) Held in the pretty grounds of Riccarton House, this excellent farmers market offers a tasty array of organic fruit and veggies, South Island cheeses and salmon, local craft beer and ethnic treats.

Caffeine Laboratory   Cafe $

(www.caffeinelab.co.nz; 1 New Regent St; snacks $4-12, meals $14-26; ◷8am-late Wed-Sat, to 4pm Tue & Sun; 🍴) The small-scale, corner C-lab is hooked on coffee, but also cooks up addictive deliciousness such as house-smoked salmon, smashed broad beans, and burgers with homemade patties. In the evening go for craft beer and tapas.

C1 Espresso   Cafe $

(www.c1espresso.co.nz; 185 High St; mains $10-21; ◷7am-10pm; 🛜) 🌿 C1 sits pretty in a grand former post office that somehow escaped the cataclysm. Recycled materials fill the interior (Victorian oak panelling, bulbous 1970s light fixtures) and tables spill onto a little square. Eggy brekkies and bagels are available all day, while sliders slip onto the afternoon/evening menu.

Bodhi Tree   Burmese $$

(☎03-377 6808; www.bodhitree.co.nz; 399 Ilam Rd, Bryndwr; dishes $13-21; ◷6-10pm Tue-Sat; 🍴) Bodhi Tree has been wowing locals with the nuanced flavours of Burmese cuisine for more than a decade. Their feel-good food comes in sharing-sized dishes and sings with zing. Standouts include *le pet thoke* (pickled tea-leaf salad) and *ameyda nut* (slow-cooked beef curry).

Kinji   Japanese $$

(☎03-359 4697; www.kinjirestaurant.com; 279b Greers Rd, Bishopdale; mains $16-24; ◷5.30-10pm Mon-Sat) Despite being hidden away in suburbia, this acclaimed Japanese restaurant has a loyal following, so it's wise to book. Tuck into the likes of sashimi, grilled ginger squid and venison tataki, but save room for the green tea tiramisu, a surprising highlight.

Twenty Seven Steps   Modern NZ $$$

(☎03-366 2727; www.twentysevensteps.co.nz; 16 New Regent St; mains $30-40; ◷5pm-late Tue-

Sat) Upstairs on the Edwardian New Regent St strip, the pared-back interior of this elegant restaurant puts the focus firmly on a menu showcasing local produce. Mainstays include modern renditions of lamb, beef, venison and seafood, but there's also outstanding risotto and desserts such as caramelised lemon tart.

King of Snake   Asian $$$

(☑03-365 7363; www.kingofsnake.co.nz; 145 Victoria St; mains $27-43; ☺11am-late Mon-Fri, 4pm-late Sat & Sun) Dark wood, gold tiles and purple skull-patterned wallpaper fill this hip restaurant and cocktail bar with just the right amount of sinister opulence. The exciting menu gainfully plunders the cuisines of Asia – from India to Korea – to delicious, if pricey, effect.

🍸 DRINKING & NIGHTLIFE

Smash Palace   Bar

(☑03-366 5369; www.thesmashpalace.co.nz; 172 High St; ☺4pm-late Mon-Fri, noon-late Sat & Sun) Epitomising the spirit of transience, tenacity and number-eight wire that

Christchurch is now known for, this deliberately downcycled and ramshackle beer garden is an intoxicating mix of grease-monkey garage, trailer-trash park, and proto-hipster hang-out complete with a psychedelic school bus, edible garden and blooming roses. There's craft beer, chips and cereal, and burgers ($11 to $15).

Pomeroy's Old Brewery Inn   Pub

(☑03-365 1523; www.pomspub.co.nz; 292 Kilmore St; ☺3-11pm Tue-Thu, noon-11pm Fri-Sun) For fans of great beer, there's no better place than Pomeroy's for supping a drop or two alongside a plate of pork crackling. Among this British-style pub's many other endearing features are regular live music, a snug, sunny courtyard and Victoria's Kitchen, serving comforting pub food (mains $24 to $30). The newest addition, pretty **Little Pom's** cafe, serves super-fine fare (meals $14 to $22) til mid afternoon.

Dux Central   Bar

(☑03-943 7830; www.duxcentral.co.nz; 6 Poplar St; ☺11am-late) Pumping a whole lot of heart back into the flattened High St precinct, the

Cashell St Mall

epic new Dux comprises a brew bar serving their own and other crafty drops, the Emerald Room wine bar, Upper Dux restaurant and the Poplar Social Club cocktail bar, all within a lovingly restored old building.

The Brewery Craft Beer
(www.casselsbrewery.co.nz; 3 Garlands Rd, Woolston; ⊙7am-late) An essential destination for beer-loving travellers, the Cassels & Sons' brewery crafts beers using a wood-fired brew kettle, resulting in big, bold ales. Tasting trays are available for the curious and the indecisive, live bands perform regularly, and the food – including wood-fired pizzas ($20 to $24) – is top-notch, too.

⊛ ENTERTAINMENT

Court Theatre Theatre
(⊡03-963 0870; www.courttheatre.org.nz; Bernard St, Addington) Christchurch's original Court Theatre was an integral part of the city's Arts Centre, but it was forced to relocate to this warehouse after the earthquakes. The new premises are much more spacious; it's a great venue to see popular international plays and works by NZ playwrights.

darkroom Live Music
(www.darkroom.bar; 336 St Asaph St; ⊙7pm-late Wed-Sun) A hip combination of live-music venue and bar, darkroom has lots of Kiwi beers and great cocktails. Live gigs are frequent – and frequently free.

❶ INFORMATION

Christchurch i-SITE (⊡03-379 9629; www.christchurchnz.com; Botanic Gardens, Rolleston Ave; ⊙8.30am-5pm, extended hours summer) This ever-helpful and eternally busy i-SITE also now has an outpost in the Re:START Mall, open daily from November to March.

❶ GETTING THERE & AWAY

AIR

Christchurch Airport (p305) is the South Island's main international gateway. **Air New**

Zealand (⊡0800 737 000; www.airnewzealand.co.nz) flies to/from Auckland, Wellington, Dunedin and Queenstown; **Jetstar** (⊡0800 800 995; www.jetstar.com) flies to/from Auckland and Wellington. There are international connections with Australia, Singapore and Guangzhou in China.

BUS

There are regular buses and shuttles linking Christchurch to destinations including Lake Tekapo, Akaroa, Picton, Queenstown and Te Anau.

TRAIN

Christchurch Railway Station (www.kiwirailscenic.co.nz; Troup Dr, Addington; ⊙ticket office 6.30am-3pm) is the terminus for the TranzAlpine, crossing the Southern Alps west to Greymouth (p230), and the *Coastal Pacific,* running daily from September to April north up the east coast via Kaikoura to Picton.

❶ GETTING AROUND

Christchurch's flat topography and gridlike structure make getting around on foot or by bike a breeze. To hire a funky vintage bicycles, see the **Vintage Peddler Bike Hire Co** (⊡03-365 6530; www.thevintagepeddler.co.nz; 7/75 Peterborough St; per hour/day from $15/30).

Akaroa

Akaroa ('Long Harbour' in Māori) was the site of the country's first French settlement and descendants of the original French pioneers still reside here. It's a charming town that strives to recreate the feel of a French provincial village, down to the names of its streets and houses

◉ SIGHTS

Akaroa Museum Museum
(www.akaroamuseum.org.nz; cnr Rues Lavaud & Balguerie; ⊙10.30am-4.30pm) An arduous post-quake revamp has rewarded Akaroa with one of the smartest regional museums in the land. Learn about

Akaroa

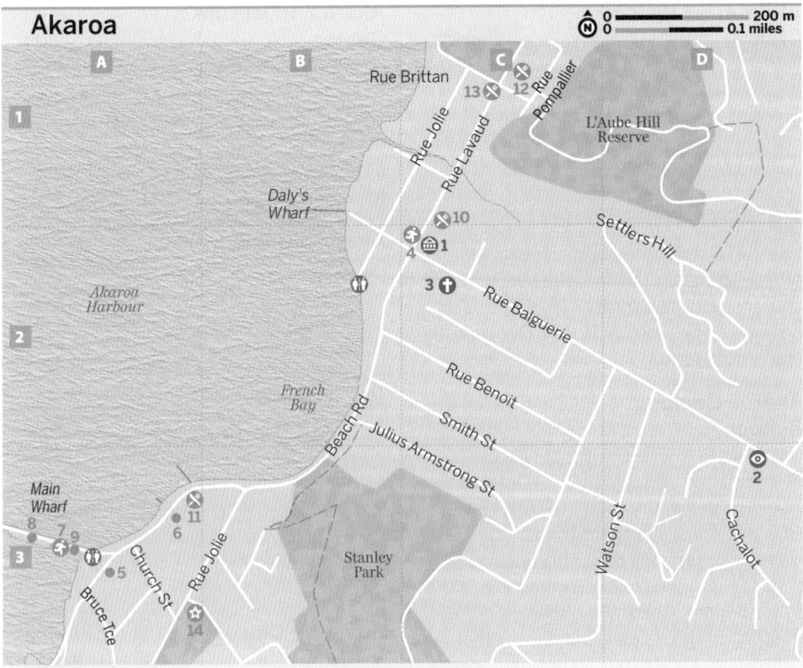

0 200 m
0 0.1 miles
A
B
C
D
1
2
3
Rue Brittan
Rue Pompallier
L'Aube Hill Reserve
Rue Jolie
Rue Lavaud
Daly's Wharf
Settlers Hill
Akaroa Harbour
Rue Balguerie
Rue Benoit
French Bay
Smith St
Beach Rd
Julius Armstrong St
Main Wharf
Stanley Park
Watson St
Cachalot
Church St
Rue Jolie
Bruce Tce

Akaroa

Sights

1 Akaroa Museum C2
2 Giant's House D3
3 St Peter's Anglican Church C2

Activities, Courses & Tours

4 Akaroa Adventure Centre C2
5 Akaroa Cooking School A3
6 Akaroa Dolphins A3
7 Akaroa Sailing Cruises A3
8 Black Cat Cruises A3
9 Coast Up Close A3

Eating

10 Akaroa Butchery & Deli C1
11 Akaroa Fish & Chips A3
12 Little Bistro C1
13 Peninsula General Store C1

Entertainment

14 Akaroa Cinema & Café A3

Information

Akaroa i-SITE & Adventure Centre .... (see 4)

the various phases of the peninsula's settlement and its fascinating natural and industrial history, and hear stories of old characters including Pompey the penguin. A 20-minute film fills in some gaps while several adjacent historic buildings keep it real. Note the donation box.

Giant's House Gardens

(www.thegiantshouse.co.nz; 68 Rue Balguerie; adult/child $20/10; ⌚noon-5pm Jan-Apr, 2-4pm May-Dec) An ongoing labour of love by local artist Josie Martin, this playful and whimsical combination of sculpture and mosaics cascades down a hillside garden above Akaroa. Echoes of Gaudí and Miró can be found in the intricate collages of mirrors, tiles and broken china, and there are many surprising nooks and crannies to discover.

St Peter's Anglican Church
Church

(46 Rue Balguerie) Graciously restored in 2015, this 1864 Anglican gem features extensive exposed timbers, stained glass and an historic organ, and it has a few stories to tell. Well worth a look.

✈ ACTIVITIES

The i-SITE stocks booklets on walks around Akaroa township, taking in the old cottages, churches and gardens that lend Akaroa its character. The six-hour Skyline Circuit also starts from town.

Akaroa Cooking School
Cooking

(☏021 166 3737; www.akaroacooking.co.nz; 81 Beach Rd; per person from $225) Options include popular 'Gourmet in a Day' sessions (10am to 4pm) and specialised barbecue classes. All sessions end with consuming your self-prepared feast, accompanied by local wines. Check the website for the school's occasional forays into other cuisines, including Thai, French and Spanish.

Akaroa Adventure Centre
Adventure Sports

(☏03-304 7784; www.akaroa.com; 74a Rue Lavaud; ⊘9am-6pm) Rents out sea kayaks and stand-up paddle boards (per hour/day $20/60), paddle boats (per hour $30), bikes (per hour/day $15/65), and fishing rods (per day $10). Based at the i-SITE.

Akaroa Sailing Cruises
Boating

(☏0800 724 528; www.aclasssailing.co.nz; Main Wharf; adult/child $75/37.50) Set sail for a 2½-hour hands-on cruise on a gorgeous 1946 A-Class yacht.

✈ TOURS

Akaroa Farm Tours
Tour

(☏03-304 8511; www.akaroafarmtours.com; adult/child $80/50) Tours depart from Akaroa iSITE and head to a hill-country farm near Paua Bay for shearing demonstrations, sheepdog shenanigans, gardens and home-made scones; allow 2¾ hours.

Coast Up Close
Boating

(☏0800 126 278; www.coastupclose.co.nz; Main Wharf; adult/child from $75/25; ⊘departs

Banks Peninsula (p196)

DANE-MO/GETTY IMAGES ©

10.15am & 1.45pm Oct-Apr) Scenic boat trips with an emphasis on wildlife watching. Fishing trips can be arranged.

Eastern Bays Scenic Mail Run
Driving

(☑03-304 8526; tours $80; ☺9am Mon-Fri) Travel along with the postie to visit isolated communities and bays on this 120km, five-hour mail delivery service. Departs from the i-SITE; bookings are essential as there are only eight seats available.

Pohatu Plunge
Wildlife Watching

(☑03-304 8542; www.pohatu.co.nz) Runs evening tours from Akaroa to the Pohatu white-flippered penguin colony (adult/child $75/55), with a self-drive option available (adult /child $25/12). Viewing is best during breeding season, August to January, but is possible throughout the year. Sea kayaking and 4WD nature tours are also available, as is the option of staying overnight in a secluded cottage.

EATING

Akaroa Butchery & Deli
Deli $

(67 Rue Lavaud; ☺10am-5.30pm Mon-Fri, 9am-4pm Sat) This sharp butchery champions all manner of local produce from bread, salmon, cheese and pickles, to great pies, smallgoods and meat for the barbecue.

Akaroa Fish & Chips
Fish & Chips $

(59 Beach Rd; meals $8-18; ☺11am-8pm)A seaside location for tucking into blue cod, scallops, oysters and other assorted deep-fried goodies, whether you eat in or take them across the road to the harbour's edge. Either way, expect seagulls.

Peninsula General Store
Cafe, Deli $

(www.peninsulageneralstore.co.nz; 40 Rue Lavaud; ☺9am-4pm Mon-Sat) ✔ Not only does this darling little corner store sell fresh bread, organic local produce and groceries, it also does the best espresso in the village.

Hilltop Tavern
Pub Food $$

(☑03-325 1005; www.thehilltop.co.nz; 5207 Christchurch-Akaroa Rd; pizzas $24-26, mains

$23-30; ☺10am-late, reduced hours in winter) Killer views, craft beer, proper wood-fired pizzas and a pool table. Occasional live music seals the deal for locals and visitors alike at this historic pub. Enjoy grandstand views of Akaroa harbour backdropped by the peninsula.

Little Bistro
French $$$

(☑03-304 7314; www.thelittlebistro.co.nz; 33 Rue Lavaud; mains $22-40; ☺11am-2pm & 5pm-late Tue-Sat) A decent bet for refined food, this place serves a classic bistro-style menu featuring local seafood, South Island wines and Canterbury craft beers. The menu changes seasonally, but usually includes favourites such as crusted lamb or Akaroa salmon terrine.

✪ ENTERTAINMENT

Akaroa Cinema & Café
Cinema

(☑03-304 8898; www.cinecafe.co.nz; cnr Rue Jolie & Selwyn Ave; adult/child $15/13; 📶) Grab a beer and settle in to watch an art-house, classic or foreign flick with high-quality sound and projection.

❶ INFORMATION

Akaroa i-SITE & Adventure Centre (☑03-304 8600; www.akaroa.com; 74a Rue Lavaud; ☺9am-5pm) A helpful little hub offering info and bookings for local activities, transport, et al. Doubles as the post office.

❶ GETTING THERE & AWAY

From November to April the **Akaroa Shuttle** (☑0800 500 929; www.akaroashuttle.co.nz; one way/return $35/50) run daily services from Christchurch to Akaroa (departs 8.30am), returning to Christchurch at 3.45pm. Check the website for Christchurch pick-up options. Scenic tours from Christchurch exploring Banks Peninsula are also available.

French Connection (☑0800 800 575; www.akaroabus.co.nz; return $45) has a year-round daily departure from Christchurch at 9am, returning from Akaroa at 4pm.

Lake Tekapo

Lake Tekapo

Heading to Queenstown and the southern lakes from Christchurch takes you through the heart of the spectacular Mackenzie Country. Lake Tekapo combines incredible alpine and lake views with easy access to Aoraki/Mt Cook National Park.

Great For...

☑ Don't Miss

The 360-degree view across the entire Mackenize Basin from Mt John's **Astro Café** (Mt John University Observatory; mains $7-12; ◷9am-5pm).

Beautiful Lake Tekapo is the travellers' hub of the Mackenzie Country, the plateau from which the scenic peaks of Aoraki/Mt Cook National Park escalate. The area was named after the legendary James 'Jock' McKenzie who ran his stolen flocks in this then-uninhabited region in the 1840s.

In 2012 the Aoraki Mackenzie area was declared an International Dark Sky Reserve, and Tekapo's pollution-free Mt John is the ultimate place to experience the region's glorious night sky.

Other activities around Lake Tekapo include horse riding with **Mackenzie Alpine Horse Trekking** (☎0800 628 269; www.maht.co.nz) and relaxing and recharging in the hot pools, saunas and day spa at **Tekapo Springs**. (☎03-680 6550; www.tekaposprings.co.nz; 6 Lakeside Dr; ◷10am-9pm)

View towards Aoraki/Mt Cook

MATTEO COLOMBO/GETTY IMAGES ©

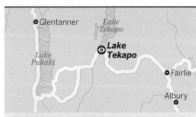

❶ Need to Know

Visit www.mtcooknz.com for a show-case of the Mackenzie Country and Aoraki/Mt Cook National Park.

✕ Take a Break

Frosty beers combine with lake views at **Mackenzie's Bar & Grill** (SH8; ⊘11.30am-late Mon-Fri, 10am-late Sat & Sun).

★ Did You Know?

Lake Tekapo's turquoise hue is due to a glacial sediment known as 'rock flour.'

Church of the Good Shepherd   Church

(Pioneer Dr; ⊘9am-5pm) The prime dis-gorging point for tour buses, this lakeside church was built of stone and oak in 1935. A picture window behind the altar gives churchgoers a distractingly divine view of lake and mountain majesty; needless to say, it's a firm favourite for weddings. Come early in the morning or late afternoon to avoid the peace-shattering masses.

Earth & Sky   Tour

(☑03-680 6960; www.earthandsky.co.nz; SH8) 🚩 If you've ever wanted to tour an obser-vatory and survey the night sky, this is the place to do it. Nightly tours head up to the University of Canterbury's observatory on Mt John (adult/child $145/80). Day tours of the facility are given on demand in win-ter, while in summer there's usually a guide

available at the observatory from around midday to 3pm (adult/child $20/10).

What's Nearby

At the northern end of slender Lake Pukaki – and 124km from Lake Tekapo – Aoraki/Mt Cook (3754m) is the tallest peak in Australasia. The **Aoraki/Mt Cook National Park Visitor Centre** (☑03-435 1186; www.doc.govt.nz; 1 Larch Grove; ⊘8.30am-4.30pm, to 5pm Oct-Apr) FREE can advise on short walks in the immediate area. Just beware the weather can be highly change-able. Located in the Hermitage, an iconic NZ hotel, the **Sir Edmund Hillary Alpine Centre** (www.hermitage.co.nz; The Hermitage, Terrace Rd; adult/child $20/10; ⊘7am-8.30pm Oct-Mar, 8am-7pm Apr-Sep) features Hillary memorabilia and displays about mountain-eering, and a fascinating 75-minute film about Sir Ed's pioneering conquest of Mt Everest in 1953. Other activities at Aoraki/Mt Cook include exploring the terminal lake of the Tasman Glacier by kayak or inflatable boat.

WEST COAST

West Coast at a glance...

Hemmed in by the Tasman Sea and the Southern Alps, the West Coast is like nowhere else in New Zealand, it's history built on the wavering fortunes of gold, coal and timber. The biggest drawcards here are the Franz Josef and Fox glaciers. Nowhere else at this latitude do glaciers come so close to the ocean. Their breathtaking existence is largely due to the West Coast's ample rain, with snow falling in the glaciers' broad accumulation zones and then fusing into 20m-depths of ice.

Two days on the West Coast

Focus your time on the West Coast's spectacular glaciers. The best way to see the incredible scale of **Franz Josef** (p216) and **Fox** (p220) – and to understand how incredibly close they are to the ocean – is to take a sightseeing flight. The weather can close in suddenly, so be prepared to be flexible with your schedule if need be.

Four days on the West Coast

After experiencing the glaciers – ideally incorporating a guided walk with **Franz Josef Glacier Guides** (p217) – head to nearby **Okarito** (p222) for after-dark kiwi spotting and kayaking on **Okarito Lagoon** (p222). Literary and history buffs should then check out **Hokitika** (p228), and if you're self-driving the South Island, definitely make time to visit the stunning **Pancake Rocks** (p224).

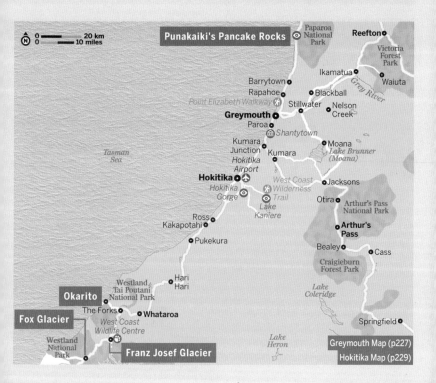

N
0 ——— 20 km
0 ——— 10 miles

Punakaiki's Pancake Rocks ◉ Paparoa National Park
Reefton ◉
Victoria Forest Park
Ikamatua ◉ ◉ Waiuta
Barrytown ◉ Grey River
Rapahoe ◉ ◉ Blackball
Point Elizabeth Walkway 🚶 Stillwater ◉ Nelson Creek
Greymouth ◉
Paroa ◉ 🏠 Shantytown
Kumara Junction ◉ ◉ Moana Lake Brunner (Moana)
Kumara ◉
Hokitika Airport ✈
Hokitika ◉ ✈ West Coast Wilderness Trail ◉ Jacksons
Hokitika Gorge ◉ ◉ Lake Kaniere Otira ◉ Arthur's Pass National Park
Ross ◉ **Arthur's Pass** ◉
Kakapotahi ◉
◉ Pukekura Bealey ◉ ◉ Cass
Craigieburn Forest Park
Tasman Sea
Hari Hari ◉
Westland Tai Poutini National Park Lake Coleridge
Okarito The Forks ◉ ◉ Whataroa
Fox Glacier *West Coast Wildlife Centre* 🏛
Springfield ◉
Westland National Park **Franz Josef Glacier** Lake Heron

Greymouth Map (p227)
Hokitika Map (p229)

Arriving in the West Coast

Greymouth Railway Station One of the world's great train journeys, the **TranzAlpine** (p230) traverses the Southern Alps from Christchurch to Greymouth. Buses and shuttles from Nelson, Franz Josef Glacier and Christchurch also stop here.

Hokitika Airport Flights on most days to/from Christchurch.

Hokitika i-SITE Regular buses and shuttles from Greymouth and Nelson.

Where to Stay

Accommodation in Greymouth is certainly plentiful with a good selection of hostels and holiday parks but you won't find many luxury options. Some of the West Coast's most charming accommodation is to be found in Hokitika and surrounds. Franz Josef has stacks of accommodation, but the town's popularity means booking head is recommended from November through March. Nearby Fox Glacier, 24km to the south, also has accommodation.

Helicopter on the glacier snowfield

MATTHEW MICAH WRIGHT/GETTY IMAGES ©

Franz Josef Glacier

The early Māori knew Franz Josef as Ka Roimata o Hine Hukatere (Tears of the Avalanche Girl). Legend tells of a girl losing her lover and her tears freezing into the glacier.

Great For...

☑ Don't Miss

Landing on the snow at the head of the glacier – pricey but priceless.

Independent Walks

Walks start from the glacier car park, all rewarding way beyond a view of the ice. A concise option is **Sentinel Rock** (20 minutes return), while **Ka Roimata o Hine Hukatere Track** (1½ hours return), the main glacier valley walk, leads to the best permissible view of the terminal face. DOC's *Region Walks* booklet ($2) outlines other local trails and incorporates maps.

An alternative to driving the 5km to the glacier car park is taking the rainforested **Te Ara a Waiau Walkway/Cycleway**, starting from near the fire station at the southern end of town. It's a one-hour walk (each way) or half that by bicycle – which are available for hire from **Across Country Quad Bikes** (p218) or the **YHA** (☑03-752 0754; www.yha.co.nz; 2-4 Cron St; dm $26-33, s $85, d $107-135; ☎). Leave your bikes at the

Hiker in an ice cave

ⓘ Need to Know

Check out www.glaciercountry.co.nz for more information on both the Franz Josef and Fox glaciers.

✕ Take a Break

Warm up with burgers, steaks and pizza at the **Landing Bar & Restaurant** (p219).

★ Top Tip

The weather can be changeable, so factor in leeway if you're planning some aerial sightseeing.

car park – you can't cycle on the glacier walkways.

Guided Walks

Small group walks with experienced guides (boots, jackets and equipment supplied) are offered by **Franz Josef Glacier Guides** (☏0800 484 337, 03-752 0763; www.franz josefglacier.com; 63 Cron St). Both standard tours require helicopter transfers on to the ice: the 'Ice Explorer' ($339) is bookended by a four-minute flight, with around three hours on the ice; the easier 'Heli Hike' ($435) explores higher reaches of the glacier, requiring a 10-minute flight with around two hours on the ice. Taking around three hours, the 'Glacier Valley Walk' ($75) follows the Waiho River up to the moraine, offering close-up views of the ice. All trips are $10 to $30 cheaper for children.

Aerial Sightseeing

Forget sandflies and mozzies. The buzzing you're hearing is a swarm of aircraft in the skies around the glaciers and just beyond in the realm of Aoraki/Mt Cook. A common heliflight ($220 to $240) goes for 20 minutes, and flies to the head of Franz Glacier with a snow landing up top. A 'twin glacier' flight – taking in Fox as well as Franz in around 30 minutes – costs in the region of $300, with a 40-minute trip (swooping around Aoraki/Mt Cook) from $420. Fares for children under 12 years cost between 50% and 70% of the adult price. Shop around: most operators are situated on the main road in Franz Josef Village.

Sights

West Coast Wildlife Centre Wildlife (www.wildkiwi.co.nz; cnr Cron & Cowan Sts; day pass adult/child/family $35/20/85, incl backstage pass $55/35/145) ⌀ The purpose of this feel-good attraction is breeding two of the world's rarest kiwi – the rowi and Haast tokoeka. The entry fee is well worthwhile by the time you've viewed the conservation, glacier and heritage displays, and hung out with real, live kiwi in their ferny enclosure. The additional backstage pass into the incubating and rearing area is a rare opportunity to learn how a species can be brought back from the brink of extinction.

Activities

Glacier Hot Pools   Hot Spring

(☑03-752 0099; www.glacierhotpools.co.nz; 63 Cron St; adult/child $26/22; ☺1-9pm, last entry 8pm) In a pretty rainforest setting on the edge of town, this stylish and well-maintained outdoor hot-pool complex is perfect après-hike or on a rainy day. Massage and private pools also available.

Glacier Valley Eco Tours   Ecotour

(☑0800 999 739, 03-752 0699; www.glacier valley.co.nz) Offers leisurely three- to eight-hour walking tours around local sights ($75 to $170), packed with local knowledge; plus regular shuttle services to the glacier car park ($12.50 return).

Glacier Country Kayaks   Kayaking

(☑0800 423 262, 03-752 0230; www.glacier kayaks.com; 64 Cron St; 3hr kayak $115) Take a guided kayak trip on Lake Mapourika (7km north of Franz), with fascinating commentary, birdlife, mountain views, a serene channel detour and an additional bushwalk on offer. Ask about the new boat cruises.

Across Country
Quad Bikes   Quad-Biking

(☑0800 234 288, 03-752 0123; www.across countryquadbikes.co.nz; Air Safaris Bldg,

Path leading towards Franz Josef Glacier

Main Rd) Quad-bike outings through the rainforest (rider/passenger $160/70, two hours), with 'buggy' options for smaller folks. Mountain-bike hire available (half-/full day $25/40).

Eco-Rafting
Rafting

(☏03-755 4254, 021 523 426; www.ecorafting.co.nz; family trip adult/child $135/110, 7hr trip $450) Rafting adventures throughout the coast, from gentle family trips, to the seven-hour 'Grand Canyon' trip on the Whataroa River with its towering granite walls, which includes a 15-minute helicopter ride.

★ Did You Know?

The glacier was first explored by Europeans in 1865, with Austrian Julius Haast naming it after the Austrian emperor.

STOCKPHOTO MANIA/SHUTTERSTOCK ©

Eating
Alice May
Modern NZ $$

(☏03-752 0740; www.alicemay.co.nz; cnr Cowan & Cron Sts; mains $20-32; ⏰4pm-late) A faux Tudor corner pub with pastoral chic, mellow vibe and family-friendly attitude, Alice May serves up meaty meals with $20 options, including a daily roast, pasta, and venison burger, with sirloin steak and fish at the upper end.

Landing Bar & Restaurant
Pub Food $$

(☏03-752 0229; www.thelandingbar.co.nz; Main Rd; mains $20-42; ⏰7.30am-late; 🛜) This busy but well-run pub offers an inordinately huge menu of crowd-pleasing food such as burgers, steaks and pizza. The patio – complete with sunshine and gas heaters – is a good place to warm up after a day on the ice.

ℹ️ INFORMATION
Franz Josef i-SITE
Tourist Information

(www.glaciercountry.co.nz; 63 Cron St) Helpful local centre offering advice and booking service for activities, accommodation and transport in the local area and beyond.

Westland Tai Poutini National Park Visitor Centre
Tourist Information

(☏03-752 0360; www.doc.govt.nz; 69 Cron St; ⏰8.30am-6pm summer, to 5pm winter) Housed in its flash new quarters, the national park visitor centre has insightful exhibits, weather information, maps, and vital track updates and weather forecasts.

ℹ️ GETTING THERE & AWAY
Buses and shuttles track north for Hokitika and Nelson and south to Fox Glacier and Queenstown.

ℹ️ GETTING AROUND
Glacier Valley Eco Tours (p218) runs scheduled shuttle services to the glacier car park (return trip $12.50).

Hiking on Fox Glacier

Fox Glacier

Fox Glacier is relatively small and quiet, with a farmy feel and open aspect. Beautiful Lake Matheson is a highlight, as are the salty walks down at Gillespies Beach.

Great For...

☑ Don't Miss

Keeping your fingers crossed for a perfect reflection of Aoraki/Mt Cook at Lake Matheson.

Independent Walks

It's 1.5km from Fox Village to the glacier turn-off, and a further 2km to the car park, which you can reach under your own steam via Te Weheka Walkway/Cycleway, a pleasant rainforest trail starting just south of the Bella Vista motel. It's just over an hour each way to walk, or 30 minutes to cycle (leave your bikes at the car park – you can't cycle on the glacier walkways). Hire bikes from the **Westhaven** (☑0800 369 452, 03-751 0084; www.thewesthaven.co.nz; SH6; d $145-185; ☎) motel.

From the car park, the terminal-face viewpoint is around 40 minutes' walk, depending on current conditions. Obey all signs: this place is dangerously dynamic.

Short walks near the glacier include the Moraine Walk (over a major 18th-century advance) and Minnehaha Walk. The fully

🛈 Need to Know

There's no ATM in Fox Glacier (which means no cash out south until Wanaka), and Fox Glacier Motors is your last chance for fuel before Haast, 120km away.

✗ Take a Break

Next to Lake Matheson, the **Matheson Cafe** combines mountain views, strong coffee and craft beers.

★ Top Tip

Find info about accommodation and activities at www.glaciercountry.co.nz

accessible River Walk Lookout Track (20 minutes return) starts from the Glacier View Rd car park and allows people of all abilities the chance to view the glacier. Pick up a copy of DOC's excellent *Glacier Region Walks* booklet ($2).

Guided Walks

The only way on to the ice is by taking a helihiking trip, run by **Fox Glacier Guiding** (☑03-751 0825, 0800 111 600; www.foxguides. co.nz; 44 Main Rd). Independent walks, however, offer a chance to explore the valley – raw and staggeringly beautiful even in its iceless lower reaches – and get as close to the glacier's terminal face as safety allows.

Aerial Sightseeing

A common heliflight ($220 to $240) is 20 minutes' long, and goes to the head of

Fox Glacier with a snow landing up top. A 'twin glacier' flight – taking in Franz as well as Fox in around 30 minutes – costs in the region of $300, with a 40-minute trip (swooping around Aoraki/Mt Cook) from $420. Fares for children under 12 years cost between 50% and 70% of the adult price. Shop around: most operators are on the main road in Fox Glacier Village.

What's Nearby

The famous 'mirror lake' – reflecting Aoraki/Mt Cook on a good day – **Lake Matheson** can be found about 6km down Cook Flat Rd. Wandering slowly it will take 1½ hours to complete a circuit of the lake. The best time to visit is early morning, or when the sun is low in the late afternoon, although the presence of the **Matheson Cafe** (☑03-751 0878; www.lakematheson.com; Lake Matheson Rd; breakfast & lunch $10-21, dinner $17-33; ◷8am-late Nov-Mar, to 4pm Apr-Oct) means that any time is a good time.

Okarito Lagoon

MATTHEW WILLIAMS-ELLIS/GETTY IMAGES ©

Okarito

Overlooked by many West Coast visitors, the coastal settlement of Okarito offers travellers a great chance so see a kiwi in the wild. Also look forward to excellent kayaking.

The magical seaside hamlet of Okarito sits alongside Okarito Lagoon, the largest unmodified wetland in New Zealand and a superb place for spotting birds, including rare kiwi and the majestic kotuku. Travelling by car, the turn-off to the Forks is 15km south of Whataroa, which branches west for 13km to Okarito.

Okarito Kiwi Tours Wildlife Watching
(☑03-753 4330; www.okaritokiwitours.co.nz; 3hr tours $75) Runs nightly expeditions to spot the rare bird (95% success rate) with an interesting education along the way. Numbers are limited to eight,

Okarito Boat Tours Wildlife Watching
(☑03-753 4223; www.okaritoboattours.co.nz) Okarito Boat Tours runs bird-spotting lagoon tours, the most fruitful of which is the 'early bird' ($80, 1½ hrs, 7.30am). The

Great For...

☑ **Don't Miss**

Heading out on an after-dark expedition to spot New Zealand's beloved kiwi.

Kiwi

NEIL FARRIN/GETTY IMAGES ©

Hari Hari

Tasman Sea

Okarito ⊙
The Forks

● **Whataroa**

Franz
Josef
● Glacier

ⓘ Need to Know

To reach Okarito you''ll need your own wheels.

✕ Take a Break

Stock up on on-the-road picnic goodies in Hokitika or Franz Josef.

popular two-hour 'ecotour' offers deeper insight into this remarkable natural area ($90, 9am and 11.30am). Cheery, long-time Okaritians Paula and Swade can also fix you up with accommodation in the village.

Andris Apse Okarito Gallery
Gallery

(☑03-753 4241; www.andrisapse.com; 109 The Strand) Okarito is home to world-class landscape photographer Andris Apse. His gallery showcases his beautiful works, printed on-site and available to purchase, as well as infinitely more affordable books.

What's Nearby

A dot of a town strung out along SH6, Whataroa – around 24km east inland from Okarito – is the departure point for tours to the Kotuku Sanctuary, New Zealand's only nesting site for the kotuku (white heron), which roosts here between November and February. The only way to visit the nesting site is with **White Heron Sanctuary Tours** (☑0800 523 456, 03-753 4120; www.whiteheron tours.co.nz; SH6, Whataroa; adult/child $120/55; ⊙4 tours daily late Aug-Mar) on an enjoyable 2½-hour tour involving a gentle jetboat ride and short boardwalk to a viewing hide. Seeing the scores of birds perched in the bushes is a magical experience.

Glacier Country Scenic Flights (☑03-753 4096, 0800 423 463; www.glacier adventures.co.nz; SH6, Whataroa; flights $195-435) offers a range of scenic flights and helihikes, lifting off from Whataroa Valley. These guys give you more mountain-gawping for your buck than many of the operators flying from the glacier townships.

If it's open, call in to the **Peter Hlavacek Gallery** (☑03-753 4199; www.nzicescapes.com; SH6, Whataroa; ⊙9am-5pm Mon-Fri) on the highway. Many regard him as one of NZ's finest landscape photographers.

Pancake Rocks

Punakaiki's Pancake Rocks

Nature's power is showcased amid the spectacular geological display of Punakaiki's Pancake Rocks. The surrounding coastal scenery is also wildly beautiful, and walking tracks carefully negotiate verdant forest.

Great For

☑ **Don't Miss**

The exciting Fox River Cave Walk (three hours return), 12km north of Punakaiki; BYO torch.

Reached via a stunning coast road, Punakaiki is 45km north of Greymouth. The area's claim to fame is Dolomite Point, where a layering-weathering process called stylobedding has carved the limestone into what looks like piles of thick pancakes. Aim for high tide when the sea surges into caverns and booms menacingly through blowholes (tide timetables are posted in town; hope that it coincides with sunset). See it on a wild day and be reminded that Mother Nature really is the boss. An easy 15-minute walk loops from the highway out to the rocks and blowholes.

Most travellers just stop off at the highway to see the Pancake Rocks, but active types are encouraged to spend longer and explore the stunning forest and coastal scenery of the area and the nearby Paparoa National Park.

❶ Need to Know

Paparoa National Park Visitor Centre
(☑03-731 1895; www.doc.govt.nz; SH6;
☻9am-5pm Oct-Nov, to 6pm Dec-Mar, to
4.30pm Apr-Sep)

✕ Take a Break

Shelter from the sometimes rugged
weather at the **Pancake Rocks Cafe**
(☑03-731 1122; www.pancakerockscafe.com;
4300 Coast Rd, Punakaiki; meals $10-22;
☻8am-5pm).

★ Top Tip

Buses traversing the West Coast via
Westport and Franz Josef stop for passengers to admire the Pancake Rocks.

Punakaiki Canoes (☑03-731 1870; www.
riverkayaking.co.nz; SH6; canoe hire 2hr/full day
$40/60, family rates available) rents canoes
near the Pororari River bridge for gentle,
super-scenic paddling for all abilities, while
Punakaiki Horse Treks (☑03-731 1839;
www.pancake-rocks.co.nz; SH6; 2½hr ride $170;
☻Nov-May), based at Hydrangea Cottages,
conducts treks in the beautiful Punakaiki
Valley, with river crossings, finishing at the
beach.

Tramps around Punakaiki include the
Truman Track (30 minutes return) and the
Punakaiki–Porari Loop (3½ hours), which
goes up the spectacular limestone Pororari
River gorge before popping over a hill and
coming down the bouldery Punakaiki River
to rejoin the highway.

Other tramps in the national park are
detailed in the DOC *Paparoa National*

Park pamphlet ($1). Note that many of
Paparoa's inland walks are susceptible to
river flooding so it is vital that you obtain
updates from the Paparoa National Park
Visitor Centre in Punakaiki .

What's Nearby

The highway between Punakaiki and Greymouth is flanked by white-capped waves
and rocky bays on one side, and the steep,
bushy Paparoa Ranges on the other.

At Barrytown, 17km south of Punakaiki,
Steve and Robyn run **Barrytown Knife-
making** (☑0800 256 433, 03-731 1053; www.
barrytownknifemaking.com; 2662 SH6, Barrytown; classes $150; ☻closed Mon), where you
can make your own knife – from hand-
forging the blade to crafting a handle from
native rimu timber. The day-long course
features lunch, archery, axe-throwing and
a stream of entertainingly bad jokes from
Steve. Bookings are essential, and transport from Punakaiki can be arranged.

Greymouth

Welcome to the 'Big Smoke,' crouched at the mouth of the imaginatively named Grey River. Known to Māori as Mawhera, the West Coast's largest town has gold in its veins, and today its fortunes still ebb and flow with the tide of mining. Tourism and dairy farming, however, are increasingly vital to the economy. The town is well geared for travellers, offering all the necessary services and the odd tourist attraction, the most famous of which is Shantytown.

 SIGHTS

Left Bank Art Gallery   Gallery
(www.leftbankarts.org.nz; 1 Tainui St; admission by donation; ⊙11am-4.30pm Tue-Fri, 11am-2pm Sat) This 95-year old former bank houses contemporary NZ jade carvings, prints, paintings, photographs and ceramics. The gallery also fosters and supports a wide society of West Coast artists.

Monteith's Brewing Co   Brewery
(☑03-768 4149; www.monteiths.co.nz; cnr Turumaha & Herbert Sts; guided tour $22; ⊙11am-8pm) The original Monteith's brewhouse may simply be brand HQ for mainstream product largely brewed elsewhere, but it still delivers heritage in spades through its excellent-value guided tour (25 minutes, includes generous samples; four tours daily). The flash tasting room-cum-bar is now Greymouth's most exciting watering hole (tasty snacks $9 to $22) – shame it shuts up shop so early.

Shantytown   Museum
(www.shantytown.co.nz; Rutherglen Rd, Paroa; adult/child/family $33/16/78; ⊙8.30am-5pm) Eight kilometres south of Greymouth and 2km inland from SH6, Shantytown evocatively presents and preserves local history through a recreated 1860s gold-mining town, complete with steam-train rides, pub and Rosie's House of Ill Repute. There's also gold panning, a sawmill, a gory

hospital, and short holographic movies in the Princess Theatre.

History House Museum   Museum
(www.greydc.govt.nz; 27 Gresson St; adult/child $6/2; ⊙10am-4pm Mon-Fri) Housed in an historic building, this museum is predominantly pictorial and, although old fashioned, provides endless background on the region's trials and tribulations. A good place to pull up a chair on a rainy day.

 ACTIVITIES

Floodwall Walk   Walking
Take a 10-minute riverside stroll along Mawhera Quay – the start of the West Coast Wilderness Trail (www.westcoast wildernesstrail.co.nz) – or keep going for an hour or so, taking in the fishing boat harbour, Blaketown Beach and breakwater – a great place to experience the ocean and savour a famous West Coast sunset.

Point Elizabeth Walkway   Walking
(www.doc.govt.nz) Accessible from Dommett Esplanade in Cobden, 6km north of Greymouth, this enjoyable walkway (three hours return) skirts around a richly forested headland in the shadow of the Rapahoe Range to an impressive ocean lookout, before continuing on to the northern trailhead at Rapahoe (11km from Greymouth) – small town, big beach, friendly local pub.

 EATING

DP1 Cafe   Cafe $
(104 Mawhera Quay; meals $7-23; ⊙8am-5pm Mon-Fri, 9am-5pm Sat & Sun; 🛜) A stalwart of the Greymouth cafe scene, this hip joint serves great espresso, along with good-value grub. Groovy tunes, wi-fi, local art and quayside tables make this a welcoming spot to linger. Swing in for the $6 morning muffin and coffee special.

Recreation Hotel   Restaurant $$
(☑03-768 5154; www.rechotel.co.nz; 68 High St; mains $17 to $26; ⊙11am-late) A strong local following fronts up to 'the Rec' for its smart

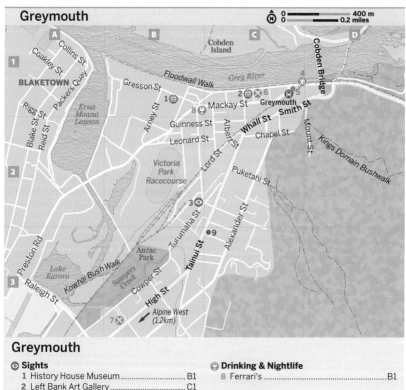

Greymouth

public bar serving good pub grub, such as a daily roast, burgers and local fish and chips amid pool tables and the TAB. Out the back, Buccleugh's dining room offers fancier fare such as venison backstrap and pork fillet wrapped in parma ham (mains $18 to $34).

⊖ DRINKING & NIGHTLIFE

Ferrari's   Bar
(☏03-768 4008; www.ferraris.co.nz; 6 Mackay St; ☺5pm-late Thur-Sat, noon-6pm Sun)

Valiantly trying to capture the sophistication and glamour of golden-era Hollywood in good old Greymouth, this bar inside the Regent Cinema is an atmospheric and comfortable place to plonk yourself down in a leather sofa for a drink or two.

ⓘ INFORMATION

Greymouth i-SITE (☏03-768 5101, 0800 473 966; www.westcoasttravel.co.nz; 164 Mackay St, Greymouth Train Station; ☺9am-5pm Mon-Fri,

9.30am-4pm Sat & Sun; 📶) The helpful crew at the train station can assist with all manner of advice and bookings, including those for DOC huts and walks. See also www.westcoastnz.com.

West Coast Travel Centre (📞03-768 7080; www.westcoasttravel.co.nz; 164 Mackay St, Greymouth Train Station; ⊙9am-5pm Mon-Fri, 10am-4pm Sat & Sun; 📶) Sharing the old train station with the i-SITE, West Coast Travel Centre books all forms of transport, including buses, trains and inter-island ferries, and has luggage-storage facilities. It also doubles as the bus depot.

❶ GETTING THERE & AWAY

As well as the i-SITE at the train station, the West Coast Travel Centre books local and national transport. Buses and shuttles link Greymouth to Nelson, Christchurch and south to the Franz Josef and Fox glaciers.

❶ GETTING AROUND

Several car-hire company desks are located in the train station. Local companies include **Alpine West** (📞0800 257 736, 03-768 4002; www.alpinerentals.co.nz; 11 Shelley St) and **NZ Rent-a-Car** (📞03-768 0379; www.nzrentacar.co.nz; 170 Tainui St).

Hokitika

Popular with history buffs and the setting for numerous New Zealand novels – including the 2013 Man Booker–award winning *The Luminaries* by Eleanor Catton – Hokitika's riches come in many forms. Founded on gold, today the town is the stronghold of indigenous *pounamu* (greenstone), which jostles for attention amid many other arts and crafts, drawing rafts of visitors to its wide open streets.

◎ SIGHTS

Hokitika Museum　　Museum
(www.hokitikamuseum.co.nz; 17 Hamilton St; adult/child $6/3; ⊙10am-5pm Nov-Mar, 10am-2pm Apr-Oct) Housed in the imposing

Carnegie Building (1908), this is an exemplary provincial museum, with intelligently curated exhibitions presented in a clear, modern style. Highlights include the fascinating *Whitebait!* exhibition, and the Pounamu room – the ideal primer before you hit the galleries looking for greenstone treasures.

Glowworm Dell　　Natural Feature
On the northern edge of town, a short stroll from SH6 leads to this glowworm dell, an easy opportunity to enter the other-worldly home of NZ's native fungus gnat larvae (so not even a worm at all). An information panel at the entrance will further illuminate your way.

Hokitika Glass Studio　　Gallery
(www.hokitikaglass.co.nz; 9 Weld St; ⊙8.30am-5pm) Glass art covering a continuum from garish to glorious; watch the blowers at the furnace on weekdays.

Hokitika Craft Gallery　　Gallery
(www.hokitikacraftgallery.co.nz; 25 Tancred St; ⊙8.30am-5pm) The town's best one-stop shop, this co-op showcases a wide range of local work, including *pounamu*, jewellery, textiles, ceramics and woodwork.

Waewae Pounamu　　Gallery
(www.waewaepounamu.co.nz; 39 Weld St; 8am-5pm) This stronghold of NZ *pounamu* displays traditional and contemporary designs in its main-road gallery.

Hokitika Gorge　　Gorge
(www.doc.govt.nz) A picturesque 35km drive leads to Hokitika Gorge, a ravishing ravine with unbelievably turquoise waters coloured by glacial 'flour'. Photograph the scene from every angle via the short forest walkway and swingbridge. The gorge is well signposted from Stafford St (past the dairy factory). En route, you will pass Kowhitirangi, the site of NZ's first mass murder and a massive 12-day manhunt (immortalised in the 1982 classic film *Bad Blood*). A poignant roadside monument lines up the farmstead site through a stone shaft.

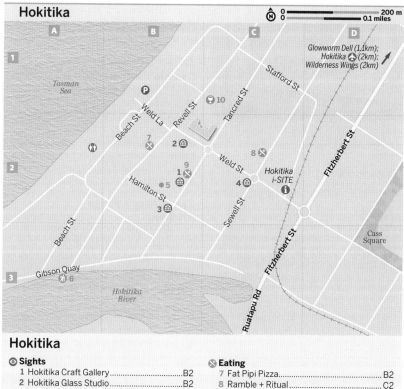

Hokitika

⊙ Sights
1 Hokitika Craft Gallery	B2
2 Hokitika Glass Studio	B2
3 Hokitika Museum	B2
4 Waewae Pounamu	C2

⊕ Activities, Courses & Tours
5 Bonz 'N' Stonz	B2
6 Hokitika Heritage Walk	A3

⊗ Eating
7 Fat Pipi Pizza	B2
8 Ramble + Ritual	C2
9 Sweet Alice's Fudge Kitchen	B2

⊕ Drinking & Nightlife
10 West Coast Wine Bar	C1

Lake Kaniere　　　　　　Lake

(www.doc.govt.nz) Lying at the heart of a
7000-hectare scenic reserve, beautiful
Lake Kaniere is 8km long, 2km wide, 195m
deep, and freezing cold as you'll discover if
you swim. You may, however, prefer simply
to camp or picnic at Hans Bay or undertake
one of numerous walks in the surrounds,
ranging from the 15-minute Canoe Cove
Walk to the seven-hour return gut-buster
up Mt Tuhua. The historic **Kaniere Water
Race Walkway** (3½ hours one way) forms
part of the West Coast Wilderness Trail
(p226).

⊕ ACTIVITIES

Bonz 'N' Stonz　　　　　　Carving

(www.bonz-n-stonz.co.nz; 16 Hamilton St; full-day
workshop $85-180) Design, carve and polish
your own *pounamu*, bone or paua (shell-
fish) masterpiece, with tutelage from Steve.
Prices vary with materials and design
complexity. Bookings recommended.

Hokitika Heritage Walk　　　　Walking

Ask staff at the i-SITE for the worthy 50c
leaflet before wandering the old wharf
precinct, or ask them about a guided walk
with Mr Verrall. Another map details the

The TranzAlpine

The **TranzAlpine** (☑0800 872 467, 03-341 2588; www.kiwirailscenic.co.nz; one way adult/child from $99/69; ⊘departs Christchurch 8.15am, Greymouth 1.45pm) is one of the world's great train journeys, traversing the Southern Alps between Christchurch (p191) and Greymouth, from the Pacific Ocean to the Tasman Sea, passing through Arthur's Pass National Park.

En route is a sequence of dramatic landscapes, from the flat, alluvial Canterbury Plains, through narrow alpine gorges, an 8.5km tunnel, beech-forested river valleys and alongside a lake fringed with cabbage trees. The 4½-hour journey is unforgettable, even in bad weather (if it's raining on one coast, it's probably fine on the other).

It can be done as a day trip, departing Christchurch at 8.15am and returning east from Greymouth at 1.45pm, but it is also a great way to get to the West Coast and then travel down to the glaciers by car or bus.

CLAVER CARROLL/GETTY IMAGES ©

Hokitika Heritage Trail, an 11km (two- to three-hour) loop taking in historic sites and interesting town views.

 TOURS

Wilderness Wings Scenic Flights
(☑0800 755 8118; www.wildernesswings.co.nz; Hokitika Airport; flights from $285) A highly regarded operator running scenic flights over Hokitika and further afield to Aoraki/ Mt Cook and the glaciers.

 EATING

Ramble + Ritual Cafe $
(☑03-755 6347; 51 Sewell St; snacks $3-8, meals $8-15; ⊘8am-4pm Mon-Fri, 9am-1pm Sat; ☑) Tucked away near the Clock Tower, this gallery-cum-cafe is a stylish little spot to linger over great espresso, delicious fresh baking and simple, healthy salads made to order. The ginger oaty may well be the best in the land.

Sweet Alice's Fudge Kitchen Sweets $
(27 Tancred St; fudge per slice $7; ⊘10am-5pm) Treat yourself with a slice of Alice's hand-made fudge, real fruit ice cream or a bag of boiled lollies– or maybe all three.

Fat Pipi Pizza Pizza $$
(89 Revell St; pizzas $20-30; ⊘12-2.30pm Wed-Sun, 5-9pm daily; ☑) Vegetarians, carnivores and everyone in between will be salivating for the pizza (including a whitebait version) made with love right before your eyes. Lovely cakes, honey buns and Benger juices, too. Best enjoyed in the garden bar – one of the town's (in fact the West Coast's) best dining spots.

 DRINKING & NIGHTLIFE

West Coast Wine Bar Wine Bar
(www.westcoastwine.co.nz; 108 Revell St; ⊘8am-late Tue-Sat, 8am-2pm Mon) Upping Hoki's sophistication factor, this weeny joint with a cute garden bar packs a fridge full of fine wine and craft beer, with the option of ordering up pizza from Fat Pipi Pizza, down the road.

ℹ INFORMATION

Hokitika i-SITE (☑03-755 6166; www.hokitika. org; 36 Weld St; ⊘8.30am-6pm Mon-Fri, 9am-5pm Sat & Sun) One of NZ's best i-SITEs offers extensive bookings, including all bus services. Also holds DOC info, although you'll need to book

Swing bridge at Hokitika Gorge (p228)

online or at DOC Visitor Centres further afield. See also www.westcoastnz.com.

ⓘ GETTING THERE & AWAY

Hokitika Airport (www.hokitikaairport.co.nz; Airport Dr, off Tudor St) is 1.5km east of the town centre. **Air New Zealand** (☏0800 737 000; www.airnz.co.nz) has three flights most days to/from Christchurch.

ⓘ GETTING AROUND

Car hire is available in town from **NZ Rent A Car** (☏027 294 8986, 03-755 6353; www.nzrentacar. co.nz); there are a couple of other options at Hokitika Airport.

QUEENSTOWN

Queenstown at a glance...

Surrounded by the indigo heights of the Remarkables and framed by the meandering coves of Lake Wakatipu, Queenstown wears its 'Global Adventure Capital' badge proudly. But then there's the other Queenstown with the cosmopolitan restaurant and arts scene, excellent vineyards and five golf courses. Go ahead and jump off a bridge or out of a plane, but also take time to slow down find a lakeside bench and immerse yourself in one of NZ's most beautiful views.

Queenstown in two days

Settle the nerves with brunch at **Bespoke Kitchen** (p252) before embarking on an exciting time experiencing the legendary **Kawarau Bridge bungy** (p236). Afterwards get your holiday mojo back at the relaxing **Onsen Hot Pools** (p250). The following day embark on a wine-tinged discovery of the **Gibbston Valley** with **Cycle de Vine** (p239) before dinner back in town at the lakeside **Public Kitchen & Bar** (p252).

Queenstown in four days

On day three explore **Lake Wakatipu**, either on the **TSS Earnslaw** (p242) to Walter Peak Farm or admiring the flash real estate on the **Million Dollar Cruise** (p242). If you've got time, rent a car and drive up the lake to beautiful **Glenorchy** (p243). Spend the morning of day four in **Arrowtown** (p244), before squeezing in more thrills in the afternoon with **Ziptrek Ecotours** (p249).

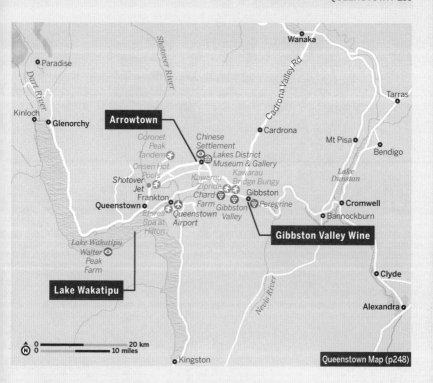

Queenstown Map (p248)

Arriving in Queenstown

Queenstown Airport Located 7km east of the town centre with flights to/from Auckland, Wellington and Christchurch. Australian destinations include Sydney, Melbourne, Brisbane and the Gold Coast.

Queenstown i-SITE Most buses and shuttles stop here or on nearby Athol St. Destinations include Christchurch, Te Anau, Lake Tekapo and Franz Josef.

Where to Stay

Queenstown has endless accommodation options, but midrange rooms are hard to come by. The hostels, however, are extremely competitive, offering ever-more extras to win custom – they're worth considering even if it's not usually your thing. Places book out and prices rocket during the peak summer (Christmas to February) and ski (June to September) seasons; book well in advance.

Bungy jumping at Kawarau Bridge

NICRAM SABOD/SHUTTERSTOCK ©

Extreme Queenstown

Most visitors do crazy things that they've never done before here – often surrounded by stunning Central Otago scenery. Look forward to a good collection of souvenir T-shirts.

Great For...

☑ Don't Miss

Jumping off the Kawarau Bridge, the site in 1988 of the world's first commercial bungy.

For adventure completists, jetboating, skydiving and paragliding are also popular around Queenstown.

AJ Hackett Bungy Adventure Sports
(☎03-450 1300, 0800 286 4958; www.bungy.co.nz; The Station, cnr Camp & Shotover Sts)
The bungy originators offer jumps from three sites in the Queenstown area, with giant swings available at two of them. Most popular is the 1880 **Kawarau Bridge** (Gibbston Hwy; adult/child $190/145), 23km from Queenstown (transport included).

Near the Kawarau Bridge site is the **Kawarau Zipride** (Gibbston Hwy; adult/child $50/40, 3-/5-ride pack $105/150), three 130m zip-lines targeted at kids, but also a thrill for adults. Multi-ride packs can be split between groups, making it a cheaper alternative to the bungy.

Rafting on the Shotover River

WILL SALTER/GETTY IMAGES ©

The closest options to Queenstown are the **Ledge Bungy** (adult/child $195/145) and **Ledge Swing** (adult/child $160/110) at the top of the Skyline Gondola; the drop is only 47m, but it's 400m above town. In winter you can even leap into the dark.

Last but most pant-wetting is the **Nevis Bungy** (per person $275) – the highest bungy in Australasia. 4WD buses will transport you onto private farmland where you can jump from a specially constructed pod, 134m above the Nevis River. The **Nevis Swing** (solo/tandem $195/350) starts 160m above the river and cuts a 300m arc across the canyon on a rope longer than a rugby field.

❶ Need to Know

Most operators can provide transport from central Queenstown to jump sites. Check when you book.

✖ Take a Break

Recount all the exciting action over a craft ale at the **Atlas Beer Cafe** (p252).

★ Top Tip

If you're planning several activities, combination tickets are available at booking offices around Queenstown.

Shotover Canyon Swing   Adventure Sports

(✆03-442 6990; www.canyonswing.co.nz; 35 Shotover St; per person $219, additional swings $45) Be released loads of different ways – backwards, in a chair, upside down. From there it's a 60m free fall and a wild swing across the canyon at 150km/h. The price includes the transfer to/from their Queenstown booking office.

Queenstown Rafting   Rafting

(✆03-442 9792; www.rafting.co.nz; 35 Shotover St; rafting/helirafting $209/309) Rafts year-round on the choppy Shotover River (Grade III to V) and calmer Kawarau River (Grade II to III). Trips take four to five hours with two to three hours on the water. Helirafting trips are an exciting alternative. Participants must be at least 13 years old and weigh more than 40kg.

Serious Fun River Surfing   Adventure Sports

(✆03-442 5262; www.riversurfing.co.nz; per person $215) The only company to surf the infamous Chinese Dogleg section of the Kawarau River, on what's basically a glorified boogie board.

Wine cave at Gibbston Valley

Gibbston Valley Wine

As thrill-seeking bungy jumpers plunge towards the Kawarau River, they might not realise they're in the heart of the Gibbston Valley, one of Central Otago's main wine subregions.

Great For...

☑ Don't Miss

The drive to picturesque Chard Farm along a precipitous 2km gravel road.

Gung-ho visitors to Queenstown might be happiest dangling off a giant rubber band, but the surrounding Gibbston Valley area also offers superb food and wine experiences. Almost opposite the bungy jumping at Kawarau Bridge, a precipitous 2km gravel road leads to **Chard Farm** (☎03-441 8452; www.chardfarm.co.nz; Chard Rd, Gibbston; ⏰11am-5pm), the most picturesque of the Gibbston wineries. A further 800m along the Gibbston Hwy (SH6) is **Gibbston Valley** (☎03-442 6910; www.gibbstonvalley.com; 1820 Gibbston Hwy (SH6), Gibbston; tastings $5-12, tour incl tastings $15; ⏰10am-5pm), which makes excellent pinot noir and has a large visitor complex with a restaurant and a 'cheesery.' Take a tour of the winery and their impressive wine cave.

A further 3km along SH6, **Peregrine** (☎03-442 4000; www.peregrinewines.co.nz;

Pruning vines, Gibbston Valley

❶ Need to Know

Enquire at the **Queenstown i-SITE** (p253) for details of Gibbston Valley mountain-biking trails.

✕ Take a Break

At the rustic **Gibbston Tavern** (☎03-409 0508; www.gibbstontavern.co.nz; Coal Pit Rd, Gibbston; ⊙11.30am-7pm Sun-Thu, to 10.30pm Fri & Sat Oct-Apr, closed Mon May-Sep), ask to try their very own Moon-shine Wines.

★ Top Tip

Gibbston is showcased every March at the Gibbston Wine & Food Festival (gibbstonwineandfood.co.nz) at Queenstown Gardens.

2127 Gibbston Hwy (SH6), Gibbston; ⊙10am-5pm) is one of Gibbston's top wineries, producing excellent sauvignon blanc, pinot gris, riesling and, of course, pinot noir. Also impressive is the winery's architecture – a bunker-like building with a roof reminiscent of a falcon's wing in flight.

Tours

Appellation Central
Wine Tours   Wine
(☎03-442 0246; www.appellationcentral.co.nz; tours $185-230) ⚐ Tours visit wineries in Gibbston, Bannockburn and Cromwell, and include platter lunches at a winery.

Cycle de Vine   Cycling
(☎0800 328 897; www.cycledevine.co.nz; tour $155; ⊙Oct-May) Cruise on a retro bicycle around Gibbston. Tours include three differ-ent wineries and a picnic snack beside the meandering Kawarau River.

What's Nearby

Cromwell – 60km east of Queenstown – lies at the very heart of the prestigious Central Otago wine region (www.cowa.org. nz), known for its extraordinarily good pinot noir and, to a lesser extent, riesling, pinot gris and chardonnay. The Cromwell Basin accounts for over 70% of Central Otago's total wine production. Pick up the *Central Otago Wine Map* for details of upwards of 50 local wineries.

Crafting a wonderful pinot noir, **Mt Difficulty** (☎03-445 3445; www.mt difficulty.co.nz; 73 Felton Rd, Bannockburn; mains $30-35; ⊙tastings 10.30am-4.30pm, restaurant noon-4pm) is a lovely spot for a leisurely lunch looking down over the valley. There are large wine-friendly platters to share, but save room for the decadent desserts.

Lake Wakatipu seen from the Remarkables range

Lake Wakatipu

Shaped like a perfect cartoon thunderbolt and framed on its southeastern edge by the spectacular Remarkables mountain range, beautiful Lake Wakatipu offers lake cruises, and easygoing adventures at sleepy Glenorchy.

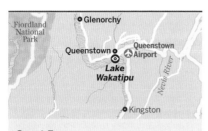

Great For...

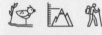

ℹ Need to Know

Glenorchy Information Centre & Store (☏03-409 2049; www.glenorchy-nz. co.nz; 42-50 Mull St, Glenorchy; ⊗8.30am-6pm)

★ **Top Tip**

Most Glenorchy operators offer shuttles to/from Queenstown for a small surcharge.

This gorgeous lake has a 212km shoreline and reaches a depth of 379m (the average depth is over 320m). Five rivers flow into it but only one (the Kawarau) flows out, making it prone to sometimes quite dramatic floods.

If the water looks clean, that's because it is. Scientists have rated it as 99.9% pure – making it the second-purest lake water in the world. In fact, you're better off dipping your glass in the lake than buying bottled water. It's also very cold. That beach by Marine Parade may look tempting on a scorching day, but trust us, you won't want to splash about in water that hovers at around 10°C year-round.

Lake Cruises

TSS Earnslaw — Boat Tour

(☑0800 656 501; www.realjourneys.co.nz; Steamer Wharf, Beach St; adult/child $57/22) The stately, steam-powered TSS *Earnslaw* celebrated a centenary of continuous service in 2012. Once the lake's major means of transport, now its ever-present cloud of black soot seems a little incongruous in such a pristine setting. Climb aboard for the standard 1½-hour Lake Wakatipu tour or take a 3½-hour excursion to the high-country **Walter Peak Farm** (1 Mount Nicholas-Beach Bay Rd; sheep show incl cruise adult/child $77/22) for sheepdog and shearing demonstrations.

Million Dollar Cruise — Boat Tour

(☑03-442 9770; www.milliondollarcruise.co.nz; cruise $35; ☉11am, 2pm & 4pm) Good-value,

Queenstown lakefront

informative, 90-minute cruises heading up the Frankton end of the lake, past the multi-million-dollar real estate of Kelvin Heights.

What's Nearby

Set in achingly beautiful surroundings, postage-stamp-sized **Glenorchy** is the perfect low-key antidote to Queenstown. An expanding range of adventure operators will get you active on the lake and in nearby mountain valleys by kayak, horse or jetboat, and if you prefer to strike out on two legs,

MATTHEW MICAH WRIGHT/GETTY IMAGES ©

the mountainous region at the northern end of Lake Wakatipu is the setting for some of the South Island's finest tramps.

Glenorchy lies at the head of Lake Wakatipu, a scenic 40-minute (46km) drive northwest from Queenstown. With sweeping vistas and gem-coloured waters, the sealed road is wonderfully scenic, although its constant hills are a killer for cyclists. There are no bus services but there are trampers' shuttles during the Great Walks season (late October to March).

Those with sturdy wheels can explore the superb valleys north of Glenorchy. The gravel road to Paradise runs through beautiful farmland fringed by majestic mountains. You might recognise it from T*he Lord of the Rings* movies as the approach to both Isengard and Lothlórien

Horse riding with **Dart Stables** (☏03-442 5688; www.dartstables.com; Coll St) includes treks traversing many locations familiar from Sir Peter Jackson's Tolkien adaptations, including a two-hour 'River Wild' ride ($145) and a 1½-hour 'Ride of the Rings' ($165).

Journeys with **Dart River Wilderness Jet** (☏03-442 9992; www.dartriver.co.nz; 45 Mull St; adult/child $229/129; ⊘departs 9am & 1pm) ✈ travel into the heart of spectacular wilderness, including a short walk through beech forest and a back-road excursion. The round trip from Glenorchy takes three hours. It also offers jetboat rides combined with a river descent in an inflatable three-seater 'funyak' (departs 8.30am, adult/child $330/230). Prices include Queenstown pick-ups.

Other activities on offer include farm tours, fly fishing, guided photography tours and cookery classes; enquire at the Queenstown i-SITE (p253).

MJ PROTOTYPE/SHUTTERSTOCK ©

Arrowtown

Quaint Arrowtown sprang up in the 1860s following the discovery of gold in the Arrow River. Today its pretty, tree-lined avenues retain more than 60 of their original gold-rush buildings.

Great For...

☑ Don't Miss

A cold beer at the classic **New Orleans Hotel** (03-442 1748; www.neworleans hotel.co.nz; 27 Buckingham St; ⊙8am-11pm;), the local favourite since 1866.

Consider using Arrowtown as a base for exploring Queenstown and the wider region. That way you can enjoy its history, charm and excellent restaurants when the tour buses have gone back to Queenstown.

Sights

Chinese Settlement   Historic Site
(Buckingham St; ⊙24hr) **FREE** Arrowtown has NZ's best example of an early Chinese settlement. Interpretive signs explain the lives of Chinese diggers during and after the gold rush (the last resident died in 1932), while restored huts and shops make the story more tangible. Subjected to significant racism, the Chinese often had little choice but to rework old tailings rather than seek new claims.

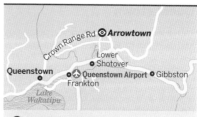

ℹ Need to Know

Arrowtown Visitor Information Centre (☎03-442 1824; www.arrowtown. com; 49 Buckingham St; ⊙8.30am-5pm)

✕ Take a Break

Try one of the deservedly famous sticky buns at **Provisions** (☎03-445 4048; www. provisions.co.nz; 65 Buckingham St; mains $8.50-24; ⊙8.30am-5pm; 🛜).

★ Top Tip

Catch Connectabus 10 from Queenstown to Frankton and change to bus 11 to Arrowtown.

Lakes District Museum & Gallery   Museum

(www.museumqueenstown.com; 49 Buckingham St; adult/child $10/3; ⊙8.30am-5pm) Exhibits cover the gold-rush era and the early days of Chinese settlement around Arrowtown. You can also rent pans here to try your luck panning for gold on the Arrow River ($3); you're more likely to find some traces if you head away from the town centre.

Activities

Arrowtown Time Walks   Walking

(☎021 782 278; www.arrowtowntimewalks. com; adult/child $20/12; ⊙1.30pm Oct-Apr) Guided walks (90 minutes) depart from the museum daily, tracing a path through the township, pointing out places of interest along the way and delving into Arrowtown's gold-rush history.

Arrowtown Bike Hire   Mountain Biking

(☎0800 224 473; www.arrowtownbikehire.co.nz; 59 Buckingham St; half-/full-day rental $38/55) Hires bikes and provides great advice on local trails. If you fancy tackling the Arrow River Bridges Ride and then indulging in tastings at some of the Gibbston wineries, they'll collect you and your bikes for $60. Multiday rentals are also available.

Dudley's Cottage   Gold Panning

(☎03-409 8162; www.dudleyscottagenz.com; 4 Buckingham St; ⊙9am-5pm) Call into this historical cottage for a gold-panning lesson ($10, plus an extra $5 if you're keen to rent a pan and give it go). If you've already got the skills, rent a pan and shovel ($6) or sluice box ($25) and head out on your own.

Spa at Millbrook   Spa

(☎03-441 7017; www.millbrook.co.nz; Malaghans Rd; treatments from $79) Located at the Millbrook Resort, this spa has been rated one of NZ's best.

Queenstown

With a cinematic background of mountains and lakes, and a 'what can we think of next?' array of adventure activities, it's little wonder Queenstown tops the itineraries of many travellers. Factor in easy access to some of New Zealand's most beautiful vineyards, excellent restaurants and quite probably the South Island's most energetic night life, and this improbably scenic town framed by Lake Wakatipu and the Remarkables is an essential NZ highlight.

◉ SIGHTS

Queenstown Gardens   Park

(Park St) Set on its own little tongue of land framing Queenstown Bay, this pretty park was laid out in 1876 by those garden-loving Victorians as a place to promenade. The clothes may have changed (they've certainly shrunk), but people still flock to this leafy peninsula to stroll, picnic and laze about. Less genteel types head straight for the frisbee golf course (www.queenstowndiscgolf. co.nz; Queenstown Gardens) `FREE`.

Skyline Gondola   Cable Car

(☏03-441 0101; www.skyline.co.nz; Brecon St; adult/child return $32/20; ☺9am-late) ✎ Hop aboard for fantastic views. At the top there's the inevitable cafe, restaurant, souvenir shop and observation deck, as well as the **Queenstown Bike Park** (p247), **Skyline Luge** (p247), **Ledge Bungy** (p237), **Ledge Swing** (p237) and **Ziptrek Ecotours** (p249). At night there are Māori culture shows from **Kiwi Haka** (p253) and stargazing tours (including gondola adult/child $85/45).

Kiwi Birdlife Park   Zoo

(☏03-442 8059; www.kiwibird.co.nz; Brecon St; adult/child $45/23; ☺9am-5pm, shows 11am & 3pm) These five acres are home to 10,000 native plants, tuatara and scores of birds, including kiwi, kea, moreporks, parakeets and extremely rare black stilts. Stroll around the aviaries, watch the conservation show, and tiptoe quietly into the darkened kiwi houses.

View over Queenstown from the Skyline Gondola

St Peter's Anglican Church
Church

(☏03-442 8391; www.stpeters.co.nz; 2 Church St) This pretty wood-beamed stone building (1932) has colourful stained glass and an impressive gilded and painted organ. Take a look at the eagle-shaped cedar lectern, carved and donated in 1874 by Ah Tong, a Chinese immigrant.

Underwater Observatory
Viewpoint

(☏03-409 0000; www.kjet.co.nz; main jetty; adult/child $10/5; ⏱9am-7pm Nov-Mar, to 5pm Apr-Oct) Six windows showcase life under the lake in this reverse aquarium (the people are behind glass). Large brown trout abound, and look out for freshwater eels and scaup (diving ducks), which cruise right past the windows – especially when the coin-operated food-release box is triggered.

✪ ACTIVITIES

If you're planning on tackling several activities, various combination tickets are available, including those offered by **Queenstown Combos** (☏03-442 7318; www.combos.co.nz; The Station, cnr Shotover & Camp Sts).

Coronet Peak Tandem
Paragliding

(☏0800 467 325; www.tandemparagliding.com; from $199) Offering spectacular paragliding and hang-gliding takeoffs from Coronet Peak, with free pickups from Queenstown accommodation.

Skyline Luge
Adventure Sports

(☏03-441 0101; www.skyline.co.nz; Skyline; 2/3/4/5 rides incl gondola $45/48/49/55; ⏱10am-8pm Oct-Mar, to 5pm Apr-Sep) 🚲 Ride the gondola to the top, then hop on a three-wheeled cart to ride the 800m track. Nail the Blue Track once and you're allowed on the more advanced Red Track, with its banked corners and tunnel.

 ## Gibbston River Trail

The Gibbston River Trail is a scenic walking and mountain-biking track that follows the Kawarau River from the Kawarau Bridge to Peregrine winery (one to two hours, 5km). From Peregrine, walkers (but not cyclists) can continue on the Wentworth Bridge Loop (one hour, 2.7km), which crosses over old mining works on various timber and steel bridges.

Kawarau River
OLGA KATRYCHENKO/GETTY IMAGES ©

Queenstown Bike Park
Mountain Biking

(☏03-441 0101; www.skyline.co.nz; Skyline; half-/full day incl gondola $60/85; ⏱10am-6pm, extended to 8pm as light permits Oct-Apr) Over 20 different trails – from easy (green) to extreme (double black) – traverse Bob's Peak high above the lake. Once you've descended on two wheels, simply jump on the gondola and do it all over again. The best trail for novice riders is the 6km-long Hammy's Track, which is studded with lake views and picnic spots. BYO bike.

Ben Lomond Track
Hiking

(www.doc.govt.nz) The track to the summit of Ben Lomond (1748m, six to eight hours return) is a steep tramp requiring a high level of fitness and shouldn't be underestimated. Snow and ice can make it even more difficult; in winter, check at DOC or the i-SITE before setting out. It starts at the top of the gondola.

Queenstown

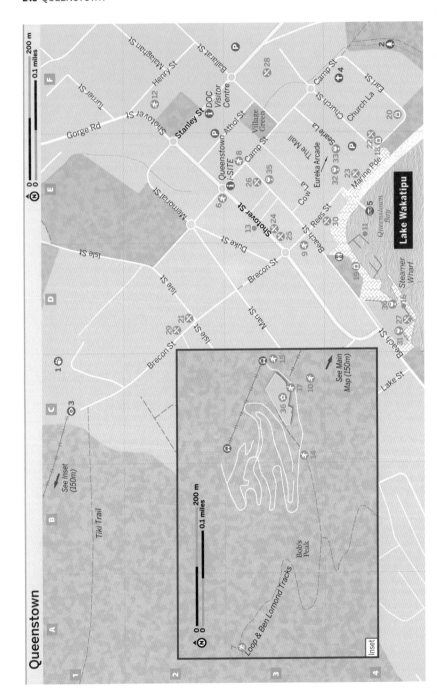

Queenstown

Sights

1 Kiwi Birdlife Park C1
2 Queenstown Gardens F4
3 Skyline Gondola C1
4 St Peter's Anglican Church F4
5 Underwater Observatory E4

Activities, Courses & Tours

6 AJ Hackett Bungy E2
7 Ben Lomond Track A3
8 Canyoning Queenstown E3
9 Hush Spa D3
10 Ledge Bungy C3
Ledge Swing .... (see 10)
11 Million Dollar Cruise E4
12 Mobile Massage Company F2
13 Nomad Safaris E3
NZone .... (see 13)
14 Queenstown Bike Park C3
Queenstown Combos .... (see 6)
Queenstown Rafting .... (see 13)
Shotover Canyon Swing .... (see 13)
15 Skyline Luge C3
16 TSS Earnslaw D4
17 Ziptrek Ecotours C3

Shopping

18 Artbay Gallery E4
19 Arts & Crafts Market D4
20 Vesta F4

Eating

21 Bespoke Kitchen D2
22 Blue Kanu E4
23 Eichardt's Bar E4
24 Fergbaker E3
25 Fergburger E3
26 Fishbone E3
27 Public Kitchen & Bar D4
28 Rata F3
29 Taco Medic D2
30 Vudu Cafe & Larder E4

Drinking & Nightlife

31 Atlas Beer Cafe D4
32 Ballarat Trading Company E4
33 Bardeaux E4
34 Little Blackwood D4
35 The Winery E3

Entertainment

36 Kiwi Haka C3

Canyoning Queenstown Adventure Sports
(☎03-441 3003; www.canyoning.co.nz; 39 Camp St) Canyoning expeditions in the nearby 12-Mile Delta Canyons ($199) or in the remote Routeburn ($299) and Dart River ($450) valleys.

Shotover Jet Boating
(☎03-442 8570; www.shotoverjet.com; Gorge Rd, Arthurs Point; adult/child $135/75) Half-hour jetboat trips through the rocky Shotover Canyon, with lots of thrilling 360-degree spins.

NZone Adventure Sports
(☎03-442 5867; www.nzoneskydive.co.nz; 35 Shotover St; from $299) Jump out of a perfectly good airplane – with a tandem-skydiving expert.

Ziptrek Ecotours Adventure Sports
(☎03-441 2102; www.ziptrek.co.nz; Skyline) Incorporating a series of zip-lines (flying foxes), this harness-clad thrill-ride takes you from treetop to treetop high above Queenstown. Ingenious design and eco-friendly values are a bonus. Choose from the two-hour four-line 'Moa' tour (adult/child $135/85) or the gnarlier three-hour six-line 'Kea' option ($185/135).

Family Adventures Rafting
(☎03-442 8836; www.familyadventures.co.nz; adult/child $179/120) Gentler (Grade I to II) trips on the Shotover suitable for children three years and older. Operates in summer only.

Guided Walks New Zealand Hiking
(☎03-442 3000; www.nzwalks.com; adult/child from $107/67) Excellent walks in the Queenstown area, ranging from half-day nature walks to the full three-day Hollyford Track. They also offer snowshoeing in winter.

Top Five
Ways to Relax

Here's our pick of the best experiences to slow down, recharge and remind your body that there's more to the travelling life than scaring yourself silly. You're on holiday, remember?

Onsen Hot Pools (03-442 5707; www. onsen.co.nz; 160 Arthurs Point Rd, Arthurs Point; 1/2/3/4 people $46/88/120/140; ⊙11am-10pm) Private Japanese-style hot tubs with mountain views. Book ahead and one will be warmed up for you.

Mobile Massage Company (0800 426 161; www.queenstownmassage.co.nz; 2c Shotover St; 1hr from $120; ⊙9am-9pm) To reboot your system after a few days of skiing, biking and jetboating, ease into in-room massage and spa treatments.

Hush Spa (03-442 9656; www.hushspa. co.nz; 1st fl, 32 Rees St; 30/60min massage from $70/128; ⊙9am-6pm Fri-Mon, to 9pm Tue-Thu) Slow down even more by checking in for a massage or pedicure.

Spa at Millbrook (p245) For truly world-class spa treatment, make the short trek to Millbrook near Arrowtown, where you'll find one of NZ's best.

Eforea Spa at Hilton (03-450 9416; www.queenstownhilton.com; 79 Peninsula Rd, Kelvin Heights; treatments from $70; ⊙9am-late) Catch a water taxi across the lake to the luxurious Eforea Spa.

Sunrise Balloons Ballooning
(03-442 0781; www.ballooningnz.com; adult/child $495/295) One-hour sunrise

rides including a champagne breakfast; allow four hours for the entire experience.

 TOURS

Queenstown Heritage Tours Tour
(03-409 0949; www.queenstown-heritage. co.nz; adult/child $160/80) Scenic but hair-raising 4WD minibus tours head into Skippers Canyon via a narrow, winding road built by gold panners in the 1800s. The route starts near Coronet Peak and continues above the Shotover River, passing gold-rush sights along the way. Wine tours are also available.

Queenstown Wine Trail Wine
(03-441 3990; www.queenstownwinetrail. co.nz) Choose from a five-hour tour with tastings at four wineries ($155) or a four-hour 'Wine & Food Sampler' tour with lunch included ($176).

Nomad Safaris Driving
(03-442 6699; www.nomadsafaris.co.nz; 37 Shotover St; adult/child from $175/89) Take in spectacular scenery and hard-to-get-to backcountry vistas around Skippers Canyon and Macetown, or head on a 'Safari of the Scenes' through Middle-earth locations around Glenorchy and the Wakatipu Basin. You can also quad-bike through a sheep station on Queenstown Hill ($245).

🔒 SHOPPING

Artbay Gallery Arts
(03-442 9090; www.artbay.co.nz; 13 Marine Pde; ⊙11am-6pm Mon-Wed, to 9pm Thu-Sun) Occupying an attractive 1863-built Freemason's Hall on the lakefront, Artbay is always an interesting place to peruse, even if you don't have thousands to spend on a delicately carved ram's skull. It showcases the work of contemporary NZ artists, most of whom have a connection to the region.

Vesta Arts, Crafts
(03-442 5687; www.vestadesign.co.nz; 19 Marine Pde; ⊙10am-6pm) Showcasing really cool NZ-made art and craft, Vesta is full

of interesting prints, paintings, glass art and gifts. It's housed in Williams Cottage (1864), Queenstown's oldest home. It's worth visiting just to check out the 1930s wallpaper and 1920s garden.

Arts & Crafts Market Market
(www.marketplace.net.nz; Earnslaw Park; ⊘9.30am-3.30pm Sat) Locally crafted gifts and souvenirs, on the lakefront beside Steamer Wharf.

EATING

Queenstown's town centre is peppered with busy eateries. Many target the tourist dollar, but dig a little deeper and you'll discover local favourites covering a wide range of international cuisines. At the more popular places, it's wise to make a reservation.

Fergbaker Bakery $
(42 Shotover St; items $5-9; ⊘6.30am-4.30am) Fergburger's sweeter sister bakes all manner of tempting treats – and although most things look tasty with 3am beer goggles on, they withstand the daylight test admira-

bly. Goodies include meat pies, filled rolls, danish pastries and banoffee tarts. If you're after gelato, call into Mrs Ferg next door.

Taco Medic Fast Food $
(www.tacomedic.co.nz; 11 Brecon St; tacos $7; ⊘11am-9pm Nov-Apr, 10am-6.30pm May-Oct) Operating out of a food truck by the bike-hire place on Brecon St, these convivial lads dispense tacos of tasty fish, beef, pork belly and black bean to a devoted group of fans. One's a snack and two's a meal. During the ski season they move to an empty lot on the corner of Gorge Rd and Bowen St.

Fergburger Burgers $$
(☑03-441 1232; www.fergburger.com; 42 Shotover St; burgers $11-19; ⊘8.30am-5am) Queenstown's famous Fergburger has now become a tourist attraction in itself, forcing many locals to look elsewhere for their big-as-your-head gourmet burger fix. The burgers are as tasty and satisfying as ever, but is any burger worth a 30-minute wait? You decide.

Steamer Wharf

Bespoke Kitchen   Cafe $$

(☑03-409 0552; www.facebook.com/
Bespokekitchenqueenstown; 9 Isle St; mains
$11-19; ☺7.30am-5pm; ☜) Occupying a
light-filled corner site between the town
centre and the gondola, Bespoke delivers a
good selection of counter food, beautifully
presented cooked options, free wi-fi and, of
course, great coffee.

Public Kitchen
& Bar   Modern NZ $$

(☑03-442 5969; www.publickitchen.co.nz;
Steamer Wharf, Beach St; dishes $15-45; ☺9am-
11pm) The trend towards informal, shared
dining has come to Queenstown in the form
of this excellent waterfront eatery. The
meaty dishes, in particular, are excellent.

Blue Kanu   Modern NZ $$

(☑03-442 6060; www.bluekanu.co.nz; 16 Church
St; mains $27-39; ☺4pm-late) Disproving the
rule that all tiki houses are inherently tacky,
Blue Kanu somehow manages to be not
just tasteful but stylish. The menu meshes
robust Māori, Pasifika and Asian flavours
with local ingredients to come up with an
exotic blend of delicious dishes.

Vudu Cafe & Larder   Cafe $$

(☑03-441 8370; www.vudu.co.nz; 16 Rees
St; mains $14-20; ☺7.30am-6pm) Excellent
home-style baking combines with great
coffee and tasty cooked breakfasts at this
cosmopolitan cafe. Admire the huge photo
of a much less populated Queenstown from
an inside table, or head through to the rear
garden for lake and mountain views.

Eichardt's Bar   Tapas $$

(www.eichardtshotel.co.nz; 1-3 Marine Pde;
breakfast $16-18, lunch $25-26, tapas $7.50-12;
☺7.30am-late) Elegant without being stuffy,
the small bar attached to Eichardt's Private
Hotel is a wonderful refuge from the buzz
of the streets. Foodwise, tapas is the main
focus – and although the selection isn't
particularly Spanish, it is delicious.

Fishbone   Seafood $$$

(☑03-442 6768; www.fishbonequeenstown.
co.nz; 7 Beach St; mains $26-38; ☺5-10pm)

Queenstown's more than a few miles
inland, but that doesn't prevent Fishbone
from sourcing the best NZ seafood. Don't
let the kitsch shell-framed mirrors put you
off, as the food's excellent. Favourites include Sri Lankan fish curry, grilled octopus
and prawns in XO sauce.

Rata   Modern NZ $$$

(☑03-442 9393; www.ratadining.co.nz; 43
Ballarat St; mains $36-42, 2-/3-course lunch
$28/38; ☺noon-11pm) After gaining Michelin
stars for restaurants in London, New
York and LA, chef-owner Josh Emett has
brought his exceptional but surprisingly
unflashy cooking back home in the form of
this upmarket but informal back-lane eatery. Native bush, edging the windows and
in a large-scale photographic mural, sets
the scene for a short menu showcasing the
best seasonal NZ produce.

🍸 DRINKING & NIGHTLIFE

Atlas Beer Cafe   Bar

(☑03-442 5995; www.atlasbeercafe.com;
Steamer Wharf, Beach St; ☺10am-late) Perched
at the end of Steamer Wharf, this pint-sized
bar specialises in beers from Dunedin's
Emerson's Brewery, Queenstown's Altitude
and regular guest brews from further afield.
It's also one of the best places in Queenstown for a good-value meal, serving excellent cooked breakfasts and simple hearty
fare such as steaks, burgers and chicken
parmigiana (mains $10 to $20).

Little Blackwood   Cocktail Bar

(☑03-441 8066; www.littleblackwood.com;
Steamer Wharf; ☺3pm-1am) With subway
tiles on the walls, interesting art and
barmen dressed in stripy shirts looking like
old-fashioned sailors, Little Blackwood is an
appealingly quirky addition to the Steamer
Wharf complex. It's much more stylish than
it sounds, and the cocktails are good too.

Bardeaux   Wine Bar

(☑03-442 8284; www.goodgroup.co.nz; Eureka
Arcade, Searle Lane; ☺3pm-4am) This small,
low-key, cavelike wine bar is all class. Under
a low ceiling are plush leather armchairs

and a fireplace made from Central Otago schist. The wine list is extraordinary, with the price of several bottles at four digits.

The Winery   Wine Bar

(☑03-409 2226; www.thewinery.co.nz; 14 Beach St; ☺10.30am-late) Here's something different: load up cash on a smart card and then help yourself to tasting pours or glasses of over 80 NZ wines dispensed through an automated gas-closure system. There's also a whisky corner, and cheese platters are available.

Ballarat Trading Company   Pub

(☑03-442 4222; www.ballarat.co.nz; 7-9 The Mall; ☺11am-4am) Beyond the eclectic decor (stuffed bear, rampant wall-mounted ducks), Ballarat is quite a traditional spot, with gleaming beer taps, cover bands, sports on TV, quiz nights, occasional lapses into 1980s music and robust meals.

⊛ ENTERTAINMENT

Sherwood   Live Music

(☑03-450 1090; www.sherwoodqueenstown.nz; 554 Frankton Rd, Queenstown East) As well as being a brilliant spot for a meal or a drink, the Sherwood has quickly become Queenstown's go-to spot for visiting musos. Many of NZ's bigger names have performed here; check the website for coming gigs.

Kiwi Haka   Traditional Music

(☑03-441 0101; www.skyline.co.nz; Skyline; adult/child excl gondola $39/26) For a traditional Māori cultural experience, head to the top of the gondola for one of the 30-minute shows. There are usually three shows per night; bookings are essential.

❶ INFORMATION

Queenstown i-SITE (☑03-442 4100; www.queenstowninformation.com; cnr Shotover & Camp Sts; ☺8.30am-7pm) Friendly and informative despite being perpetually frantic, the saintly staff here can help with bookings and information on Queenstown, Gibbston, Lake Hayes, Arrowtown and Glenorchy.

⤵⌐ Gold Rush
⌐   Ghost Town

Macetown, 14km north of Arrowtown, is a gold-rush ghost town reached via a rugged, flood-prone road (the original miners' wagon track), which crosses the Arrow River more than 25 times.

Don't even think about taking the rental car here. A much more sensible option is the 4WD tour offered by Nomad Safaris (p250). You can also hike there from Arrowtown (16km each way, 7½ hours return), but it's particularly tricky in winter and spring; check with the information centre about conditions before heading out.

DOC Visitor Centre (☑03-442 7935; www.doc.govt.nz; 50 Stanley St; ☺8.30am-5pm) Head here to pick up confirmed bookings for the Routeburn Track and backcountry hut passes, and to get the latest weather and track updates. It can also advise on walks to suit your ability.

❶ GETTING THERE & AWAY

AIR

Air New Zealand (☑0800 737 000; www.airnewzealand.co.nz) flies to Queenstown from Auckland, Wellington and Christchurch. **Jetstar** (☑0800 800 995; www.jetstar.com) also flies to Auckland.

Various airlines offer direct flights to Queenstown from Australian destinations including Brisbane, the Gold Coast, Sydney and Melbourne.

BUS

Most buses and shuttles stop on Athol St or opposite the i-SITE. Destinations include Christchurch, Franz Josef and Te Anau.

❶ GETTING AROUND

Connectabus (☑03-441 4471; www.connectabus.com) has various colour-coded routes, including to Arrowtown. Pick up a route map and timetable from the i-SITE.

FIORDLAND

Fiordland at a glance...

Formidable Fiordland is New Zealand's most impenetrable wilderness, a jagged, mountainous, densely forested landmass ribbed with deeply recessed sounds (technically fiords) reaching inland from the Tasman Sea. Popular boat trips explore the sounds, but it's walkers who can best delve the deepest into this remote and magical area, not only on the famous, multiday Milford, Kepler and Hollyford Tracks, but even on short day walks, easily accessible from the highway.

Fiordland in two days

Begin with a day trip to **Milford Sound** (p260). Options include exploring the fiord by boat, but to really experience the area's huge expanses, soaring cliffs and verdant forest, consider a kayaking excursion. Kayaking is also popular on **Doubtful Sound** (p266), a much less-visited destination for day two. Doubtful Sound trips can also incorporate visits to the West Arm hydroelectric power station.

Fiordland in five days

For an extended Fiordland experience, undertake one of New Zealand's Great Walks for three days and four nights. Once you've conquered the **Milford Track** (p258), take time to explore **Milford Sound** (p260) by boat, before returning to lakeside **Te Anau** (p268). You'll really have earned something baked and delicious at **Miles Better Pies** (p270), or an ice-cold beer at the local pub. Cheers!

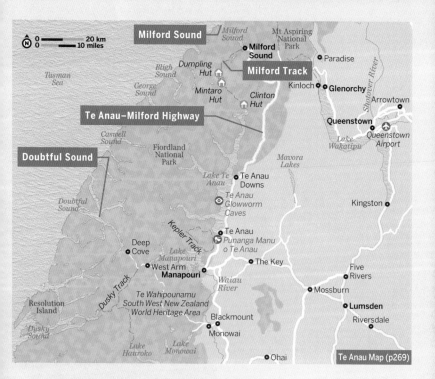

Arriving in Fiordland

Te Anau Buses from Queenstown, Dunedin and Christchurch all stop outside the Kiwi Country store in central Te Anau.

Queenstown Tour companies also offer return day trips from Queenstown to Milford Sound but it's a long day of travel with less than two hours at Milford.

Where to Stay

Te Anau has a decent array of motels, B&Bs and tramper-friendly hostels. Accommodation can get booked out in the peak season (December to February). Book early if possible.

Hiker at Mackinnon Pass, looking over Clinton Valley

ANDREW BAIN/GETTY IMAGES ©

Milford Track

Internationally renowned, the Milford Track is an absolute stunner, complete with dense rainforest, deep glaciated valleys, and an alpine pass surrounded by towering peaks and powerful waterfalls.

Great For...

☑ Don't Miss

Feeling very good about yourself after conquering the Mackinnon Pass.

New Zealand's best-known track is routinely touted as 'the finest walk in the world,' and more than 14,000 trampers complete the 54km-long track each year.

During the Great Walks season, the track can only be walked in one direction, starting from Glade Wharf. You must stay at Clinton Hut the first night, despite it being only one hour from the start of the track, and you must complete the trip in three nights and four days.

During the Great Walks season, the track is also frequented by guided tramping parties, which stay at cosy, carpeted lodges with hot showers and proper food. Contact Ultimate Hikes (p268), the only operator permitted to run guided tramps on the Milford.

ⓘ Need to Know

See www.doc.govt.nz/milfordtrack for essential pre-trip planning and booking guidelines.

✕ Take a Break

Back in Te Anau, celebrate completing the Milford Track at **Redcliff Cafe**. (p271)

★ Top Tip

Book yout hike early with DOC to avoid disappointment as the entire season fills very quickly.

Bookings & Transport

The Milford Track is officially a Great Walk. Between late October and mid-April, you need a Great Walk pass ($162) to cover your three nights in the huts: Clinton Hut, Mintaro Hut and Dumpling Hut. Passes must be obtained in advance, either online via the Department of Conservation's Great Walks Bookings or at a DOC visitor centre.

In the low season the huts revert to the Serviced category ($15), and the track can be walked in any time frame you like. This makes late April and early May a great time to tramp, weather dependent. September to late October is not recommended as there's considerable danger of spring avalanches.

The track starts at Glade Wharf on Lake Te Anau, accessible by a 1½-hour boat trip from Te Anau Downs, 29km from Te Anau on the road to Milford Sound. The track finishes at Sandfly Point, a 15-minute boat trip from Milford Sound village, from where you can return by road back to Te Anau (two hours). Connecting transport and hut tickets can all be booked online at the same time.

Tracknet (☏0800 483 262; www.tracknet. net) offers transport from Queenstown and Te Anau to meet the boats at Te Anau Downs and Milford Sound. Another option includes a float-plane hop from Te Anau to Glade Wharf with Wings & Water (p268). In Te Anau, the Fiordland i-SITE and the Fiordland National Park Visitor Centre can advise on all options.

Milford Sound

The iconic image of Mitre Peak amid Milford Sound has long dominated New Zealand tourism marketing. Opportunities to explore the fabled body of water include boat cruises, kayaking and flight-seeing.

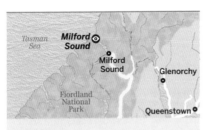

Tasman Sea
Milford Sound
Milford Sound
Glenorchy
Fiordland National Park
Queenstown

Great For...

ⓘ **Need to Know**

Gas up in Te Anau (118km) before driving to Milford Sound via the Homer Tunnel.

★ **Top Tip**

Milford Sound is one of NZ's wettest spots, but it's still beautiful in Fiordland rain.

Sydney Opera House or the Eiffel Tower – your first glimpse of a world-famous sight can really stop you in your tracks. So it is with Mitre Peak (Rahotu), the spectacular, 1692m-high mountain rising from the dark waters of Milford Sound (Piopiotahi).

From the road's end it sits dead centre of a beautiful landscape of sheer rocky cliffs anchored in inky waters. Occasionally the precarious forests clinging to the slopes relinquish their hold, causing a 'tree avalanche' into the fiord.

Milford Sound receives about half a million visitors annually, but on the water this humanity is dwarfed by nature's vastness.

Cruises

The clue is in the name: Milford Sound is all about the water, and the landforms that envelop it. It's enough to make you go misty-eyed, as an average annual rainfall of 7m fuels innumerable cascading waterfalls. The unique ocean environment – caused by freshwater sitting atop warmer seawater – replicates deep-ocean conditions, encouraging the activity of marine life such as dolphins, seals and penguins. Getting out on the water is a must.

Real Journeys   Cruise

(📞0800 656 501, 03-249 7416; www.real journeys.co.nz) 🚢 Various trips, including the popular 1¾-hour scenic cruise (adult/child from $76/22). The 2½-hour nature cruise (adult/child from $88/22) hones in on wildlife with a specialist nature guide providing commentary. Overnight cruises include kayaking and taking nature tours in small boats en route.

Cruising on Milford Sound

Overnight trips depart from the cruise terminal mid-afternoon and return around 9.30am the following day. The *Milford Wanderer,* modelled on an old trading scow, accommodates 36 passengers in two- and four-bunk cabins with shared bathrooms (dorm/single/double $305/621/710). The *Milford Mariner* sleeps 60 in more-upmarket single ($744) or double ($850) en suite cabins. Cheaper prices apply from April through to September; coach transport from Te Anau is extra.

---

❶ Need to Know

If you're driving, snow chains must be carried on ice- and avalanche-risk days from May to November (there will be signs on the road), and can be hired from service stations in Te Anau.

PICHUGIN DMITRY/SHUTTERSTOCK ©

Southern Discoveries   Cruise
(☏0800 264 536; www.southerndiscoveries.
co.nz; adult/child from $59/20) Options
include a 2¼-hour Encounter Nature cruise
on a relatively small (75-person) boat.

Cruise Milford   Cruise
(☏0800 645 367; www.cruisemilfordnz.com;
adult/child from $80/18; ⊙10.45am, 12.45pm &
2.45pm) A small boat heads out three times
a day on a 1¾-hour cruise.

Activities
One of the best perspectives you can get
of Milford Sound is from a kayak, dwarfed
by the cliffs. Two operators can get you out
on the water, both of which have booking
offices in Te Anau.

Rosco's Milford Kayaks   Kayaking
(☏03-249 8500, 0800 476 726; www.roscos
milfordkayaks.com; 72 Town Centre, Te Anau; trips
$99-199; ⊙Nov-Apr) Guided, tandem-kayak
trips including the 'Morning Glory' ($199),
a challenging paddle the full length of the
fiord to Anita Bay, and the easier 'Stirling
Sunriser' ($195), which ventures beneath
the 151m-high Stirling Falls. Among many
other options are trips 'your grandmother
could do', and kayak-walk combos on the
Milford Track.

Descend Scubadiving   Diving
(www.descend.co.nz; 2 dives incl gear $299)
Descend runs day trips with four hours
cruising on Milford Sound in a 7m cata-
maran and two dives along the way. The
marine reserve is home to unique marine
life, including a multitude of corals. Transport, equipment, hot drinks and snacks are
supplied.

✘ Take a Break

There's a perfunctory cafe at the Discover Milford Sound Information Centre
and another at Milford Sound Lodge.

The Chasm

Te Anau–Milford Highway

Milford Sound is deservedly famous, but the road linking Te Anau to the sound is also a world standout – wonderfully scenic and travelling deep into the heart of true wilderness.

Great For...

☑ Don't Miss

Taking one of the excellent walks off the main road to hidden lakes and rivers.

The 119km stretch from Te Anau to Milford Sound (SH94) offers an easily accessible experience of Fiordland, taking in beech forest, river valleys, mirror-like lakes and alpine scenery.

Depart Te Anau early (by 8am) to avoid tour buses at the sound. Make sure you fill up with petrol before setting off.

The trip takes two to 2½ hours non-stop, but take time to experience the various viewpoints and walks en route. Pick up DOC'S *Fiordland National Park Day Walks* brochure ($2) from the Fiordland i-SITE or Fiordland National Park Visitor Centre, or download it at www.doc.govt.nz.

At the 29km mark the road passes **Te Anau Downs**, where boats for the Milford Track depart. An easy 45-minute return walk leads through forest to **Lake Mistletoe**, a small glacier-formed lake. The road

Hiker on the Routeburn Track

NARUEDOM YAEMPONGSA/SHUTTERSTOCK ©

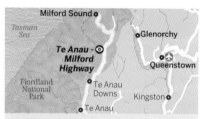

Milford Sound
Tasman Sea
Glenorchy
Te Anau - Milford Highway
Queenstown
Fiordland National Park
Te Anau Downs
Te Anau
Kingston

ℹ️ Need to Know

Chains must be carried on icy or avalanche-risk days from May to November.

✕ Take a Break

Stock up on picnic items in Te Anau and stop along this very scenic road.

★ Top Tip

Kea (alpine parrots) hang around the Homer Tunnel. Don't feed them as it's bad for their health.

then heads into the **Eglinton Valley**, reaching deeper wilderness immersion crossing into Fiordland National Park.

Just past the **Mackay Creek** campsite (at 51km) are views to Pyramid Peak (2295m) and Ngatimamoe Peak (2164m) ahead. The boardwalk at **Mirror Lakes** (at 58km) leads through beech forest and wetlands. After 77km is **Cascade Creek** and **Lake Gunn**. The **Lake Gunn Nature Walk** (45 minutes return) loops through red beech forest with side trails leading to lakeside beaches.

At 84km the vegetation changes as you pass across the **Divide**, the lowest east–west pass in the Southern Alps. From here is a good two-hour return walk along the the start of the **Routeburn Track**, climbing up through beech forest to the alpine tussock land of **Key Summit**. From the Divide,

the road falls into the beech forest of the **Hollyford Valley** – stop at Pop's View for a great outlook.

The road then climbs through a spectacular valley to the **Homer Tunnel**, 101km from Te Anau and framed by a high-walled, ice-carved amphitheatre. Opened in 1954, the tunnel is one way, with the world's most alpine set of traffic lights to direct vehicle flow. Dark and dripping with water, the 1270m-long tunnel emerges at the head of the spectacular **Cleddau Valley**. At the tunnel entrance, look forward to the company of curious and cheeky kea.

About 10km before Milford Sound, the **Chasm Walk** (20 minutes return) is well worth a stop. The forest-cloaked Cleddau River plunges through scooped-out boulders in a narrow chasm. Look out for glimpses of **Mt Tutoko** (2746m), Fiordland's highest peak.

Doubtful Sound

Milford Sound gets all the attention, but the misty expanse of Doubtful Sound is even more spectacular. The area's remoteness is especially enhanced during an overnight stay on the water.

Great For...

☑ Don't Miss

Dipping your kayak blades into silky smooth water as you negotiate Doubtful Sound's mystic coves.

Magnificent Doubtful Sound is a wilderness area of fractured and gouged mountains, dense forest and thundering waterfalls. Technically a fiord, having being carved by glaciers, Doubtful is one of New Zealand's largest sounds – three times the length and 10 times the area of Milford. It is also much less visited. If you have the time and the money and the weather's behaving, it's an essential experience.

Until relatively recently, only the most intrepid tramper or sailor ever explored Doubtful Sound. Even Captain Cook only observed it from off the coast in 1770, because he was 'doubtful' whether the winds in the sound would be sufficient to blow the ship back out to sea.

Manapouri is the jumping-off point for cruises to Doubtful Sound, and the town was the site of NZ's first major environmen-

ⓘ Need to Know

If you're staying in Te Anau, tour operators usually also include shuttle transport to Manapouri.

✕ Take a Break

Manapouri's **Lakeview Café & Bar** (☎03-249 6652; www.manapouri.com; 68 Cathedral Dr; mains $20-34; ☻11am-8.30pm; ☎) has brilliant views from the pub's front lawn.

> ★ **Top Tip**
>
> Kayaking companies usually operate double kayaks, so solo travellers will be paired with another person.

tal campaign. The original plan for the West Arm hydroelectric power station, built to supply electricity for an aluminium smelter, required raising the level of the lake by 30m. A petition gathered 265,000 signatures and the issue contributed to the downfall of the government at the following election. The win proved big for environmentalists, for not only was the power station built without the lake levels being changed, it also spawned more nationwide environmental action through the 1970s and '80s.

Guided Tours

Major considerations are the size of the boat and whether you overnight (pricey but preferable) or take a day trip. Overnight cruises include meals plus the option of fishing and kayaking. Tours can also be joined in Te Anau.

Real Journeys   Cruise

(☎0800 656 501; www.realjourneys.co.nz) ✿ The day-long 'wilderness cruise' (adult/child from $250/65) includes a three-hour journey aboard a modern catamaran with a specialist nature guide. The overnight cruise, which runs from September to May, is aboard the *Fiordland Navigator*, which sleeps 70 in en-suite cabins (quad-share per adult/child $385/193, single/double $1076/1230). Some trips include a visit to the West Arm power station.

Fiordland Expeditions   Cruise

(☎0508 888 656; www.fiordlandexpeditions. co.nz; dm/s/d from $595/1270/1350) Overnight cruise on the *Tutoko II* (maximum 14 passengers).

Adventure Kayak & Cruise   Kayaking

(☎0800 324 966; www.fiordlandadventure.co.nz; day/overnight tour $249/295; ☻Oct-Apr) Runs day trips to Doubtful Sound, or two-day trips with a night camping on a beach.

Te Anau

Peaceful, lakeside Te Anau township is the main gateway to Fiordland National Park tramps and the ever-popular Milford Sound, as well as a pleasant place to while away a few days. It's large enough to have a smattering of good eateries and accommodation, but it's much easier on the liver and wallet than attention-grabbing Queenstown.

To the east are the pastoral areas of central Southland, while west across Lake Te Anau lie the rugged mountains of Fiordland. The lake, New Zealand's second-largest, was gouged out by a huge glacier and has several arms that extend into the mountainous, forested western shore. Its deepest point is 417m, about twice the depth of Loch Ness.

◎ SIGHTS

Punanga Manu o
Te Anau   Bird Sanctuary
(www.doc.govt.nz; Te Anau–Manapouri Rd; ☺dawn-dusk) **FREE** By the lake, this set of outdoor aviaries offers a chance to see native bird species difficult to spot in the wild, including the precious icon of Fiordland, the extremely rare takahe.

Mavora Lakes
Conservation Park   Nature Reserve
(www.doc.govt.nz; Centre Hill Rd) Mavora Lakes Conservation Park, in the Snowdon State Forest, lies within the Te Wāhipounamu–South West New Zealand World Heritage Area. The heart of the park is the sublime Mavora Lakes camping area, huge golden meadows sitting alongside two lakes – North and South Mavora – fringed by forest and towered over by the impressive Thomson and Livingstone Mountains with peaks rising to more than 1600m.

Te Anau Glowworm Caves   Cave
(☏0800 656 501; www.realjourneys.co.nz; adult/child $79/22) Once present only in Māori legends, these impressive caves were rediscovered in 1948. Accessible only by boat, the 200m-long system of caves is a magical place with sculpted rocks, waterfalls small and large, whirlpools and a glittering glowworm grotto in its inner reaches. Real Journeys (p270) runs 2¼-hour guided tours, reaching the heart of the caves via a lake cruise, walkway and a short underground boat ride. Journeys depart from its office on Lakefront Dr.

❸ ACTIVITIES

Te Anau is primarily a gateway to the great wilderness of Te Wāhipounamu, which boasts such crowd-pullers as Milford Sound. However, there's plenty to keep you occupied around the town itself, as well as out on the water and up in the air.

Wings & Water   Scenic Flights
(☏03-249 7405; www.wingsandwater.co.nz; Lakefront Dr) Ten-minute local flights (adult/child $95/55), and longer flights over the Kepler Track and Dusky, Doubtful and Milford Sounds (from $310/190).

Ultimate Hikes   Tramping
(☏0800 659 255, 03-450 1940; www.ultimate hikes.co.nz; 5-day tramp incl food dm/s/d $2195/3085/5210; ☺Nov-Apr) ∕ The only operator permitted to run guided tramps of the Milford Track, Ultimate Hikes provides its walkers with cosy, carpeted wilderness lodges with hot showers and proper food.

Hollyford Track   Tramping
(☏03-442 3000; www.hollyfordtrack.com; adult/child from $1795/1395; ☺late Oct-late Apr) ∕ Ngāi Tahu–owned Hollyford Track runs excellent three-day guided trips on the Hollyford staying at private huts/lodges. The journey is shortened with a jetboat trip down the river and Lake McKerrow on day two, and it ends with a scenic flight to Milford Sound.

Luxmore Jet   Jetboating
(☏0800 253 826; www.luxmorejet.com; Lakefront Dr; adult/child $99/49) One-hour trips on the Upper Waiau River (aka the River Anduin).

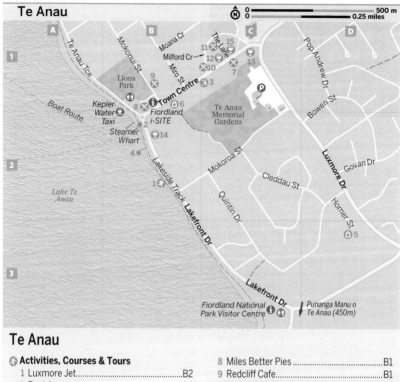

Te Anau

☉ TOURS

Southern Lakes Helicopters
Scenic Flights

(☏03-249 7167; www.southernlakeshelicopters. co.nz; Lakefront Dr) Flights over Te Anau for 30 minutes ($240), longer trips over Doubtful, Dusky and Milford Sounds (from $685), and various helihike, helibike and heliski options.

Fiordland Tours
Tour

(☏0800 247 249; www.fiordlandtours.co.nz; adult/child from $139/59) Runs small-group bus and Milford Sound cruise tours, departing from Te Anau and stopping at some interesting sights on the way. It also

Day Walks Around Te Anau

Te Anau's Lakeside Track makes for a very pleasant stroll or cycle in either direction – north to the marina and around to the Upukerora River (around one-hour return), or south past the Fiordland National Park Visitor Centre and on to the control gates and start of the Kepler Track (50 minutes).

Day tramps in the national park are readily accessible from **Te Anau. Kepler Water Taxi** (📱027 249 8365; www.facebook.com/keplerwatertaxi; each way $25) will scoot you over to Brod Bay, from where you can walk to Mt Luxmore (seven to eight hours) or back along the Lakeside Track to Te Anau (two to three hours). During summer, **Trips & Tramps** (📱03-249 7081, 0800 305 807; www.tripsandtramps.com) offers small-group, guided day hikes on the Kepler and Routeburn, among other tracks. Real Journeys runs guided day hikes (adult/child $195/127, November to mid-April) along an 11km stretch of the Milford Track. Various day walks can also be completed by linking with regular bus services run by Tracknet (p259).

For self-guided adventures, pick up DOC's *Fiordland National Park Day Walks* brochure ($2) from the Fiordland i-SITE or Fiordland National Park Visitor Centre, or download it at www.doc.govt.nz.

Hiking on the Kepler Track
NARUEDOM YAEMPONGSA/SHUTTERSTOCK ©

provides track transport and guided day walks on the Kepler Track.

Real Journeys Tour
(0800 656 501; www.realjourneys.co.nz; 85 Lakefront Dr; ⊙7.30am-8.30pm Sep-May, 8am-7pm Jun-Aug) 🚲 A major player offering a multitude of services, including cruises on Doubtful and Milford Sounds, guided day-walks on the Milford Track and tours of the Te Anau Glowworm Cave.

🛍 SHOPPING

Bev's Tramping Gear Hire Outdoor Equipment
(📱03-249 7389; www.bevs-hire.co.nz; 16 Homer St; ⊙9am-noon & 5.30-7pm Mon-Sat) Lovely Bev walks the talk, hires tramping and camping equipment, and sells dehydrated meals. From May to October she's only open by prior arrangement.

Outside Sports Outdoor Equipment
(📱03-249 8195; www.outsidesports.co.nz; 38 Town Centre; ⊙9am-9pm daily Nov-Mar, to 6pm Mon-Sat Apr-Oct) Tramping and camping equipment for sale, or hire, plus bike rental (half-/full day $30/50).

🍽 EATING

Miles Better Pies Fast Food $
(03-249 9044; www.milesbetterpies.co.nz; 19 Town Centre; pies $5-6.50; ⊙6am-3pm) The bumper selection includes venison, lamb and mint, and fruit pies. There are a few pavement tables, but sitting and munching beside the lake is nicer.

Sandfly Cafe Cafe $
(📱03-249 9529; 9 The Lane; mains $7-20; ⊙7am-4.30pm; 📶) Clocking the most local votes for the town's best espresso, simple but satisfying Sandfly is a top spot to enjoy an all-day breakfast, soup, sandwich or sweet treat, while listening to cruisy music or sunning yourself on the lawn.

Mainly Seafood Fish & Chips **$**
(☏027 516 5555; www.mainlyseafood.co.nz;
106 Town Centre; mains $7.50-18; ◷11.30am-
8.30pm) Commendable fish and chips, and
burgers with homemade patties – yippee!
If the queue stresses you out, there's a
massage chair ($2).

Ristorante Pizzeria da
Toni Italian **$$**
(☏03-249 4305; 1 Milford Cres; mains $20-29;
◷4-10pm Mon-Fri, noon-10pm Sat & Sun; ☽)
Excellent, authentic Italian fare: wood-fired
pizzas with simple, high-quality toppings
and homemade pastas are the stars of the
show, supported by thoughtful service and
a baroque soundtrack.

Redcliff Cafe Modern NZ **$$$**
(☏03-249 7431; www.theredcliff.co.nz; 12
Mokonui St; mains $38-42; ◷4-10pm) Housed
in a replica settler's cottage, relaxed
Redcliff offers generous fine-dining in a
convivial atmosphere backed by sharp
service. The predominantly locally sourced
food is truly terrific: try the wild venison or
hare. Kick off or wind it up with a drink in
the rustic front bar, which often hosts live
music.

🍷 DRINKING & NIGHTLIFE

Black Dog Bar Bar
(☏03-249 8844; www.blackdogbar.co.nz; 7
The Lane; ◷10am-late; ☽) Attached to the
Fiordland Cinema, this is Te Anau's most
sophisticated watering hole.

Fat Duck Bar
(☏03-249 8480; 124 Town Centre; ◷noon-late
Tue-Sun; ☽) This corner bar with pavement
seating is a sound choice for supping a pint
or two of Mac's beer. The kitchen dishes up
marginally trendy gastropub and cafe fare,
opening for breakfast daily in summer.

Ranch Bar & Grill Pub
(☏03-249 8801; www.theranchbar.co.nz; 111
Town Centre; ◷noon-late) Popular with locals
for its generous pub meals, head to the
Ranch for a quality Sunday roast dinner

($15), Thursday jam night or a big sports
match.

Moose Pub
(☏03-249 7100; www.themoosebarteanau.com;
84 Lakefront Dr; ◷11am-late) Head to this
rough-edged waterfront bar for a late-
afternoon beer and bar snacks on the patio.

ENTERTAINMENT

Fiordland Cinema Cinema
(☏03 249 8844; www.fiordlandcinema.co.nz; 7
The Lane; ☽) In between back-to-back show-
ings of the excellent *Ata Whenua/Fiordland
on Film* (adult/child $10/5), essentially
a 32-minute advertisement for Fiordland
scenery, Fiordland Cinema serves as the
local movie house.

ℹ️ INFORMATION

Fiordland i-SITE (☏03-249 8900; www.
fiordland.org.nz; 19 Town Centre; ◷8.30am-7pm
Dec-Mar, to 5.30pm Apr-Nov) Activity, accommodation and transport bookings.

Fiordland National Park Visitor Centre (DOC;
☏03-249 7924; www.doc.govt.nz; cnr Lakefront
Dr & Te Anau–Manapouri Rd; ◷8.30am-4.30pm)
Can assist with Great Walks bookings, general
hut tickets and information, with the bonus of
a natural history display, and a shop stocking
tramping supplies and essential topographical
maps for backcountry trips.

ℹ️ GETTING THERE & AWAY

Buses for destinations including Queenstown
and Christchurch depart outside Kiwi Country
on Miro St.

ℹ️ GETTING AROUND

For transport to trailheads including the Milford
Track and the Kepler Track, see **Tracknet**
(p259) or **Topline Tours** (03-249 8059; www.
toplinetours.co.nz).

Kaikoura (p188)

In Focus

Christ Church Cathedral (p198), damaged by the 2011 earthquake

New Zealand Today

New Zealand has had a bad run on the disaster front in recent years, with devastating earthquakes and mining and helicopter tragedies rattling the national psyche. But things are looking up: tourism is booming, the arts and local craft-beer scenes are effervescing, and the Kiwi rugby and cricket teams are in awesome form – there's plenty to put a smile on the country's collective dial.

Reasons to be Cheerful

Christchurch's recovery from the 2010 and 2011 earthquakes is ongoing, producing as much good news as bad. On one hand it is testing relationships between the citizens and government agencies, as tough decisions are made about fix-ups and payouts. On the other, Christchurch's recovery reinforces the perception Kiwis have of themselves as 'battlers' with strong communities and civic pride.

Speaking of pride, New Zealanders have been flush with it of late. Following the All Blacks' success at the 2011 Rugby World Cup at home, the beloved national team beat arch-rivals Australia 34–17 in the 2015 final in London. In doing so, NZ became the first country ever to win back-to-back Rugby World Cups, capping off a remarkable four-year

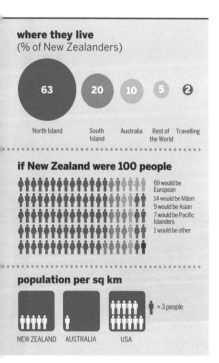

where they live
(% of New Zealanders)

63 North Island
20 South Island
10 Australia
5 Rest of the World
2 Travelling

if New Zealand were 100 people

69 would be European
14 would be Māori
9 would be Asian
7 would be Pacific Islanders
1 would be other

population per sq km

NEW ZEALAND   AUSTRALIA   USA

👤 ≈ 3 people

period in which the All Blacks lost just three (and drew one) of their 53 matches between World Cup wins.

But the depth of Kiwi sporting talent ranges beyond the rugby pitch. In 2015 the national men's cricket team, the Black Caps, made the final of the Cricket World Cup for the first time, stringing together an impressive series of test cricket results both before and afterwards. Other Kiwi sporting stars making their mark include golfing sensation Lydia Ko, who became world No 1 in 2015, aged just 17; NBA seven-footer Steven Adams (from Rotorua), currently playing with the Oklahoma City Thunder; quadruple US IndyCar champion Scott Dixon; and Valerie Adams, the greatest female shot-putter the world has ever seen (also from Rotorua – something in the water?).

On the arts front, Canadian director James Cameron has set up a rural home base near Wellington and will create three *Avatar* sequels in the capital from 2016, bringing substantial investment and cementing NZ's reputation as a world-class film-making destination.

And at the end of a long day, Kiwi craft beer is consolidating itself at the top of the global scene. You can't go anywhere in NZ these days without stumbling across these microbrewed delights: local, flavoursome, potent and passionately marketed. The NZ wine industry is looking nervously over its shoulder, wondering where all its sav blanc drinkers have gone.

The Trans-Pacific Partnership

In October 2015 after seven long years of negotiations, the Trans-Pacific Partnership (TPP) was ratified by 12 nations with Pacific interests – Australia, Brunei, Canada, Chile, Japan, Malaysia, Mexico, New Zealand, Peru, Singapore, the US and Vietnam – bringing into effect a broad raft of initiatives aimed at boosting relationships and economies within the region. For New Zealand, the new agreement will cut taxes and tariffs on NZ exports, which it's hoped will have a beneficial effect on exports, particularly in the dairy sector.

Critics of the TPP suggest that it will lead to increased costs of basic medicines in NZ, and that it grants too much freedom to large corporations to sidestep international and internal labour, environmental, health, financial and food-safety laws, angling for profit rather than social benefit. It remains to be seen whether the TPP will sink or swim – watch this space.

Māori warrior

MIKE POWELL/GETTY IMAGES ©

History

New Zealand's history is not long, but it is fast. In less than a thousand years the islands have produced two new peoples: the Polynesian Māori and European New Zealanders. The latter are often known by their Māori name, 'Pākehā' (though not all like the term). New Zealand shares some history with the rest of Polynesia, and with other European settler societies, but has unique features too.

AD 1000–1200

Possible date of the arrival of Māori in NZ. Archaeological evidence points to about AD 1200, but much earlier dates have been suggested.

1642

First European contact: Abel Tasman arrives to find the 'Great South Land'. His party leaves without landing after a sea skirmish with Māori.

1769

James Cook and Jean de Surville visit. Despite some violence, both manage to communicate with Māori.

Engraving of a warrior and his wife from *Journal of a Voyage to the South Seas* by Sydney Parkinson

Making Māori

Despite persistent myths, there is no doubt that the first settlers of NZ were the Polynesian forebears of today's Māori. Beyond that, there are a lot of question marks. Exactly where in east Polynesia did they come from – the Cook Islands, Tahiti, maybe the Marquesas? When did they arrive? Did the first settlers come in one group, or several? Some evidence, such as the diverse DNA of the Polynesian rats that accompanied the first settlers, suggests multiple founding voyages. On the other hand, only rats and dogs brought by the founders have survived, not the more valuable pigs and chickens. The survival of these cherished animals would have had high priority, and their failure to be successfully introduced suggests fewer voyages.

Prime sites for first settlement were warm coastal gardens for the food plants brought from Polynesia (kumara or sweet potato, gourd, yam and taro); sources of workable stone for knives and adzes; and areas with abundant big game. New Zealand has no native land mammals apart from a few species of bat, but 'big game' is no exaggeration: the islands

1790s	1818–36	1840
Whaling ships and sealing gangs arrive. Europeans depend on Māori contacts for essentials such as food, water and protection.	Intertribal Māori 'Musket Wars' take place: tribes acquire muskets and win bloody victories against tribes without them.	On 6 February, around 500 chiefs countrywide sign the Treaty of Waitangi. New Zealand becomes a nominal British colony.

were home to a dozen species of moa (a large flightless bird), the largest of which weighed up to 240kg, about twice the size of an ostrich. There were also other species of flightless birds and large sea mammals such as fur seals, all unaccustomed to being hunted. For people from small Pacific islands, this was like hitting the jackpot. The first settlers spread far and fast, from the top of the North Island to the bottom of the South Island within the first 100 years. High-protein diets are likely to have boosted population growth.

By about 1400, however, with big-game supply dwindling, Māori economics turned from big game to small game – forest birds and rats – and from hunting to gardening and fishing. A good living could still be made, but it required detailed local knowledge, steady effort and complex communal organisation, hence the rise of the Māori tribes. Competition for resources increased, conflict did likewise, and this led to the building of increasingly sophisticated fortifications, known as pa. Vestiges of pa earthworks can still be seen around the country (on the hilltops of Auckland, for example).

Enter Europe

New Zealand became an official British colony in 1840, but the first authenticated contact between Māori and the outside world took place almost two centuries earlier in 1642, in Golden Bay at the top of the South Island. Two Dutch ships sailed from Indonesia, to search for southern land and anything valuable it might contain. The commander, Abel Tasman, was instructed to pretend to any natives he might meet 'that you are by no means eager for precious metals, so as to leave them ignorant of the value of the same'.

When Tasman's ships anchored in the bay, local Māori came out in their canoes to make the traditional challenge: friends or foes? Misunderstanding this, the Dutch challenged back, by blowing trumpets. When a boat was lowered to take a party between the two ships, it was attacked. Four crewmen were killed. Tasman sailed away and did not come back; nor did any other European for 127 years. But the Dutch did leave a name: initially 'Statenland', which was then changed to 'Nieuw Zeeland' or 'New Sealand'.

English & French Arrivals

Contact between Māori and Europeans was renewed in 1769, when English and French explorers arrived, under James Cook and Jean de Surville. Relations were more sympathetic, and exploration continued, motivated by science, profit and power rivalry. Cook made two more visits between 1773 and 1777, and there were further French expeditions.

Unofficial visits, by whaling ships in the north and sealing gangs in the south, began in the 1790s. The first mission station was founded in 1814, in the Bay of Islands, and was followed by dozens of others: Anglican, Methodist and Catholic. Trade in flax and timber generated small European–Māori settlements by the 1820s. Surprisingly, the most numerous category of European visitor was probably American. New England whaling ships favoured the Bay of Islands for rest and recreation; 271 called there between 1833 and 1839 alone. To whalers, rest and recreation meant sex and drink. Their favourite haunt, the little town

1845	1858	1860–69
Young Ngāpuhi chief Hone Heke challenges British sovereignty. The ensuing Northland war continues until 1846.	The Waikato chief Te Wherowhero is installed as the first Māori king.	First and Second Taranaki wars, starting with the controversial swindling of Māori land by the government at Waitara.

of Kororareka (now Russell), was known to the missionaries as 'the hellhole of the Pacific'. New England visitors today might well have distant relatives among the local Māori.

Māori–European Trade

One or two dozen bloody clashes dot the history of Māori–European contact before 1840 but, given the number of visits, inter-racial conflict was modest. Europeans needed Māori protection, food and labour, and Māori came to need European articles, especially muskets. Whaling stations and mission stations were linked to local Māori groups by intermarriage, which helped keep the peace.

Europe brought such things as pigs (at last) and potatoes, which benefited Māori, while muskets and diseases had the opposite effect. Europeans expected peoples like the Māori to simply fade away at contact, and some early estimates of Māori population were overly high – up to one million. Current estimates are between 85,000 and 110,000 Māori population for 1769. The Musket Wars killed perhaps 20,000, and new diseases did considerable damage too (although NZ had the natural quarantine of distance: infected Europeans usually recovered or died during the long voyage, and smallpox, for example, which devastated indigenous North Americans, did not make it here). By 1840, Māori had been reduced to about 70,000, a decline of at least 20%. Māori bent under the weight of European contact, but they certainly did not break.

Musket Wars

Most warfare was between Māori and Māori: the terrible intertribal 'Musket Wars' of 1818–36. Because Northland had the majority of early contact with Europe, its Ngāpuhi tribe acquired muskets first. Under their great general Hongi Hika, Ngāpuhi then raided south, winning bloody victories against tribes without muskets. Once they acquired muskets, these tribes saw off Ngāpuhi, but also raided further south in their turn. The domino effect continued to the far south of the South Island in 1836. The missionaries claimed that the Musket Wars then tapered off through their influence, but the restoration of the balance of power through the equal distribution of muskets was probably more important.

Making Pākehā

By 1840 Māori tribes described local Europeans as 'their Pākehā', and valued the profit and prestige they brought. Māori wanted more of both, and concluded that accepting nominal British authority was the way to get them. At the same time, the British government was overcoming its reluctance to undertake potentially expensive intervention in NZ. It too was influenced by profit and prestige, but also by humanitarian considerations. It believed, wrongly but sincerely, that Māori could not handle the increasing scale of unofficial Euro-

1861	**1863–64**	**1893**
Gold discovered in Otago. As a result, the population of Otago climbs from less than 13,000 to over 30,000 in six months.	Waikato Land War. Despite surprising successes, Māori are defeated and much land is confiscated.	New Zealand becomes the first country in the world to grant the vote to women, following a campaign led by Kate Sheppard.

Arrowtown (p244)

MJ PROTOTYPE/SHUTTERSTOCK/GETTY IMAGES ©

pean contact. In 1840, the two peoples struck a deal, symbolised by the treaty first signed at Waitangi on 6 February that year.

The Treaty of Waitangi now has a standing not dissimilar to that of the Constitution in the US, but is even more contested. The original problem was a discrepancy between British and Māori understandings of it. The English version promised Māori full equality as British subjects in return for complete rights of government. The Māori version also promised that Māori would retain their chieftainship, which implied local rights of government. The problem was not great at first, because the Māori version applied outside the small European settlements. But as those settlements grew, conflict brewed.

Mass Migration

In 1840 there were only about 2000 Europeans in NZ, with the shanty town of Kororareka as the capital and biggest settlement. By 1850 six new settlements had been formed with 22,000 settlers between them. About half of these had arrived under the auspices of the New Zealand Company and its associates, who hoped to create 'instant civilisation'. However, from the 1850s these settlers, who included a high proportion of upper-middle-class gentlefolk, were swamped by succeeding waves of immigrants that continued to wash in until the 1880s.

These people were part of the great British and Irish diaspora that also populated Australia and much of North America, but the NZ mix was distinctive. Lowland Scots settlers were more prominent in NZ than elsewhere, for example, with the possible exception of parts of Canada. New Zealand's Irish, even the Catholics, tended to come from the north of Ireland; New Zealand's English tended to come from the counties close to London.

Māori Resistance

The Māori resistance to the central government's control was one of the most formidable ever mounted against European expansion, comparable to that of the Sioux and Seminole in the US. The first clash took place in 1843 in the Wairau Valley, now a wine-growing dis-

1901	1908	1914–18
New Zealand politely declines the invitation to join the new Commonwealth of Australia.	New Zealand physicist Ernest Rutherford is awarded the Nobel Prize in chemistry.	In WWI about 100,000 NZ men serve overseas (from a population of just over 1 million). Some 60,000 become casualties.

trict. A posse of settlers set out to enforce the myth of British control, but encountered the reality of Māori control. Twenty-two settlers were killed, along with about six Māori.

In 1845 more serious fighting broke out in the Bay of Islands, when Hone Heke sacked a British settlement. Heke and his ally Kawiti baffled three British punitive expeditions, using a modern variant of the traditional *pa* fortification. Vestiges of these innovative earthworks can still be seen at Ruapekapeka (south of Kawakawa). Governor Grey claimed victory in the north, but few were convinced at the time. Grey had more success in the south, where he arrested the formidable Ngāti Toa chief Te Rauparaha, who until then wielded great influence on both sides of Cook Strait. Pākehā were able to swamp the few Māori living in the South Island, but the fighting of the 1840s confirmed that the North Island at that time comprised a European fringe around an independent Māori heartland.

In the 1850s settler population and aspirations grew, and fighting broke out again in 1860. The wars burned on sporadically until 1872 over much of the North Island. In the early years a Māori nationalist organisation, the King Movement, was the backbone of resistance. In later years some remarkable prophet-generals, notably Titokowaru and Te Kooti, took over. Most wars were small-scale, but the Waikato war of 1863–64 was not. This conflict, fought at the same time as the American Civil War, involved armoured steamships, ultramodern heavy artillery, telegraph and 10 proud British regular regiments. Despite the odds, Māori forces won several battles, such as that at Gate Pa, near Tauranga, in 1864. But in the end they were ground down by European numbers and resources. Māori political, though not cultural, independence ebbed away in the last decades of the 19th century. It finally expired when police invaded its last sanctuary, the Urewera Mountains, in 1916.

Welfare & Warfare

From the 1850s to the 1880s, despite conflict with Māori, the Pākehā economy boomed on the back of wool exports, gold rushes and massive overseas borrowing for development. The crash came in the 1880s, when NZ experienced its Long Depression. In 1890 the Liberals came to power, and stayed there until 1912, helped by a recovering economy. The Liberals were NZ's first organised political party and the first of several governments to give NZ a reputation as 'the world's social laboratory'. New Zealand became the first country in the world to give women the vote in 1893, and introduced old-age pensions in 1898. The Liberals also introduced a long-lasting system of industrial arbitration, but this was not enough to prevent bitter industrial unrest in 1912–13. This happened under the conservative 'Reform' government, which had replaced the Liberals in 1912. Reform remained in power until 1928 and later transformed itself into the National Party. Renewed depression struck in 1929, and the NZ experience of it was as grim as any. The derelict little farmhouses still seen in rural areas often date from this era.

In 1935 a second reforming government took office: the First Labour government, led by Michael Joseph Savage, easily NZ's favourite Australian. For a time the Labour government

1931	**1939–45**	**1953**
A massive earthquake in Napier and Hastings kills 131 people.	NZ troops back Britain and the Allies during WWII; from 1942 around 100,000 Americans arrive to protect NZ from the Japanese.	New Zealander Edmund Hillary and Nepalese Tenzing Norgay become the first men to reach the summit of Mt Everest.

was considered the most socialist government outside Soviet Russia. But, when the chips were down in Europe in 1939, Labour had little hesitation in backing Britain.

Better Britons?

British visitors have long found NZ hauntingly familiar. This is not simply a matter of the Irish and British origin of most Pākehā. It also stems from the tightening of NZ links with Britain from 1882, when refrigerated cargoes of food were first shipped to London. By the 1930s, giant ships carried frozen meat, cheese and butter, as well as wool, on regular voyages taking about five weeks one way. The NZ economy adapted to the feeding of London, and cultural links were also enhanced. New Zealand children studied British history and literature, not their own. New Zealand's leading scientists and writers, such as Ernest Rutherford and Katherine Mansfield, gravitated to Britain.

This tight relationship has been described as 'recolonial', but it is a mistake to see NZ as an exploited colony. Average living standards in NZ were normally better than in Britain, as were the welfare and lower-level education systems. New Zealanders had access to British markets and culture, and they contributed their share to the latter as equals. The list of 'British' writers, academics, scientists, military leaders, publishers and the like who were actually New Zealanders is long. Indeed, New Zealanders, especially in war and sport, sometimes saw themselves as a superior version of the British – the Better Britons of the south. The NZ–London relationship was like that of the American Midwest and New York.

'Recolonial' NZ prided itself, with some justice, on its affluence, equality and social harmony. But it was also conformist, even puritanical. Until the 1950s it was technically illegal for farmers to allow their cattle to mate in fields fronting public roads, for moral reasons. The 1953 Marlon Brando movie *The Wild One* was banned until 1977. Sunday newspapers were illegal until 1969, and full Sunday trading was not allowed until 1989. Licensed restaurants hardly existed in 1960, nor did supermarkets or TV. Notoriously, from 1917 to 1967, pubs were obliged to shut at 6pm.

Coming In, Coming Out

The 'recolonial' system was shaken several times after 1935, but managed to survive until 1973, when Mother England ran off and joined the Franco–German commune now known as the EU. New Zealand was beginning to develop alternative markets to Britain, and alternative exports to wool, meat and dairy products. Wide-bodied jet aircraft were allowing the world and NZ to visit each other on an increasing scale. New Zealand had only 36,000 tourists in 1960, compared with more than two million a year now. Women were beginning to penetrate first the upper reaches of the workforce and then the political sphere. Gay people came out of the closet, despite vigorous efforts by moral conservatives to push them back in. University-educated youths were becoming more numerous and more assertive.

1981	1985	2010
Springbok rugby tour divides the nation. Many New Zealanders show a strong anti-apartheid stance by protesting the games.	*Rainbow Warrior* sunk in Auckland Harbour by French government agents.	A cave-in at Pike River coal mine on the South Island's West Coast kills 29 miners.

There were also developments in cultural nationalism, beginning in the 1930s but really flowering in the 1970s. Writers, artists and film-makers were by no means the only people who 'came out' in that era.

The Big Shift

From 1945 Māori experienced both a population explosion and massive urbanisation. In 1936 Māori were 17% urban and 83% rural. Fifty years later, these proportions had reversed. The immigration gates, which until 1960 were pretty much labelled 'whites only', widened, first to allow in Pacific Islanders for their labour, and then to allow in (East) Asians for their money. These transitions would have generated major socioeconomic change whatever happened in politics. But most New Zealanders associate the country's recent 'Big Shift' with the politics of 1984.

That year, NZ's third great reforming government was elected – the Fourth Labour government, led nominally by David Lange and in fact by Roger Douglas, the Minister of Finance. This government adopted an antinuclear foreign policy, delighting the left, and a more-market economic policy, delighting the right. New Zealand's numerous economic controls were dismantled at breakneck speed. Middle NZ was uneasy about the antinuclear policy, which threatened NZ's ANZUS alliance with Australia and the US. But in 1985 French spies sank the antinuclear protest ship *Rainbow Warrior* in Auckland Harbour, killing one crewman. The lukewarm American condemnation of the French act brought middle NZ in behind the antinuclear policy, which became associated with national independence. Other New Zealanders were uneasy about the more-market economic policy, but failed to come up with a convincing alternative. Revelling in their new freedom, NZ investors engaged in a frenzy of speculation and suffered even more than the rest of the world from the economic crash of 1987.

New Zealand in the 21st Century

The early 21st century is an interesting time for NZ. Like NZ food and wine, film and literature are flowering as never before, and the new ethnic mix is creating something very special in popular music. There are continuities, however – the pub, the sportsground, the quarter-acre section, the bush, the beach and the bach – and they too are part of the reason people like to come here.

Debate has long raged over whether New Zealand should adopt a new national flag. Those arguing for the change wanted to replace the existing flag incorporating a British Union Jack which, they said, harked back to the days when NZ was a British colony. Designs for the new flag were submitted by the public and a public referendum, to decide which of five proposed designs Kiwis preferred, happened in late 2015. A further referendum in early 2016 put the chosen design head-to-head with the old flag. The result? New Zealanders voted to retain the existing national flag, Union Jack and all.

2011	2013	2015
A severe earthquake strikes Christchurch, killing 185 people and badly damaging the central business district.	New Zealand becomes one of just 15 countries in the world to legally recognise same-sex marriage.	New Zealand's beloved All Blacks win back-to-back Rugby World Cups in England, defeating arch-rivals Australia 34–17 in the final.

Champagne Pool, Wai-O-Tapu Thermal Wonderland (p121)

CHRISTOPHER CHAN S/GETTY IMAGES ©

Environment

New Zealand is a young country – its present shape is less than 10,000 years old. Having broken away from the supercontinent of Gondwanaland (which included Africa, Australia, Antarctica and South America) some 85 million years ago, it endured continual uplift and erosion, buckling and tearing, and the slow fall and rise of the sea as ice ages came and went.

The Land

Straddling the boundary of two great colliding slabs of the earth's crust – the Pacific plate and the Indian/Australian plate – to this day NZ remains the plaything of nature's strongest forces.

The result is one of the most varied and spectacular landscapes in the world, ranging from snow-dusted mountains and drowned glacial valleys to rainforests, dunelands and an otherworldly volcanic plateau. It is a diversity of landforms you would expect to find across an entire continent rather than a small archipelago in the South Pacific.

Evidence of NZ's tumultuous past is everywhere. The South Island's mountainous spine – the 650km-long ranges of the Southern Alps – is a product of the clash of the two plates; the result of a process of rapid lifting that, if anything, is accelerating today. Despite

NZ's highest peak, Aoraki/Mt Cook, losing 10m from its summit overnight in a 1991 land-slide, the Alps are on an express elevator that, without erosion and landslides, would see them reach 10 times their present height within a few million years.

Volcanoes

On the North Island, the most impressive changes have been wrought by volcanoes. Auck-land is built on an isthmus peppered by scoria cones, on many of which you can still see the earthworks of *pa* (fortified villages) built by early Māori. The city's biggest and most recent volcano, 600-year-old Rangitoto Island, is just a short ferry ride from the down-town wharves. Some 300km further south, the classically shaped cone of snow-capped Mt Taranaki overlooks tranquil dairy pastures.

But the real volcanic heartland runs through the centre of the North Island, from the restless bulk of Mt Ruapehu in Tongariro National Park, northeast through the Rotorua lake district out to NZ's most active volcano, White Island, in the Bay of Plenty. Called the Taupo Volcanic Zone, this great 250km-long rift valley – part of a volcano chain known as the 'Pacific Ring of Fire' – has been the seat of massive eruptions that have left their mark on the country physically and culturally.

Most spectacular were the eruptions from the volcano that created Lake Taupo. Con-sidered the world's most productive volcano in terms of the amount of material ejected, Taupo last erupted 1800 years ago in a display that was the most violent anywhere on the planet within the past 5000 years.

You can experience the aftermath of volcanic destruction on a smaller scale at Te Wairoa (the Buried Village), near Rotorua on the shores of Lake Tarawera. Here, partly excavated and open to the public, lie the remains of a 19th-century Māori village overwhelmed when nearby Mt Tarawera erupted without warning. The famous Pink and White Terraces (one of several claimants to the popular title 'eighth wonder of the world') were destroyed over-night by the same upheaval.

But when nature sweeps the board clean with one hand she often rebuilds with the other: Waimangu Volcanic Valley, born of all that geothermal violence, is the place to go to experience the hot earth up close and personal amid geysers, silica pans, bubbling mud pools and the world's biggest hot spring; or you can wander around Rotorua's Whakare-warewa Village, where descendants of Māori displaced by the eruption live in the middle of steaming vents and prepare food for visitors in boiling pools.

The South Island also sees some evidence of volcanism – if the remains of the old vol-canoes of Banks Peninsula weren't there to repel the sea, the vast Canterbury Plains, built from alpine sediment washed down the rivers from the Alps, would have eroded long ago.

Earthquakes

A second by-product of movement along the tectonic plate boundary is seismic activity – earthquakes. Not for nothing has New Zealand been called 'the Shaky Isles'. Most quakes only rattle the glassware, but one was indirectly responsible for creating an internationally celebrated tourist attraction: in 1931, an earthquake measuring 7.9 on the Richter scale levelled the Hawke's Bay city of Napier, causing huge damage and loss of life. Napier was rebuilt almost entirely in the then-fashionable art-deco architectural style, and walking its streets today you can relive its brash exuberance in this mecca for lovers of art deco.

However, the North Island doesn't have a monopoly on earthquakes. In September 2010 Christchurch was rocked by a magnitude 7.1 earthquake. Less than six months later, in February 2011, a magnitude 6.3 quake destroyed much of the city's historic heart and claimed 185 lives, making it the country's second-deadliest natural disaster. New Zealand's second city continues to be jostled by aftershocks as it builds anew.

Pukeko

★ Native Birds

Tui

Kereru

Kiwi

Pukeko

Kea

Weather

In the south it is the Southern Alps themselves that dominate, dictating settlement patterns, throwing down engineering challenges and offering outstanding recreational opportunities. The island's mountainous backbone also helps shape the weather, as it stands in the path of the prevailing westerly winds that roll in, moisture-laden, from the Tasman Sea. As a result, bush-clad lower slopes of the western Southern Alps are among the wettest places on earth, with an annual precipitation of some 15,000mm. Having lost its moisture, the wind then blows dry across the eastern plains towards the Pacific coast.

The North Island has a more even rainfall and is spared the temperature extremes of the South, which can plunge when a wind blows in from Antarctica. The important thing to remember, especially if you are tramping at high altitude, is that NZ has a maritime climate. This means weather can change with lightning speed, catching out the unprepared.

Flora & Fauna

New Zealand may be relatively young, geologically speaking, but its plants and animals go back a long way. The tuatara, for instance, an ancient reptile unique to these islands, is a Gondwanaland survivor closely related to the dinosaurs, while many of the distinctive flightless birds here (ratites) have distant African and South American cousins.

Due to its long isolation, the country became a veritable warehouse of unique and varied plants, most of which are found nowhere else. And with separation of the landmass occurring before mammals appeared on the scene, birds and insects have evolved in spectacular ways to fill the gaps.

The now-extinct flightless moa, the largest of which grew to 3.5m tall and weighed over 200kg, browsed open grasslands much as cattle do today (skeletons can be seen at Auckland Museum), while the smaller kiwi still ekes out a nocturnal living rummaging among forest leaf litter for insects and worms, much as small mammals do elsewhere. One of the country's most ferocious-looking insects, the mouse-sized giant weta, meanwhile, has taken on a scavenging role elsewhere filled by rodents.

As one of the last places on earth to be colonised by humans, NZ was for millennia a safe laboratory for such risky evolutionary strategies, but with the arrival of Māori, and Europeans soon after, things went downhill fast.

Many endemic creatures, including moa and the huia, an exquisite songbird, were driven to extinction, and the vast forests were cleared for their timber and to make way for agriculture. Destruction of habitat and the introduction of exotic animals and plants have taken a terrible environmental toll and New Zealanders are now fighting a rearguard battle to save what remains.

A traditional *hongi* greeting

Māori Culture

*'Māori' once just meant 'common' or 'everyday', but now
it means... Well, let's just begin by saying that there
is a lot of 'then' and a lot of 'now' in the Māori world.
Sometimes the cultural present follows on from the
past quite seamlessly; sometimes things have changed
hugely; sometimes we just want to look to the future.*

Māori Then

Some three millennia ago people began moving eastward into the Pacific, sailing against the prevailing winds and currents (hard to go out, easier to return safely). Some stopped at Tonga and Samoa, and others settled the small central East Polynesian tropical islands.

The Māori colonisation of Aotearoa began from an original homeland known to Māori as Hawaiki. Skilled navigators and sailors travelled across the Pacific, using many navigational tools – currents, winds, stars, birds and wave patterns – to guide their large, double-hulled ocean-going craft to a new land. The first of many was the great navigator Kupe, who arrived, the story goes, chasing an octopus named Muturangi. But the distinction of giving New Zealand its well-known Māori name – Aotearoa – goes to his wife, Kuramarotini, who cried out, '*He ao, he ao tea, he ao tea roa!*' (A cloud, a white cloud, a long white cloud!).

Auckland Museum (p38)

JOHN ELK/GETTY IMAGES ©

Kupe and his crew journeyed around the land, and many places around Cook Strait (between the North and South Islands) and the Hokianga in Northland still bear the names that the crew gave them and the marks of their passage. Kupe returned to Hawaiki, leaving from (and naming) Northland's Hokianga. He gave other seafarers valuable navigational information. And then the great *waka* (ocean-going craft) began to arrive.

The *waka* that the first settlers arrived on, and their landing places, are immortalised in tribal histories. Well-known *waka* include *Tākitimu, Kurahaupō, Te Arawa, Mataatua, Tainui, Aotea* and *Tokomaru*. There are many others. Māori trace their genealogies back to those who arrived on the *waka* (and further back as well).

What would it have been like making the transition from small tropical islands to a much larger, cooler land mass? Goodbye breadfruit, coconuts, paper mulberry; hello moa, fernroot, flax – and immense space (relatively speaking). New Zealand has over 15,000km of coastline. Rarotonga, by way of contrast, has a little over 30km. There was land, lots of it, and a flora and fauna that had developed more or less separately from the rest of the world for 80 million years. There was an untouched, massive fishery. There were great seaside mammalian convenience stores – seals and sea lions – as well as a fabulous array of birds.

The early settlers went on the move, pulled by love, by trade opportunities and greater resources; pushed by disputes and threats to security. When they settled, Māori established *mana whenua* (regional authority), whether by military campaigns, or by the peaceful methods of intermarriage and diplomacy. Histories were carried by the voice, in stories, songs and chants. Great stress was placed on accurate learning – after all, in an oral culture, the past is always a generation or two away from oblivion.

Māori lived in *kainga* (small villages), which often had associated gardens. Housing was quite cosy by modern standards – often it was hard to stand upright while inside. From time to time people would leave their home base and go to harvest seasonal foods. When peaceful life was interrupted by conflict, the people would withdraw to *pa* (fortified dwelling places).

And then Europeans began to arrive.

Māori Today

Māori today are a diverse people. Some are engaged with traditional cultural networks and pursuits; others are occupied with adapting tradition and placing it into a dialogue with globalising culture. The Māori concept of *whanaungatanga* (family relationships) is central to the culture: families spread out from the *whānau* (extended family) to the *hapū* (sub-tribe) and *iwi* (tribe) and even, in a sense, beyond the human world and into the natural and spiritual worlds.

Māori are New Zealand's *tangata whenua* (people of the land); once a predominantly rural people, many Māori now live in urban centres, away from their traditional home base. But it's still common practice in formal settings to introduce oneself by referring to home: an ancestral mountain, river, sea or lake, or an ancestor. Today's culture is marked by new developments in the arts, business, sport and politics. Many historical grievances still stand, but some *iwi* (Ngāi Tahu and Tainui, for example) have settled historical grievances and are major forces in the NZ economy. Māori have also addressed the decline in Māori language use by establishing *kohanga reo, kura kaupapa Māori* and *wananga* (Māori-medium preschools, schools and universities). There is now a generation of people who speak Māori as a first language. There is a network of Māori radio stations, and Māori TV attracts a committed viewership.

Religion

Christian churches and denominations are important in the Māori world: televangelists, mainstream churches for regular and occasional worship, and two major Māori churches (Ringatu and Ratana).

But in the (non-Judeo-Christian) beginning there were the *atua Māori,* the Māori gods, and for many Māori the gods are a vital and relevant force still. It is common to greet the earth mother and sky father when speaking formally at a *marae* (meeting-house complex). The gods are represented in art and carving, sung of in *waiata* (songs), invoked through *karakia* (prayer and incantation) when a meeting house is opened, when a *waka* is launched, even (more simply) when a meal is served. They are spoken of on the *marae* and in wider Māori contexts. The traditional Māori creation story is well known and widely celebrated.

 Visiting Marae

As you travel around NZ, you will see many *marae* (meeting house)complexes. Often *marae* are owned by a descent group. They are also owned by urban Māori groups, schools, universities and church groups, and they should only be visited by arrangement with the owners. A good *marae* for visitors is at Te Papa museum in Wellington.

Marae complexes include a *wharenui* (meeting house), which often embodies an ancestor. Its ridge is the backbone, the rafters are ribs, and it shelters the descendants. There is a clear space in front of the *wharenui* (ie the *marae atea*). Sometimes there are other buildings: a *wharekai* (dining hall); a toilet and shower block; perhaps even classrooms, play equipment and the like.

Hui (gatherings) are held at *marae*. Issues are discussed, classes conducted, milestones celebrated and the dead farewelled. Te reo Māori (the Māori language) is prominent and sometimes the only language used.

Visitors sleep in the meeting house if a *hui* goes on for longer than a day. Mattresses are placed on the floor, someone may bring a guitar, and stories and jokes always go down well as the evening stretches out.

The Arts

Stay up to date with what's happening in the Māori arts by reading *Mana* magazine (available from most newsagents), listening to *iwi* stations (www.irirangi.net) or weekly podcasts from Radio New Zealand (www.radionz.co.nz). Māori TV also has regular features on the Māori arts – check out www.maoritelevision.com.

Māori TV went to air in 2004, an emotional time for many Māori who could at last see their culture, concerns and language in a mass medium. Over 90% of content is NZ made, and programs are in both Māori and English: they're subtitled and accessible to everyone. If you want to really get a feel for the rhythm and metre of spoken Māori, switch to Te Reo (www.maoritelevision.com/tv/te-reo-channel), a Māori-language-only channel.

Māori performers

Arts & Music

It took a hundred years for post-colonial New Zealand to develop its own distinctive artistic identity. In the early 20th century it was writers and visual artists who led the charge. The 1970s and '80s saw NZ pub rockers and indie music flourish. However, it took the success of the film industry in the 1990s to catapult the nation's creativity into the global consciousness.

Literature

In 2013 New Zealanders rejoiced to hear that 28-year-old Eleanor Catton had become only the second NZ writer to ever win the Man Booker Prize, one of the world's most prestigious awards for literature. Lloyd Jones had come close in 2007 when his novel *Mister Pip* was shortlisted, but it had been a long wait between drinks since Keri Hulme took the prize in 1985. Interestingly, both Catton's epic historical novel *The Luminaries* and Hulme's *The Bone People* were set on the numinous West Coast of the South Island – both books capturing something of the raw and mysterious essence of the landscape.

Catton and Hulme continue in a proud line of NZ women writers, starting in the early 20th century with Katherine Mansfield. Mansfield's work began a Kiwi tradition in short fiction, and for years the standard was carried by novelist Janet Frame, whose dramatic life was depicted in Jane Campion's film of her autobiography, *An Angel at My Table*. Frame's novel *The Carpathians* won the Commonwealth Writers' Prize in 1989.

Less recognised internationally, Maurice Gee has gained the nation's annual top fiction gong six times, most recently with *Blindsight* (2005). His much-loved children's novel *Under the Mountain* (1979) was made into a seminal NZ TV series in 1981, and then a major motion picture in 2009. In 2004 the adaptation of another of his novels, *In My Father's Den* (1972), won major awards at international film festivals and is one of the country's highest-grossing films.

Maurice is an auspicious name for NZ writers, with the late Maurice Shadbolt achieving much acclaim for his many novels, particularly those set during the NZ Wars. Try *Season of the Jew* (1987) or *The House of Strife* (1993).

Cinema & TV

If you first became interested in New Zealand by watching it on the silver screen, you're in good company. Sir Peter Jackson's NZ-made *The Lord of the Rings* and *The Hobbit* trilogies were the best thing to happen to NZ tourism since Captain Cook.

Yet NZ cinema is hardly ever easygoing. In his BBC-funded documentary, *Cinema of Unease,* NZ actor Sam Neill described the country's film industry as producing bleak, haunted work. You need only watch Lee Tamahori's harrowing *Once Were Warriors* (1994) to see what he means.

You could add to this list Jane Campion's *The Piano* (1993) and *Top of the Lake* (2013), Brad McGann's *In My Father's Den* (2004) and Jackson's *Heavenly Creatures* (1994) – all of which use magically lush scenery to couch disturbing violence. It's a land-mysticism constantly bordering on the creepy.

Even when Kiwis do humour it's as resolutely black as their rugby jerseys; check out Jackson's early splatter-fests and Taika Waititi's *Boy* (2010). Exporting NZ comedy hasn't been easy, yet the HBO-produced TV musical parody *Flight of the Conchords* – featuring a mumbling, bumbling Kiwi folk-singing duo trying to get a break in New York – found surprising international success.

It's the Polynesian giggle-factor that seems likeliest to break down the bleak house of NZ cinema, with feel-good-through-and-through *Sione's Wedding* (2006) netting the second-biggest local takings of any NZ film.

New Zealanders have gone from never seeing themselves in international cinema to having whole cloned armies of Temuera Morrisons invading the universe in *Star Wars*. Familiar faces such as Cliff Curtis and Karl Urban seem to constantly pop up playing Mexican or Russian gangsters in action movies. Many of them got their start in long-running soap opera *Shortland Street* (7pm weekdays, TV2).

Visual Arts

The NZ 'can do' attitude extends to the visual arts. If you're visiting a local's home, don't be surprised to find one of the owner's paintings on the wall or one of their mate's sculptures in the back garden.

This is symptomatic of a flourishing local art and crafts scene cultivated by lively tertiary courses churning out traditional carvers and weavers, jewellery-makers, multimedia boffins, and moulders of metal and glass. The larger cities have excellent dealer galleries representing interesting local artists working across all media.

It shouldn't be surprising that in a nation so defined by its natural environment, landscape painting constituted the first post-European body of art. John Gully and Petrus van

Hobbiton film set (p106)

★ **New Zealand Oscar Winners**

Anna Paquin (Best Supporting Actress; *The Piano*)

Russell Crowe (Best Actor; *Gladiator*)

Peter Jackson (Best Director; *The Lord of the Rings: The Return of the King*)

Bret McKenzie (Best Music – Original Song; 'Man or Muppet,' *The Muppets*)

der Velden were among those to arrive and paint memorable (if sometimes overdramatised) depictions of the land.

A little later, Charles Frederick Goldie painted a series of compelling, realist portraits of Māori, who were feared to be a dying race. Debate over the political propriety of Goldie's work raged for years, but its value is widely accepted now: not least because Māori themselves generally acknowledge and value them as ancestral representations.

From the 1930s NZ art took a more modern direction and produced some of the country's most celebrated artists, including Rita Angus, Toss Woollaston and Colin McCahon. McCahon is widely regarded to have been the country's most important artist. His paintings might seem inscrutable, even forbidding, but even where McCahon lurched into Catholic mysticism or quoted screeds from the Bible, his spirituality was rooted in geography. His bleak, brooding landscapes evoke the sheer power of NZ's terrain.

Music

New Zealand music began with the *waiata* (singing) developed by Māori following their arrival in the country. The main musical instruments were wind instruments made of bone or wood, the most well known of which is the *nguru* (also known as the 'nose flute'), while percussion was provided by chest- and thigh-slapping. These days, the liveliest place to see Māori music being performed is at *kapa haka* competitions in which groups compete with their own routines of traditional song and dance: track down the Te Matatini National Kapa Haka Festival (www.tematatini.co.nz), which happens in March in odd-numbered years at different venues (it's at Kahungunu in Hawke's Bay in 2017). In a similar vein, Auckland's Pasifika Festival (www.aucklandnz.com/pasifika) represents each of the Pacific Islands. It's a great place to see both traditional and modern forms of Polynesian music: modern hip-hop, Cook Island drums, or island-style guitar, ukulele and slide guitar.

Classical & Opera

Early European immigrants brought their own styles of music and gave birth to local variants during the early 1900s. In the 1950s Douglas Lilburn became one of the first internationally recognised NZ classical composers. The country has produced a number of world-renowned musicians including opera singer Dame Kiri Te Kanawa, pop diva Hayley Westenra, composer John Psathas (who created music for the 2004 Olympic Games) and composer/percussionist Gareth Farr (who also performs in drag under the name Lilith).

Rock

New Zealand has a strong rock scene, its most acclaimed exports being the revered indie label Flying Nun and the music of the Finn Brothers.

In 1981 Flying Nun was started by Christchurch record-store owner Roger Shepherd. Many of the early groups came from Dunedin, where local musicians took the DIY attitude of punk but used it to produce a lo-fi indie-pop that received rave reviews from the likes of *NME* in the UK and *Rolling Stone* in the US.

Many of the musicians from the Flying Nun scene still perform live to this day, including David Kilgour (from the Clean) and Shayne Carter (from the Straitjacket Fits, and subsequently Dimmer and the Adults). The Bats are still releasing albums, and Martin Phillipps' band the Chills released a comeback album *Silver Bullets* in 2015.

 Traditional Māori Art

Traditional Māori art has a distinctive visual style with well-developed motifs that have been embraced by NZ artists of every race. In the painting medium, these include the cool modernism of the work of Gordon Walters and the more controversial pop-art approach of Dick Frizzell's *Tiki* series. Likewise, Pacific Island themes are common, particularly in Auckland. An example is the work of Niuean-born, Auckland-raised John Pule.

Reggae, Hip-Hop & Dance

The genres of music that have been adopted most enthusiastically by Māori and Polynesian New Zealanders have been reggae (in the 1970s) and hip-hop (in the 1980s), which has led to distinct local forms. In Wellington a thriving jazz scene took on a reggae influence to create a host of groups that blended dub, roots and funky jazz – most notably Fat Freddy's Drop.

The local hip-hop scene has its heart in the suburbs of South Auckland which is home to one of New Zealand's foremost hip-hop labels, Dawn Raid. The label's most successful artist is Savage, who sold a million copies of his single 'Swing' after it was featured in the movie *Knocked Up*. Within New Zealand, the most well-known hip-hop acts are Scribe, Che Fu and Smashproof (whose song 'Brother' held number one on the NZ singles charts longer than any other local act).

Dance music gained a foothold in Christchurch in the 1990s, spawning dub/electronica outfit Salmonella Dub and its offshoot act, Tiki Taane. Drum 'n' bass remains popular and has spawned internationally renowned acts such as Concord Dawn and Shapeshifter.

New Music

Since 2000, the NZ music scene has developed new vitality after the government convinced commercial radio stations to adopt a voluntary quota of 20% local music. Rock groups such as Shihad, the Feelers and Op-shop have thrived in this environment, as have a set of soulful female solo artists (who all happen to have Māori heritage): Bic Runga, Anika Moa and Brooke Fraser (daughter of All Black Bernie Fraser). New Zealand also produced two internationally acclaimed garage rock acts: the Datsuns and the D4.

Current Kiwis garnering international recognition include the gifted songstress Kimbra (who sang on Gotye's global smash 'Somebody That I Used To Know'); indie anthem alt-rockers the Naked & Famous; multi-talented singer-songwriter Ladyhawke; the arty Lawrence Arabia; and the semi-psychedelic Unknown Mortal Orchestra.

The big news in Kiwi music recently has been the success of Lorde, a singer-songwriter who cracked the number-one spot on the US Billboard charts in 2013 with her schoolyard-chant-evoking hit 'Royals'. Aaradhna is a much-touted R&B singer who made a splash with her album *Treble & Reverb*, which won Album of the Year at the 2013 New Zealand Music Awards. The 2015 awards were dominated by Broods, a brother-sister alt-pop duo from Nelson, and Marlon Williams, a Christchurch singer with Jeff Buckley–like gravitas.

Coronet Peak ski field, near Queenstown

DOUG PEARSON/GETTY IMAGES ©

Survival Guide

Directory A–Z

Accommodation

Book your beds well in advance during peak tourist times: summer holidays from Christmas to late January, at Easter and during winter in snowy resort towns like Queenstown and Wanaka.

Holiday parks A top choice if you're camping or touring in a campervan, with myriad options from unpowered tent sites to family en suite cabins.

Hostels Backpacker hostels range from beery, party-prone joints to classy family-friendly 'flashpackers'.

Hotels NZ hotels range from small-town pubs to slick global-chain operations – with commensurate price ranges.

Book Your Stay Online

For more accommodation reviews by Lonely Planet authors, check out http://hotels.lonely planet.com/new zealand. You'll find independent reviews, as well as recommendations on the best places to stay. Best of all, you can book online.

Motels Most towns have decent, low-rise, midrange motels on their outskirts.

Price ranges generally increase by 20% to 25% in Auckland, Wellington and Christchurch. Here you can still find budget accommodation at up to $120 per double, but midrange stretches from $120 to $250, with top-end rooms more than $250.

B&Bs

B&B accommodation in NZ pops up in the middle of cities, in rural hamlets and on stretches of isolated coastline, with rooms on offer in everything from suburban bungalows to stately manors.

Breakfast may be 'continental' (cereal, toast and tea or coffee), 'hearty continental' (add yoghurt, fruit, home-baked bread or muffins) or a stomach-loading cooked meal (eggs, bacon, sausages...). Some B&B hosts may also cook dinner for guests and advertise dinner, bed and breakfast (DB&B) packages.

B&B tariffs are typically in the $120 to $200 bracket (per double), though some places cost upwards of $300 per double. Off-street parking is often a bonus in the big cities.

Booking Services

Local visitor information centres around NZ provide reams of local accommodation information, sometimes in the form of folders detailing facilities and up-to-date prices; many can also make bookings on your behalf.

Lonely Planet (www.lonely planet.com/new-zealand/ hotels) The full range of NZ accommodation, from hostels to hotels.

Automobile Association (www. aa.co.nz) Online accommodation bookings (especially good for motels, B&Bs and holiday parks).

Bed & Breakfast New Zealand (www.bed-and-breakfast.co.nz) B&B and self-contained accommodation listings.

Book a Bach (www.bookabach. co.nz) Apartment and holiday-house bookings (and maybe even a bach or two!).

Holiday Houses (www.holiday houses.co.nz) Holiday-house rentals NZ-wide.

Jasons (www.jasons.com) Long-running travel service with myriad online booking options.

New Zealand Apartments (www.nzapartments.co.nz) Rental listings for upmarket apartments of all sizes.

New Zealand Bed & Breakfast (www.bnb.co.nz) The name says it all.

Rural Holidays NZ (www.rural-holidays.co.nz) Farmstay and home-stay listings across NZ.

Camping & Holiday Parks

Campers and campervan drivers alike converge on NZ's hugely popular 'holiday parks', slumbering peacefully in powered and unpowered sites, cheap bunk rooms (dorm rooms), cabins and self-contained units (often called motels or tourist flats). Well-equipped communal kitchens, dining areas, and games and TV rooms often feature. In cities, holiday parks are usually a fair way from the action, but in smaller towns they can be impressively central or near lakes, beaches, rivers and forests.

The nightly cost of camping in a holiday park is usually between $15 and $20 per adult, with children charged half price; powered sites are a couple of dollars more. Cabin/unit accommodation normally ranges from $70 to $120 per double. Unless noted otherwise, Lonely Planet lists campsite, campervan site, hut and cabin prices for two people.

Farmstays

Farmstays open the door to the agricultural side of NZ life, with visitors encouraged to get some dirt beneath their fingernails at orchards and dairy, sheep and cattle farms. Costs can vary widely, with bed-and-breakfast generally ranging from $80 to $140. Some farms have separate cottages where you can fix your own food; others offer low-cost, shared, backpacker-style accommodation.

Farm Helpers in NZ (www.fhinz. co.nz) Produces a booklet ($25) that lists around 350 NZ farms providing lodging in exchange for four to six hours' work per day.

Rural Holidays NZ (www.rural holidays.co.nz) Lists farmstays and home-stays throughout the country.

Pubs, Hotels & Motels

The least expensive form of NZ hotel accommodation is the humble pub. Some are full of character; others are grotty, ramshackle places that are best avoided (especially by women travelling solo). In the cheapest pubs, singles/doubles might cost as little as $30/60 (with a shared bathroom down the hall); $50/80 is more common.

At the top end of the hotel scale are five-star international chains, resort complexes and splendorous boutique hotels, all of which charge a hefty premium for their mod cons, snappy service and/or historic opulence.

New Zealand's towns have a glut of nondescript, low-rise motels and 'motor lodges', charging between $80 and $180 for double rooms. These tend to skulk by highways on the edges of towns. Most are modernish (though decor is often mired in the early 2000s) and have similar facilities, namely tea- and coffee-making equipment,

Climate

Auckland

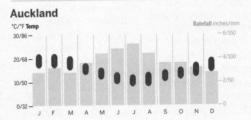

Christchurch

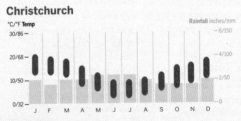

Queenstown

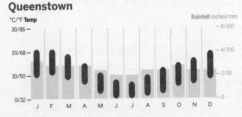

fridge and TV. Prices vary with standard.

Rental Accommodation

The basic Kiwi holiday home is called a 'bach' (short for 'bachelor', as they were historically used by single men as hunting and fishing hideouts); in Otago and Southland they're known as 'cribs'. These are simple self-contained cottages that can be rented in rural and coastal areas, often in isolated locations. Prices are typically $80 to $150 per night, which isn't bad for a whole house. For more upmarket holiday houses, expect to pay anything from $150 to $400 per double.

Good online resources include:

- www.bookabach.co.nz
- www.holidayhomes.co.nz
- www.holidayhouses.co.nz
- www.nzapartments.co.nz

Customs Regulations

For the low-down on what you can and can't bring into NZ, see the New Zealand Customs Service (www.customs.govt.nz) website. Duty-free allowances per person:

- three 1125mL (max) bottles of spirits or liqueur
- 4.5L of wine or beer

- 50 cigarettes, or 50g of tobacco or cigars
- dutiable goods up to the value of $700

It's a good idea to declare any unusual medicines. Tramping gear (boots, tents etc) will be checked and may need to be cleaned before being allowed in. You must declare any plant or animal products (including anything made of wood) and food of any kind.

Weapons and firearms are either prohibited or require a permit and safety testing. Don't take these rules lightly – non-compliance penalties will really hurt your hip pocket.

Electricity

230-240V/50Hz

The electricity supply (230V AC, 50Hz) uses a three-pin adaptor (the same as in Australia; different to British three-pin adaptors).

Food

Book top-end restaurants as far in advance as possible.

Cafes Locally roasted beans, expert baristas, savvy breakfast-to-lunch food and very family-friendly.

Pubs & bars At most Kiwi bars and pubs you can get a bite to eat too, from delicately wrought tapas to farmer-sized steaks.

Restaurants Open for dinner and lunch, plating up cuisine from the four corners of the globe. 'Modern NZ' equals local, top-quality, creative fusion.

Supermarkets Everywhere – often open til 9pm.

Takeaways Fish and chips, kebabs, burgers etc... The big internationals are here, but quality local outfits give them a run for their money.

The following price ranges refer to the average price of a main course:

$ less than $15
$$ $15–32
$$$ more than $32

Health

New Zealand is one of the healthiest countries in the world in which to travel. Diseases such as malaria and typhoid are unheard of, and the absence of poisonous snakes or other dangerous animals makes outdoor adventures here less risky than in neighbouring Australia.

Before You Go

Health Insurance

Health insurance is essential for all travellers. While health care in NZ is of a high quality and not overly expensive by international standards, considerable costs can be built up and repatriation can be pricey.

If your current health insurance doesn't cover you for medical expenses incurred overseas, consider extra insurance – for more information see www.lonelyplanet.com/travel-insurance. Find out in advance if your insurance plan will make payments directly to providers or reimburse you later for overseas health expenditures.

Medications

Bring any prescribed medications for your trip in their original, clearly labelled containers. A signed and dated letter from your physician describing your medical conditions and medications (including generic names) and any requisite syringes or needles is also wise.

Vaccinations

New Zealand has no vaccination requirements for any traveller, but the World Health Organisation recommends that all travellers should be covered for diphtheria, tetanus, measles, mumps, rubella, chickenpox and polio, as well as hepatitis B, regardless of their destination. Ask your doctor for an *International Certificate of Vaccination* (or 'the yellow booklet') in which they will list all the vaccinations you've received.

In New Zealand

Availability & Cost of Health Care

New Zealand's public hospitals offer a high standard of care (free for residents). All travellers are covered for medical care resulting from accidents that occur while in NZ (eg motor-vehicle accidents, adventure-activity accidents) by the Accident Compensation Corporation (www.acc.co.nz). Costs incurred due to treatment of a medical illness that occurs while in NZ will only be covered by travel insurance. For more details, see www.health.govt.nz.

The 24-hour, free-call **Healthline** (☑0800 611 116) offers health advice throughout NZ.

Environmental Hazards

There's very little that can bite, sting or eat you in NZ, but hypothermia and drowning are genuine threats.

Hypothermia

Hypothermia is a significant risk, especially during winter and year-round at altitude. Mountain ranges and/or strong winds produce a high chill factor, which can cause hypothermia even in moderate temperatures. Early signs include the inability to perform fine movements (such as doing up buttons), shivering and a bad case of the 'umbles' (fumbles, mumbles, grumbles, stumbles).

To treat, minimise heat loss: remove wet clothing, add dry clothes with wind- and waterproof layers, and consume water and carbohydrates to allow shivering to build the internal temperature. In severe hypothermia cases, shivering actually stops; this is a medical emergency requiring rapid evacuation in addition to the above measures.

Drowning

New Zealand has exceptional surf beaches. The power of the surf can fluctuate as a result of the varying slope of the seabed: rips and undertows are common, and drownings do happen. Check with local surf-lifesaving organisations before jumping in the sea and be aware of your own limitations and expertise.

Infectious Diseases

Aside from the usual sexually transferred discomforts (take normal precautions), giardiasis does occur in NZ.

Giardiasis

The giardia parasite is widespread in NZ waterways: drinking untreated water from streams and lakes is not recommended.

Using water filters and boiling or treating water with iodine are effective ways of preventing the disease. Symptoms consist of intermittent diarrhoea, abdominal bloating and wind. Effective treatment is available (tinidazole or metronidazole).

Pharmaceuticals

Over-the-counter medications are widely available in NZ through private chemists (pharmacies). These include painkillers, antihistamines, skin-care products and sunscreen. Some medications, such as antibiotics and the contraceptive pill, are only available via a prescription obtained from a general practitioner. If you take regular medications, bring an adequate supply and details of the generic name, as brand names differ country to country.

Tap Water

Tap water throughout New Zealand is generally safe to drink. New Zealand has strict standards about drinking water, applicable across the country.

Insurance

○ A watertight travel-insurance policy covering theft, loss and medical problems is essential. Some policies specifically exclude designated 'dangerous activities' such as diving,

bungy jumping, white-water rafting, skiing and even tramping. If you plan on doing any of these things (a distinct possibility in NZ!), make sure your policy covers you fully.

○ It's worth mentioning that under NZ law, you cannot sue for personal injury (other than exemplary damages). Instead, the country's Accident Compensation Corporation (www.acc.co.nz) administers an accident compensation scheme that provides accident insurance for NZ residents and visitors to the country, regardless of fault. This scheme, however, does not negate the necessity for your own comprehensive travel-insurance policy, as it doesn't cover you for such things as income loss, treatment at home or ongoing illness.

○ Consider a policy that pays doctors or hospitals directly, rather than you paying on the spot and claiming later. If you have to claim later, keep all documentation. Some policies ask you to call (reverse charges) to a centre in your home country where an immediate assessment of your problem is made. Check that the policy covers ambulances and emergency medical evacuations by air.

○ Worldwide travel insurance is available at www.lonelyplanet.com/travel-insurance. You can buy, extend and claim online

anytime – even if you're already on the road.

Internet Access

Getting online in NZ is easy in all but the most remote locales. In Lonely Planet's New Zealand reviews, we use the wi-fi and internet icons to indicate the availability of wireless access or actual computers on which you can get online.

Wi-Fi & Internet Service Providers

Wi-fi You'll be able to find wi-fi access around the country, from hotel rooms and hostel dorms to pub beer gardens. Usually you have to be a guest or customer to log in; you'll be issued with an access code. Sometimes it's free, sometimes there's a charge.

Hotspots The country's main telecommunications company is Spark New Zealand (www.spark.co.nz), which has wireless hotspots around the country where you can purchase prepaid access cards. Alternatively, purchase a prepaid number from the login page at any wireless hotspot using your credit card. See the Spark website for hotspot listings.

Equipment & ISPs If you've brought your tablet or laptop, consider buying a prepay USB modem (aka a 'dongle') with a local SIM card: both Spark and Vodafone (www.vodafone.co.nz) sell these from around $100. If you want to get connected via a local internet service provider (ISP), options include the following:

Clearnet (☑0508 888 800; www.clearnet.co.nz) Affiliated with Vodafone.

Earthlight (☑03-479 0303; www.earthlight.co.nz)

Slingshot (☑0800 892 000; www.slingshot.co.nz)

Legal Matters

Marijuana is widely indulged in but illegal: anyone caught carrying this or other illicit drugs will be in big trouble.

Drink-driving is a serious offence and remains a significant problem in NZ. The legal blood alcohol limit is 0.05% for drivers over 20, and zero for those under 20.

If you are arrested, it's your right to consult a lawyer before any formal questioning begins.

LGBT Travellers

The gay tourism industry in NZ isn't as high profile as it is in other developed nations, but LGBT communities are prominent in Auckland and Wellington and there are myriad support organisations across both islands. New Zealand has progressive laws protecting human rights: same-sex marriage was legalised here in 2013, while the legal minimum age

for sex between consenting persons is 16. Generally speaking, Kiwis are fairly relaxed and accepting about gender fluidity, but that's not to say that homophobia doesn't exist. Rural communities tend to be more conservative and may be uncomfortable with public displays of affection.

Resources

There are loads of websites dedicated to gay and lesbian travel in NZ. Gay Tourism New Zealand (www.gaytourismnewzealand.com) is a good starting point, with links to various sites. Other worthwhile websites include the following:

○ www.gaynz.com

○ www.gaynz.net.nz

○ www.lesbian.net.nz

○ www.gaystay.co.nz

Check out the nationwide monthly magazine *express* (www.gayexpress.co.nz) for the latest happenings, reviews and listings on the NZ gay scene.

Festivals & Events

Auckland Pride Festival (www.aucklandpridefestival.org.nz) Over two weeks of rainbow-hued celebrations in February.

Big Gay Out (www.biggayout.co.nz) Free festival (food, drink, entertainment) held every February in Auckland.

Gay Ski Week (www.gayskiweekqt.com) Annual Queenstown snow-fest in August/September.

Out Takes (www.outtakes.org.nz) G&L film festival staged in Auckland and Wellington in May/June.

Maps

New Zealand's **Automobile Association** (AA; ☑0800 500 444; www.aa.co.nz/travel) produces excellent city, town, regional, island and highway maps, available from its local offices. The AA also produces a detailed *New Zealand Road Atlas*. Other reliable countrywide atlases, available from visitor information centres and bookshops, are published by Hema, KiwiMaps and Wises.

Land Information New Zealand (www.linz.govt.nz) publishes several exhaustive map series, including street, country and holiday maps, national park and forest park maps, and topographical trampers' maps. Scan the larger bookshops, or try the nearest DOC office or visitor information centre, for topo maps.

Online, visit AA Maps (www.aamaps.co.nz) or Wises (www.wises.co.nz) to pinpoint exact NZ addresses.

Money

ATMs are widely available in cities and larger towns. Credit cards are accepted in most hotels and restaurants.

ATMs & Eftpos

Branches of the country's major banks across both islands have ATMs, but you won't find them everywhere (eg not in small towns).

Many NZ businesses use Eftpos (electronic funds transfer at point of sale), allowing you to use your credit or debit card to make direct purchases and often withdraw cash as well. Eftpos is available practically everywhere: just like at an ATM, you'll need a personal identification number (PIN).

Credit & Debit Cards

Credit cards (Visa, Master-Card) are widely accepted for everything from a hostel bed to a bungy jump, and are pretty much essential for car hire. They can also be used for over-the-counter cash advances at banks and from ATMs, but be aware that such transactions incur charges. Diners Club and American Express cards are not as widely accepted.

Debit cards enable you to draw money directly from your home bank account using ATMs, banks or Eftpos facilities. Any card connected to the international banking network (Cirrus, Maestro, Visa Plus and Eurocard) should work with your PIN. Fees will vary depending on your home bank; check before you leave. Alternatively, companies such as Travelex offer debit cards with set withdrawal fees and a balance you can

top up from your personal bank account while on the road.

Currency

New Zealand's currency is the NZ dollar, comprising 100 cents. There are 10c, 20c, 50c, $1 and $2 coins, and $5, $10, $20, $50 and $100 notes. Prices are often still marked in single cents and then rounded to the nearest 10c when you hand over your money.

Money hangers

Changing foreign currency (and to a lesser extent old-fashioned travellers cheques) is usually no problem at NZ banks or at licensed money changers (eg Travelex) in major tourist areas, cities and airports.

Taxes & Refunds

The Goods and Services Tax (GST) is a flat 15% tax on all domestic goods and services. New Zealand prices listed by Lonely Planet include GST. There's no GST refund available when you leave NZ.

Tipping

Tipping is completely optional in NZ – the total at the bottom of a restaurant bill is all you need to pay (note that sometimes there's an additional service charge). That said, it's totally acceptable to reward good service – between 5% and 10% of the bill is fine.

Opening Hours

Opening hours vary seasonally (eg Dunedin is quiet during winter), but use the following as a general guide. Note that most places close on Christmas Day and Good Friday.

Banks 9.30am to 4.30pm Monday to Friday, some also 9am to noon Saturday

Cafes 7am to 4pm

Post offices 8.30am to 5pm Monday to Friday; larger branches also 9.30am to 1pm Saturday

Pubs & bars noon to late ('late' varies by region and by day)

Restaurants noon to 2.30pm and 6.30 to 9pm

Shops & businesses 9am to 5.30pm Monday to Friday, 9am to noon or 5pm Saturday

Supermarkets 8am to 7pm, often 9pm or later in cities

Public Holidays

New Zealand's main public holidays:

New Year 1 and 2 January

Waitangi Day 6 February

Easter Good Friday and Easter Monday; March/April

Anzac Day 25 April

Queen's Birthday First Monday in June

Labour Day Fourth Monday in October

Christmas Day 25 December

Boxing Day 26 December

In addition, each NZ province has its own

Practicalities

o **DVDs** Kiwi DVDs are encoded for Region 4, which includes Australia, the Pacific, Mexico, Central America, the Caribbean and South America.

o **Newspapers** Check out Auckland's *New Zealand Herald* (www.nzherald.co.nz), Wellington's *Dominion Post* (www.stuff.co.nz/dominion-post) or Christchurch's *The Press* (www.stuff.co.nz/the-press).

o **Radio** Tune in to Radio New Zealand (www.radionz.co.nz) for news, current affairs, classical and jazz. Radio Hauraki (www.hauraki.co.nz) cranks out rock.

o **TV** Watch one of the national government-owned TV stations – including TV One, TV2, Māori TV or the 100% Māori language Te Reo – or subscriber-only Sky TV (www.skytv.co.nz).

o **Weights & measures** New Zealand uses the metric system.

anniversary-day holiday. The dates of these provincial holidays vary: when they fall on Friday to Sunday, they're usually observed on the following Monday; if they fall on Tuesday to Thursday, they're held on the preceding Monday.

Provincial anniversary holidays:

Southland 17 January
Wellington 22 January
Auckland 29 January
Northland 29 January
Nelson 1 February
Otago 23 March
Taranaki 31 March
South Canterbury 25 September
Hawke's Bay 1 November
Marlborough 1 November
Chatham Islands 30 November
Westland 1 December
Canterbury 16 December

School Holidays

The Christmas holiday season, from mid-December to late January, is part of the summer school vacation: expect transport and accommodation to book out in advance, and queues at tourist attractions. There are three shorter school-holiday periods during the year: from mid- to late April, early- to mid-July, and mid-September to early October. For exact dates see the Ministry of Education (www.education.govt.nz) website.

Safe Travel

It's no more dangerous than any other developed country, but violent crime does happen in NZ. Play it safe on the streets after dark and in remote areas.

o Avoid leaving valuables in vehicles: theft from cars is a problem.

o New Zealand's climate is unpredictable: hypothermia is a risk in high-altitude areas.

o At the beach, beware of rips and undertows, which can drag swimmers out to sea.

o Kiwi roads are often made hazardous by map-distracted tourists, wide-cornering campervans and traffic-ignorant sheep.

o In the annoyances category, NZ's sandflies are a royal (and intensely itchy) pain. Lather yourself with insect repellent in coastal areas.

Telephone

Key phone service providers include the following:

2 Degrees (www.2degrees mobile.co.nz) Mobile-network option.

Skinny Mobile (www.skinny. co.nz) Mobile-network option.

Spark New Zealand (www.spark.co.nz) The key domestic player, also with a stake in the local mobile (cell) market.

Vodafone (www.vodafone.co.nz) Mobile-network option.

Mobile Phones

Most NZ mobile phone numbers are preceded by

the prefix 021, 022 or 027. Mobile phone coverage is good in cities and towns and most parts of the North Island, but can be a bit patchy away from urban centres on the South Island.

If you want to bring your own phone and use a pre-paid service with a local SIM card (rather than pay for expensive global roaming on your home network), Vodafone (www.vodafone. co.nz) is a practical option. Any Vodafone shop (in most major towns) will set you up with a NZ Travel SIM and a phone number (from around $30; valid for 30, 60 or 90 days). Top-ups can be purchased at newsagencies, post offices and petrol stations all over the country.

Alternatively, you can rent a phone from Vodafone, with pick-up and drop-off outlets at Auckland, Christchurch and Queenstown international airports. Phone Hire New Zealand (www. phonehirenz.com) also rents out mobiles, SIM cards, modems and GPS systems.

Local Calls

Local calls from private phones are free! Local calls from payphones cost $1 for the first 15 minutes and 20c per minute thereafter, though coin-operated payphones are scarce (and if you do find one, chances are the coin slot will be gummed up); you'll generally need a phonecard. Calls to mobile phones attract higher rates.

International Calls

To make international calls from NZ (which is possible on payphones), you need to dial the international access code 00, then the country code and the area code (without the initial '0'). So for a London number, for example, you'd dial 00-44-20, then the number.

If dialling NZ from overseas, the country code is 64, followed by the appropriate area code minus the initial '0'.

Long-Distance Calls & Area Codes

New Zealand uses regional two-digit area codes for long-distance calls, which can be made from any payphone. If you're making a local call (ie to someone else in the same town), you don't need to dial the area code. But if you're dialling within a region (even if it's to a nearby town with the same area code), you do have to dial the area code.

Information & Toll-Free Calls

Numbers starting with 0900 are usually recorded information services, charging upwards of $1 per minute (more from mobiles). These numbers cannot be dialled from payphones, and sometimes not from prepay mobile phones.

Toll-free numbers in NZ have the prefix 0800 or 0508 and can be called from anywhere in the country, though they

may not be accessible from certain areas or from mobile phones. Numbers beginning with 0508, 0800 or 0900 cannot be dialled from outside NZ.

Phonecards

New Zealand has a wide range of phonecards, which can be bought at hostels, newsagencies and post offices for a fixed-dollar value (usually $5, $10, $20 and $50). These can be used with any public or private phone by dialling a toll-free access number and then the PIN number on the card. Shop around – rates vary from company to company.

Time

New Zealand is 12 hours ahead of GMT/UTC and two hours ahead of Australian Eastern Standard Time. The Chathams are 45 minutes ahead of NZ's main islands.

In summer, NZ observes daylight saving time, where clocks are wound forward by one hour on the last Sunday in September; clocks are wound back on the first Sunday of the following April.

Toilets

Toilets in NZ are sit-down Western style. Public toilets are plentiful and usually reasonably clean with working locks and plenty of toilet paper.

See www.toiletmap.co.nz for public toilet locations around the country.

Tourist Information

The website for the official national tourism body, Tourism New Zealand (www.newzealand.com), is the best place for pretrip research. Emblazoned with the hugely successful 100% Pure New Zealand branding, the site has information in several languages, including German, Spanish, French, Chinese and Japanese.

Local Tourist Offices

Almost every Kiwi city or town seems to have a visitor information centre. The bigger centres stand united within the outstanding i-SITE network (www.newzealand.com/travel/i-sites) – around 80 info centres affiliated with Tourism New Zealand. These i-SITEs have trained staff, information on local activities and attractions, and free brochures and maps. Staff can also book activities, transport and accommodation.

Bear in mind that some information centres only promote accommodation and tour operators who are paying members of the local tourist association, and that

sometimes staff aren't supposed to recommend one activity or accommodation provider over another.

There's also a network of Department of Conservation (DOC; www.doc.govt.nz) visitor centres to help you plan activities and make bookings. DOC visitor centres – in national parks, regional centres and major cities – usually also have displays on local lore, flora, fauna and biodiversity.

Travellers with Disabilities

Kiwi accommodation generally caters fairly well for travellers with disabilities, with many hostels, hotels, motels and B&Bs equipped with wheelchair-accessible rooms. Many tourist attractions similarly provide wheelchair access, with wheelchairs often available.

Tour operators with accessible vehicles operate from most major centres. Key cities are also serviced by 'kneeling' buses (buses that hydraulically stoop down to kerb level to allow easy access), and taxi companies offer wheelchair-accessible vans. Large car-hire firms (Avis, Hertz etc) provide cars with hand controls at no extra charge (but advance notice is required). Air New Zealand is also very well equipped to accommodate travellers in wheelchairs.

Activities

Out and about, the Department of Conservation maintains plenty of tracks that are wheelchair accessible, categorised as 'easy access short walks': the Cape Reinga Lighthouse Walk and Milford Foreshore Walk are two prime examples.

If cold-weather activity is more your thing, see the Disabled Snowsports NZ website (www.disabledsnowsports.org.nz).

Resources

Blind Foundation (www.blindfoundation.org.nz)

Mobility Parking (www.mobilityparking.org.nz) Info on mobility parking permits and online applications.

National Foundation for the Deaf (www.nfd.org.nz)

Weka (www.weka.net.nz) Good general information, with categories including transport and travel.

Visas

Citizens of Australia, the UK and 58 other countries don't need visas for NZ (length-of-stay allowances vary).

Citizens of other countries must obtain a visa before entering NZ. Visitor's visas allow stays of up to nine months within an 18-month period, and cost between $170 and $220, depending on where in the world the application

is processed. See www.
immigration.govt.nz.

Women Travellers

New Zealand is generally a
very safe place for female
travellers, although the
usual sensible precautions
apply (for both sexes): avoid
walking alone at night; never
hitchhike alone; if you're
out on the town have a plan
on how to get back to your
accommodation safely.
Sexual harassment is not
a widely reported problem
in NZ, but of course that
doesn't mean it doesn't
happen. See www.women-
travel.co.nz for tours aimed
at solo women.

Transport

Getting There &
Away

New Zealand is a long way
from almost everywhere –
most travellers jet in from
afar. Flights, cars and tours
can be booked online at
lonelyplanet.com/bookings.

Entering the Country

Disembarkation in New Zealand is generally a straight-

forward affair, with only the
usual customs declarations
and the luggage-
carousel scramble to
endure. Under the Orwellian
title of 'Advance Passenger
Screening', documents that
used to be checked after
you touched down in NZ
(passport, visa etc) are now
checked before you board
your flight – make sure all
your documentation is in
order so that your check-in
is stress-free.

Air

New Zealand's abundance
of year-round activities
means that airports here are
busy most of the time: if you
want to fly at a particularly
popular time of year (eg
over the Christmas period),
book well in advance.

The high season for
flights into NZ is during
summer (December to
February), with slightly
less of a premium on fares
over the shoulder months
(October/November and
March/April). The low
season generally tallies with
the winter months (June to
August), though this is still a
busy time for airlines ferry-
ing ski bunnies and powder
hounds.

Airlines Flying To &
From New Zealand

New Zealand's international
carrier is Air New Zealand
(www.airnewzealand.co.nz),
which flies to runways
across Europe, North
America, eastern Asia, Australia and the Pacific, and
has an extensive network
across NZ.

Winging in from Australia,
Virgin Australia (www.
virginaustralia.com), Qantas
(www.qantas.com.au),
Jetstar (www.jetstar.com)
and Air New Zealand are the
key players.

Joining Air New Zealand
from North America,
other operators include Air
Canada (www.aircanada.
com) and American Airlines
(www.aa.com).

From Europe, the options
are a little broader, with British Airways (www.british
airways.com), Lufthansa
(www.lufthansa.com) and
Virgin Atlantic (www.virgin
atlantic.com) entering the
fray, and plenty of others
stopping in NZ on broader
round-the-world routes.

From Asia and the Pacific
there are myriad options,
with direct flights from
China, Japan, Singapore,
Malaysia, Thailand and
Pacific Island nations.

International Airports

A number of NZ airports
handle international flights,
with Auckland receiving the
most traffic:

Auckland Airport (AKL; ☎09-
275 0789; www.aucklandairport.
co.nz; Ray Emery Dr, Mangere)

Christchurch Airport (CHC;
☎03-358 5029; www.
christchurchairport.co.nz; 30
Durey Rd)

Dunedin Airport (DUD; ☎03-
486 2879; www.dnairport.co.nz;
25 Miller Rd, Momona)

Queenstown Airport (ZQN;
☎03-450 9031; www.queen-
stownairport.co.nz; Sir Henry
Wrigley Dr, Frankton)

Wellington Airport (WLG; Map p155; ☏04-385 5100; www.wellingtonairport.co.nz; Stewart Duff Dr, Rongotai)

Note that Hamilton, Rotorua and Palmerston North airports are capable of handling direct international arrivals and departures, but are not currently doing so.

Sea

Cargo ship Alternatively, a berth on a cargo ship or freighter to/from New Zealand is a quirky way to go: check out websites such as www.freightercruises.com and www.freighterexpeditions.com.au for more info.

Cruise ship If you're looking for something with a slower pace, plenty of passenger cruise liners stop in NZ on the South Pacific legs of their respective schedules: try P&O Cruises (www.pocruises.com.au) for starters.

Yacht It is possible (though by no means straightforward) to make your way between NZ,

Australia and the Pacific islands by crewing on a yacht. Try asking around at harbours, marinas, and yacht and sailing clubs. Popular yachting harbours in NZ include the Bay of Islands and Whangarei (both in Northland), Auckland and Wellington. March and April are the best months to look for boats heading to Australia. From Fiji, October to November is a peak departure season to beat the cyclones that soon follow in that neck of the woods.

Getting Around

Air

Those who have limited time to get between NZ's attractions can make the most of a widespread (and very reliable and safe) network of intra- and inter-island flights.

Airlines in New Zealand

The country's major domestic carrier, Air New Zealand, has an aerial network covering most of the country, often operating under the Air New Zealand Link moniker on less popular routes. Australia-based Jetstar also flies between main urban areas. Between them, these two airlines carry the vast majority of domestic passengers in NZ. Beyond this, several small-scale regional operators provide essential transport services to outlying islands such as Great Barrier Island in the Hauraki Gulf, to Stewart Island and the Chathams. There are also plenty of scenic- and charter-flight operators around NZ, not listed here. Operators include the following:

Air Chathams (☏03-305 0209; www.airchathams.co.nz) Services to the remote Chatham Islands from Wellington, Christchurch and Auckland. Auckland–Whakatane flights also available.

Air New Zealand (☏0800 737 000; www.airnewzealand.co.nz) Offers flights between 20-plus domestic destinations, plus myriad overseas hubs.

Air2there.com (☏0800 777 000; www.air2there.com) Connects destinations across Cook Strait, including Paraparaumu, Wellington, Nelson and Blenheim.

Barrier Air (☏0800 900 600; www.barrierair.kiwi) Plies the skies over Great Barrier Island, Auckland, Tauranga, Whitianga, Kaitaia and Whangarei.

FlyMySky (📞0800 222 123; www.flymysky.co.nz) At least three flights daily from Auckland to Great Barrier Island.

Golden Bay Air (📞0800 588 885; www.goldenbayair. co.nz) Flies regularly between Wellington and Takaka in Golden Bay. Also connects to Karamea for Heaphy Track trampers.

Jetstar (📞0800 800 995; www.jetstar.com) Joins the dots between key tourism centres: Auckland, Wellington, Christchurch, Dunedin, Queenstown, Nelson, Napier, New Plymouth and Palmerston North.

Kiwi Regional Airlines (📞07-444 5020; www.flykiwiair.co.nz) Operator with services linking Nelson with Dunedin, Hamilton and Tauranga.

Soundsair (📞0800 505 005; www.soundsair.co.nz) Numerous flights each day between Picton and Wellington, plus flights from Wellington to Blenheim, Nelson, Westport and Taupo. Also flies Blenheim to Paraparaumu and Napier, and Nelson to Paraparaumu.

Stewart Island Flights (📞03-218 9129; www.stewartisland-flights.com) Flies between Invercargill and Stewart Island.

Sunair (📞0800 786 247; www.sunair.co.nz) Flies to Whitianga from Ardmore (near Auckland), Great Barrier Island and Tauranga, plus numerous other North Island connections between Hamilton, Rotorua, Gisborne and Whakatane.

Air Passes

Available exclusively to travellers from the USA or Canada who have bought an Air New Zealand fare to NZ from the USA or Canada,

Australia or the Pacific Islands, Air New Zealand offers the good-value **New Zealand Explorer Pass** (www.airnewzealand.com/explorer-pass). The pass lets you fly between up to 27 destinations in New Zealand, Australia and the South Pacific islands (including Norfolk Island, Tonga, New Caledonia, Samoa, Vanuatu, Tahiti, Fiji, Niue and the Cook Islands). Fares are broken down into four discounted, distance-based zones: zone one flights start at US$99 (eg Auckland to Christchurch); zone two from US$129 (eg Auckland to Queenstown); zone three from US$214 (eg Wellington to Sydney); and zone four from US$295 (eg Tahiti to Auckland). You can buy the pass before you travel, or after you arrive in NZ.

Bicycle

Touring cyclists proliferate in NZ, particularly over summer. The country is clean, green and relatively uncrowded, and has lots of cheap accommodation (including camping) and abundant fresh water. The roads are generally in good nick, and the climate is usually not too hot or cold. Road traffic is the biggest danger: trucks overtaking too close to cyclists are a particular threat. Bikes and cycling gear are readily available to rent or buy in the main centres, and bicycle-repair shops are common.

By law all cyclists must wear an approved safety helmet (or risk a fine); it's also vital to have good reflective safety clothing. Cyclists who use public transport will find that major bus lines and trains only take bicycles on a 'space available' basis and charge up to $10. Some of the smaller shuttle bus companies, on the other hand, make sure they have storage space for bikes, which they carry for a surcharge.

If importing your own bike or transporting it by plane within NZ, check with the relevant airline for costs and the degree of dismantling and packing required.

See www.nzta.govt.nz/traffic/ways/bike for more bike safety and legal tips, and the New Zealand Cycle Trail (Nga Haerenga) – a network of 23 off-road 'Great Rides' across NZ (www.nzcycletrail.com).

Hire

Rates offered by most outfits for renting road or mountain bikes are usually around $20 per hour to $60 per day. Longer-term rentals may be available by negotiation. You can often hire bikes from your accommodation (hostels, holiday parks, etc) or rent more reputable machines from bike shops in the larger towns.

Boat

New Zealand may be an island nation but there's virtually no long-distance water transport around the country. Obvious exceptions include the boat services between Auckland and various islands in the Hauraki Gulf, the inter-island ferries that cross the Cook Strait between Wellington and Picton, and the passenger ferry that negotiates Foveaux Strait between Bluff and the town of Oban on Stewart Island.

If you're cashed-up, consider the cruise liners that chug around the NZ coastline as part of broader South Pacific itineraries: P&O Cruises (www.pocruises. com.au) is a major player.

Bus

Bus travel in NZ is easygoing and well organised, with services transporting you to the far reaches of both islands (including the start/end of various walking tracks)...but it can be expensive, tedious and time-consuming.

New Zealand's main bus company is InterCity (www. intercity.co.nz), which can drive you to just about anywhere on the North and South Islands. Naked Bus (www.nakedbus.com) has similar routes and remains the main competition. Both bus lines offer fares as low as $1(!).

InterCity also has a South Island sightseeing arm called Newmans Coach Lines (www.newmanscoach. co.nz), travelling between Queenstown, Christchurch and the West Coast glaciers.

Seat Classes & Smoking

There are no allocated economy or luxury classes on NZ buses (very democratic), and smoking on the bus is a definite no-no.

Naked Bus has, however, introduced a sleeper class on overnight services between Auckland and Wellington (stopping at Hamilton and Palmerston North) where you can lie flat in a 1.8m-long bed (bring earplugs). See www. nakedbus.com/nz/bus/ nakedbus-sleeper for details.

Reservations

Over summer, school holidays and public holidays, book well in advance on popular routes (a week or two if possible). At other times a day or two ahead is usually fine. The best prices are generally available online, booked a few weeks in advance.

Bus Passes

If you're covering a lot of ground, both InterCity and Naked Bus offer bus passes that can be cheaper than paying as you go, but they do of course lock you into using their respective networks. Passes are usually valid for 12 months.

On fares other than bus passes, InterCity offers a discount of around 10% for YHA, ISIC, Nomads, BBH or VIP backpacker card holders.

Nationwide Passes

Flexipass A hop-on/hop-off InterCity pass, allowing travel to pretty much anywhere in NZ, in any direction, including the Interislander ferry across Cook Strait. The pass is purchased in blocks of travel time: minimum 15 hours ($119), maximum 60 hours ($449). The average cost of each block becomes cheaper the more hours you buy. You can top up the pass if you need more time.

Aotearoa Explorer, Tiki Tour & Island Loop Hop-on/hop-off, fixed-itinerary nationwide passes offered by InterCity. These passes link up tourist hotspots and range in price from $738 to $995. See www.intercity. co.nz/bus-pass/travel pass for details.

Naked Passport (www.naked passport.com) A Naked Bus pass that allows you to buy trips in blocks of five, which you can add to any time, and book each trip as needed. Five/15/30 trips cost $151/318/491. An unlimited pass costs $597 – great value if you're travelling NZ for many moons.

North Island Passes

InterCity offers six hop-on/hop-off, fixed-itinerary North Island bus passes, ranging from short $119 runs between Auckland and Paihia, to $384 trips from Auckland to Wellington via the big sights in between. See www.intercity.co.nz/ bus-pass/travelpass for details.

South Island Passes

On the South Island, Inter-City offers six hop-on/hop-off, fixed-itinerary passes, ranging from $119 runs along the West Coast between Picton and Queenstown, to a $509 loop around the whole island. See www.intercity.co.nz/bus-pass/travelpass for details.

Shuttle Buses

As well as InterCity and Naked Bus, regional shuttle buses fill in the gaps between the smaller towns. Operators include the following (see www.tourism.net.nz/transport/bus-and-coach-services for a complete list), offering regular scheduled services and/or bus tours and charters:

Abel Tasman Travel (www.abeltasmantravel.co.nz) Traverses the roads between Nelson, Motueka, Golden Bay and Abel Tasman National Park.

Alpine Scenic Tours (www.alpinescenictours.co.nz) Runs tours around Taupo and into Tongariro National Park, plus the ski fields around Mt Ruapehu and Mt Tongariro.

Atomic Shuttles (www.atomictravel.co.nz) Has services throughout the South Island, including to Christchurch, Dunedin, Invercargill, Picton, Nelson, Greymouth, Hokitika, Queenstown and Wanaka.

Catch-a-Bus South (www.catchabussouth.co.nz) Invercargill and Bluff to Dunedin and Queenstown.

Cook Connection (www.cookconnect.co.nz) Triangulates between Mt Cook, Twizel and Lake Tekapo.

East West Coaches (www.eastwestcoaches.co.nz) Offers a service between Christchurch and Westport via Lewis Pass.

Go Kiwi Shuttles (www.go-kiwi.co.nz) Links Auckland with Whitianga on the Coromandel Peninsula daily.

Hanmer Connection (www.hanmerconnection.co.nz) Daily services between Hanmer Springs and Christchurch.

Manabus (www.manabus.com) Runs in both directions daily between Auckland and Wellington via Hamilton, Rotorua, Taupo and Palmerston North. Also runs to Tauranga, Paihia and Napier. Some services operated by Naked Bus.

Tracknet (www.tracknet.net) Summer track transport (Milford, Routeburn, Kepler) with Queenstown, Te Anau and Invercargill connections.

Trek Express (www.trekexpress.co.nz) Shuttle services to all tramping tracks in the top half of the South Island.

Waitomo Wanderer (www.travelheadfirst.com) Does a loop from Rotorua or Taupo to Waitomo.

West Coast Shuttle (www.westcoastshuttle.co.nz) Daily bus from Greymouth to Christchurch and back.

Car

The best way to explore NZ in depth is to have your own wheels. It's easy to hire cars and campervans at good rates. Alternatively, if you're in NZ for a few months, you might consider buying your own vehicle.

Automobile Association (AA)

New Zealand's **Automobile Association** (AA; ☑0800 500 444; www.aa.co.nz/travel) provides emergency breakdown services, maps and accommodation guides (from holiday parks to motels and B&Bs).

Members of overseas automobile associations should bring their membership cards – many of these bodies have reciprocal agreements with the AA.

Driving Licences

International visitors to NZ can use their home country driving licence – if your licence isn't in English, it's a good idea to carry a certified translation with you. Alternatively, use an International Driving Permit (IDP), which will usually be issued on the spot (valid for 12 months) by your home country's automobile association.

Fuel

Fuel (petrol, aka gasoline) is available from service stations across NZ: unless you're cruising around in something from the '70s, you'll be filling up with 'unleaded', or LPG (gas). LPG is not always stocked by rural suppliers; if you're on gas, it's safer to have dual-fuel capability. Aside from remote locations like Milford Sound and Mt Cook, petrol prices don't vary much from place to place: per-litre costs at the time of research were around $2.

Hire

Campervan

Check your rear-view mirror on any far-flung NZ road and you'll probably see a shiny white campervan (aka mobile home, motor home, RV) packed with liberated travellers, mountain bikes and portable barbecues cruising along behind you.

Most towns of any size have a campground or holiday park with powered sites (where you can plug your vehicle in) for around $35 per night. There are also 250-plus vehicle-accessible Department of Conservation (DOC; www.doc.govt. nz) campsites around NZ, ranging in price from free to $15 per adult: check the website for info.

You can hire campervans from dozens of companies. Prices vary with season, vehicle size and length of rental.

A small van for two people typically has a minikitchen and foldout dining table, the latter transforming into a double bed when dinner is done and dusted. Larger 'superior' two-berth vans include shower and toilet. Four- to six-berth campervans are the size of trucks (and similarly sluggish) and, besides the extra space, usually contain a toilet and shower.

Over summer, rates offered by the main rental firms for two-/four-/six-berth vans booked six months in advance start at around $110/150/210 per day for a month-long

rental, dropping to as low as $50/70/100 per day during winter.

Major operators include the following:

Apollo (☏09-889 2976, 0800 113 131; www.apollocamper. co.nz)

Britz (☏09-255 3910, 0800 081 032; www.britz.co.nz) Also does 'Britz Bikes' (add a mountain or city bike from $12 per day).

Kea (☏09-448 8800, 0800 464 613; www.keacampers.com)

Maui (☏09-255 3910, 0800 688 558; www.maui.co.nz)

Wilderness Motorhomes (☏09-282 3606; www.wilder ness.co.nz)

Car

Competition between car-rental companies in NZ is torrid, particularly in the big cities and Picton. Remember that if you want to travel far, you need unlimited kilometres. Some (but not all) companies require drivers to be at least 21 years old – ask around.

Most car-hire firms suggest (or insist) that you don't take their vehicles between islands on the Cook Strait ferries. Instead, you leave your car at either Wellington or Picton terminal and pick up another car once you've crossed the strait. This saves you paying to transport a vehicle on the ferries and is a pain-free exercise.

International Rental Companies

The big multinational companies have offices in most

major cities, towns and airports. Firms sometimes offer one-way rentals (eg collect a car in Auckland, leave it in Wellington), but there are often restrictions and fees. On the other hand, an operator in Christchurch may need to get a vehicle back to Auckland and will offer an amazing one-way car relocation deal (sometimes free!).

The major companies offer a choice of either unlimited kilometres, or 100km (or so) per day free, plus so many cents per subsequent kilometre. Daily rates in main cities typically start at around $40 per day for a compact, late-model, Japanese car, and around $75 for medium-sized cars (including GST, unlimited kilometres and insurance).

Avis (☏09-526 2847, 0800 655 111; www.avis.co.nz)

Budget (☏09-529 7784, 0800 283 438; www.budget.co.nz)

Europcar (☏0800 800 115; www.europcar.co.nz)

Hertz (☏03-358 6789, 0800 654 321; www.hertz.co.nz)

Thrifty (☏03-359 2720, 0800 737 070; www.thrifty.co.nz)

Local Rental Companies

Local rental firms proliferate. These are almost always cheaper than the big boys – sometimes half the price – but the cheap rates may come with serious restrictions: vehicles are often older, depots might be further away from airports/ city centres, and with less formality sometimes comes a less protective legal structure for renters.

Rentals from local firms start at around $30 per day for the smallest option. It's obviously cheaper if you rent for a week or more, and there are often low-season and weekend discounts.

Affordable, independent operators with national networks include the following:

a2b Car Rentals (☎09-254 4397, 0800 545 000; www.a2b-car-rental.co.nz)

Ace Rental Cars (☎09-303 3112, 0800 502 277; www.acerentalcars.co.nz)

Apex Rentals (☎03-363 3000, 0800 500 660; www.apex rentals.co.nz)

Ezi Car Rental (☎09-254 4397, 0800 545 000; www.ezicar rental.co.nz)

Go Rentals (☎09-974 1598, 0800 467 368; www.gorentals.co.nz)

Omega Rental Cars (☎09-377 5573, 0800 525 210; www.omegarentalcars.com)

Pegasus Rental Cars (☎09-275 3222, 0800 803 580; www.rentalcars.co.nz)

Transfercar (☎09-630 7533; www.transfercar.co.nz) One-way relocation specialists.

Insurance

Rather than risk paying out wads of cash if you have an accident, you can take out your own comprehensive insurance policy, or (the usual option) pay an additional fee per day to the rental company to reduce your excess. This brings the amount you must pay in the event of an accident down from around $1500 or $2000 to around $200 or $300. Smaller operators offering cheap rates often have a compulsory insurance excess, taken as a credit-card bond, of around $900.

Most insurance agreements won't cover the cost of damage to glass (including the windscreen) or tyres, and insurance coverage is often invalidated on beaches and certain rough (4WD) unsealed roads – read the fine print.

See www.acc.co.nz for info on NZ's Accident Compensation Corporation insurance scheme (fault-free personal injury insurance).

Road Hazards

There's an unusually high percentage of international drivers involved in road accidents in NZ – something like 30% of accidents involve a non-local driver. Kiwi traffic is usually pretty light, but it's easy to get stuck behind a slow-moving truck or campervan – pack plenty of patience, and know your road rules before you get behind the wheel. There are also lots of slow wiggly roads, one-way bridges and plenty of gravel roads, all of which require a more cautious driving approach. And watch out for sheep!

To check road conditions call ☎0800 444 449 or see www.nzta.govt.nz/traffic.

Road Rules

○ Kiwis drive on the left-hand side of the road; cars are right-hand drive. Give way to the right at intersections.

○ At single-lane bridges (of which there are a surprisingly large number), a smaller red arrow pointing in your direction of travel means that *you* give way.

○ Speed limits on the open road are generally 100km/h; in built-up areas the limit is usually 50km/h. Speed cameras and radars are used extensively.

○ All vehicle occupants must wear a seatbelt or risk a fine. Small children must be belted into approved safety seats.

○ Always carry your licence when driving. Drink-driving is a serious offence and remains a significant problem in NZ, despite widespread campaigns and severe penalties. The legal blood alcohol limit is 0.05% for drivers 20 years and over, and 0% (zero) for those under 20.

Local Transport

Bus, Train & Tram

New Zealand's larger cities have extensive bus services but, with a few honourable exceptions, they are mainly daytime, weekday operations; weekend services can be infrequent or non-existent. Negotiating inner-city Auckland is made easier by Link buses; Hamilton has a free city-centre loop bus; Christchurch has a free city-shuttle service and the historic tramway. Most main cities have late-night buses for boozy Friday and Saturday nights.

The only cities with decent local train services are Auckland and Wellington, with four and five sub-urban routes respectively.

Taxi

The main cities have plenty of taxis and even small towns may have a local service. Taxis are metred, and generally reliable and trustworthy.

Train

NZ train travel is all about the journey, not about getting anywhere in a hurry.
KiwiRail Scenic Journeys (☑0800 872 467, 04-495 0775; www.kiwirailscenic.co.nz) operates four routes, listed below; reservations can be made through KiwiRail Scenic Journeys directly, or at most train stations (notably not at Palmerston North or Hamilton), travel agents and visitor information centres. All services are for day travel (no sleeper services).

Capital Connection Weekday commuter service between Palmerston North and Wellington.

Coastal Pacific Between Christchurch and Picton along the South Island's east coast.

Northern Explorer Between Auckland and Wellington: south-bound on Mondays, Thursdays and Saturdays; northbound on Tuesdays, Fridays and Sundays.

TranzAlpine Over the Southern Alps between Christchurch and Greymouth – one of the world's most famous train rides.

Train Passes

A KiwiRail Scenic Journeys Scenic Journey Rail Pass (www.kiwirailscenic.co.nz/scenic-rail-pass) allows unlimited travel on all of its rail services, including passage on the Wellington–Picton Interislander ferry. There are two types of pass, both requiring you to book your seats a minimum of 24 hours before you want to travel:

Fixed Pass Limited duration fares for one/two/three weeks, costing $599/699/799 per adult (a little bit less for kids).

Freedom Pass Affords you travel on a certain number of days over a 12-month period; a three-/seven-/10-day pass costs $417/903/1290.

Language

New Zealand has three official languages: English, Māori and NZ sign language. Although English is what you'll usually hear, Māori has been making a comeback. You can use English to speak to anyone in New Zealand, but there are some occasions when knowing a small amount of Māori is useful, such as when visiting a *marae*, where often only Māori is spoken. Some knowledge of Māori will also help you interpret the many Māori place names you'll come across.

Kiwi English

Like the people of other English-speaking countries in the world, New Zealanders have their own, unique way of speaking the language. The flattening of vowels is the most distinctive feature of Kiwi pronunciation. For example, in Kiwi English, 'fish and chips' sounds more like 'fush and chups'. On the North Island sentences often have 'eh!' attached to the end. In the far south a rolled 'r' is common, which is a holdover from that region's Scottish heritage – it's especially noticeable in Southland.

Māori

The Māori have a vividly chronicled history, recorded in songs and chants that dramatic-ally recall the migration to New Zealand from Polynesia as well as other important events. Early missionaries were the first to record the language in a written form using only 15 letters of the English alphabet.

Māori is closely related to other Polynesian languages such as Hawaiian, Tahitian and Cook Islands Māori. In fact, New Zealand Māori and Hawaiian are quite similar, even though more than 7000km separates Honolulu and Auckland.

The Māori language was never dead – it was always used in Māori ceremonies – but over time familiarity with it was definitely on the decline. Fortunately, recent years have seen a revival of interest in it, and this forms an integral part of the renaissance of *Māoritanga* (Māori culture). Many Māori people who had heard the language spoken on the *marae* for years but had not used it in their day-to-day lives, are now studying it and speaking it fluently. Māori is taught in schools throughout New Zealand, some TV programs and news reports are broadcast in it, and many English place names are being renamed in Māori. Even government departments have been given Māori names: for example, the Inland Revenue Department is also known as Te Tari Taake (the last word is actually *take*, which means 'levy', but the department has chosen to stress the long 'a' by spelling it 'aa').

In many places, Māori have come together to provide instruction in their language and culture to young children; the idea is for them to grow up speaking both Māori and English, and to develop a familiarity with Māori tradition. It's a matter of some pride to have fluency in the language. On some *marae* only Māori can be spoken.

Pronunciation

Māori is a fluid, poetic language and surprisingly easy to pronounce once you remember to split each word (some can be amazingly long) into separate syllables. Each syllable ends in a vowel. There are no 'silent' letters.

Most consonants in Māori – *h, k, m, n, p, t* and *w* – are pronounced much the same as in English. The Māori *r* is a flapped sound (not rolled) with the tongue near the front of the mouth. It's closer to the English 'l' in pronunciation.

The *ng* is pronounced as in the English words 'singing' or 'running', and can be used at the beginning of words as well as at the end. To practise, just say 'ing' over and over, then isolate the 'ng' part of it.

The letters *wh,* when occuring together, are generally pronounced as a soft English 'f'. This pronunciation is used in many place names in New Zealand, such as Whakatane and Whakapapa (all pronounced as if they begin with a soft 'f'). There is some local variation: in the region around the Whanganui River, for example, *wh* is pronounced as in the English word 'when'.

The correct pronunciation of the vowels is very important. The examples below are a rough guideline – it helps to listen carefully to someone who speaks the language well. Each vowel has both a long and a short sound, with long vowels often denoted by a line over the letter or a double vowel. We have not indicated long and short vowel forms in this book.

Vowels

a	as in 'large', with no 'r' sound
e	as in 'get'
i	as in 'marine'
o	as in 'pork'
u	as the 'oo' in 'moon'

Vowel Combinations

ae, ai	as the 'y' in 'sky'
ao, au	as the 'ow' in 'how'
ea	as in 'bear'
ei	as in 'vein'
eo	as 'eh-oh'
eu	as 'eh-oo'
ia	as in the name 'Ian'
ie	as the 'ye' in 'yet'
io	as the 'ye o' in 'ye old'
iu	as the 'ue' in 'cue'
oa	as in 'roar'
oe	as in 'toe'
oi	as in 'toil'
ou	as the 'ow' in 'how'
ua	as the 'ewe' in 'fewer'

Greetings & Small Talk

Māori greetings are becoming increasingly popular – don't be surprised if you're greeted with *Kia ora.*

Welcome!	*Haere mai!*
Hello./Good luck./ Good health.	*Kia ora.*
Hello. *(to one person)*	*Tena koe.*
Hello. *(to two people)*	*Tena korua.*
Hello. *(to three or more people)*	*Tena koutou.*
Goodbye. *(to person staying)*	*E noho ra.*
Goodbye. *(to person leaving)*	*Haere ra.*
How are you? *(to one person)*	*Kei te pehea koe?*
How are you? *(to two people)*	*Kei te pehea korua?*
How are you? *(to or three more people)*	*Kei te pehea koutou?*
Very well, thanks./ That's fine.	*Kei te pai.*

Māori Geographical Terms

The following words form part of many Māori place names in New Zealand, and indicate the meaning of these place names. For example: Waikaremoana is the Sea *(moana)* of Rippling *(kare)* Waters *(wai)*, and Rotorua means the Second *(rua)* Lake *(roto)*.

a – of
ana – cave
ara – way, path or road
awa – river or valley
heke – descend
hiku – end; tail
hine – girl; daughter
ika – fish
iti – small
kahurangi – treasured possession; special greenstone
kai – food
kainga – village
kaka – parrot
kare – rippling
kati – shut or close
koura – crayfish
makariri – cold
manga – stream or tributary
manu – bird
maunga – mountain
moana – sea or lake
moko – tattoo

motu – island

mutu – finished; ended; over

nga – the (plural)

noa – ordinary; not *tapu*

nui – big or great

nuku – distance

o – of, place of...

one – beach, sand or mud

pa – fortified village

papa – large blue-grey mudstone

pipi – common edible bivalve

pohatu – stone

poto – short

pouri – sad; dark; gloomy

puke – hill

puna – spring; hole; fountain

rangi – sky; heavens

raro – north

rei – cherished possession

roa – long

roto – lake

rua – hole in the ground; two

runga – above

tahuna – beach; sandbank

tane – man

tangata – people

tapu – sacred, forbidden or taboo

tata – close to; dash against; twin islands

tawaha – entrance or opening

tawahi – the other side (of a river or lake)

te – the (singular)

tonga – south

ure – male genitals

uru – west

waha – broken

wahine – woman

wai – water

waingaro – lost; waters that disappear in certain seasons

waka – canoe

wera – burnt or warm; floating

wero – challenge

whaka... – to act as ...

whanau – family

whanga – harbour, bay or inlet

where – house

whenua – land or country

whiti – east

GLOSSARY

Following is a list of abbreviations, 'Kiwi English', Māori and slang terms used in this book and which you may hear in New Zealand.

All Blacks – NZ's revered national rugby union team

Anzac – Australia and New Zealand Army Corps

Aoraki – Māori name for Mt Cook, meaning 'Cloud Piercer'

Aotearoa – Māori name for NZ, most often translated as 'Land of the Long White Cloud'

aroha – love

bach – holiday home (pronounced 'batch'); see also crib

bro – literally 'brother'; usually meaning mate

BYO – 'bring your own' (usually applies to alcohol at a restaurant or cafe)

choice/chur – fantastic; great

crib – the name for a bach in Otago and Southland

DOC – Department of Conservation (or Te Papa Atawhai); government department that administers national parks, tracks and huts

eh? – roughly translates as 'don't you agree?'

farmstay – accommodation on a Kiwi farm

football – rugby, either union or league; occasionally soccer

Great Walks – set of nine popular tramping tracks within NZ

greenstone – jade; *pounamu*

haka – any dance, but usually a war dance

hangi – oven whereby food is steamed in baskets over embers in a hole; a Māori feast

hapu – subtribe or smaller tribal grouping

Hawaiki – original homeland of the Māori

hei tiki – carved, stylised human figure worn around the neck; also called a *tiki*

home-stay – accommodation in a family house

hongi – Māori greeting; the pressing of foreheads and noses, and sharing of life breath

hui – gathering; meeting

i-SITE – information centre

iwi – large tribal grouping with common lineage back to the original migration from *Hawaiki*; people; tribe

jandals – contraction of 'Japanese sandals'; flip-flops; thongs; usually rubber footwear

kauri – native pine

kia ora – hello

Kiwi – New Zealander; an adjective to mean anything relating to NZ

kiwi – flightless, nocturnal brown bird with a long beak

Kiwiana – things uniquely connected to NZ life and culture, especially from bygone years

kiwifruit – small, succulent fruit with fuzzy brown skin and juicy green flesh; aka Chinese gooseberry or zespri

kumara – Polynesian sweet potato, a Māori staple food

Kupe – early Polynesian navigator from *Hawaiki*, credited with the discovery of the islands that are now NZ

mana – spiritual quality of a person or object; authority or prestige

Māori – indigenous people of NZ

Māoritanga – things Māori, ie Māori culture

marae – sacred ground in front of the Māori meeting house; more commonly used to refer to the entire complex of buildings

Maui – figure in Māori (Polynesian) mythology

mauri – life force/principle

moa – large, extinct flightless bird

moko – tattoo; usually refers to facial tattoos

nga – the (plural); see also *te*

ngai/ngati – literally, 'the people of' or 'the descendants of'; tribe (pronounced 'kai' on the South Island)

pa – fortified Māori village, usually on a hilltop

Pakeha – Māori for a white or European person

Pasifika – Pacific Island culture

paua – abalone; iridescent paua shell is often used in jewellery

pavlova – meringue cake topped with cream and kiwifruit

PI – Pacific Islander

poi – ball of woven flax

pounamu – Māori name for greenstone

powhiri – traditional Māori welcome onto a *marae*

rip – dangerously strong current running away from the shore at a beach

Roaring Forties – the ocean between 40° and 50° south, known for very strong winds

silver fern – symbol worn by the All Blacks and other national sportsfolk on their jerseys; the national netball team is called the Silver Ferns

sweet, sweet as – all-purpose term like choice; fantastic, great

tapu – strong force in Māori life, with numerous meanings; in its simplest form it means sacred, forbidden, taboo

te – the (singular); see also *nga*

te reo – literally 'the language'; the Māori language

tiki – short for *hei tiki*

tiki tour – scenic tour

tramp – bushwalk; trek; hike

tuatara – prehistoric reptile dating back to the age of dinosaurs

tui – native parson bird

wahine – woman

wai – water

wairua – spirit

Waitangi – short way of referring to the Treaty of Waitangi

waka – canoe

Behind the Scenes

Acknowledgements

Climate map data adapted from Peel MC, Finlayson BL & McMahon TA (2007) 'Updated World Map of the Koppen-Geiger Climate Classification', *Hydrology and Earth System Sciences*, 11, 163344

This Book

This book was curated by Brett Atkinson and researched and written by Brett, Sarah Bennett, Peter Dragicevich, Charles Rawlings-Way and Lee Slater.

This guidebook was produced by the following:

Destination Editor Tasmin Waby
Product Editors Tracy Whitmey, Elizabeth Jones
Senior Cartographer Diana von Holdt
Book Designer Katherine Marsh
Assisting Editors Janet Evans, Paul Harding
Cover Researcher Naomi Parker
Thanks to Victoria Harrison, Indra Kilfoyle, Kate Mathews, Kirsten Rawlings, Dianne Schallmeiner, Angela Tinson, John Taufa, Amanda Williamson, Juan Winata

Send Us Your Feedback

We love to hear from travellers – your comments keep us on our toes and help make our books better. Our well-travelled team reads every word on what you loved or loathed about this book. Although we cannot reply individually to postal submissions, we always guarantee that your feedback goes straight to the appropriate authors, in time for the next edition. Each person who sends us information is thanked in the next edition, the most useful submissions are rewarded with a selection of digital PDF chapters.

Visit lonelyplanet.com/contact to submit your updates and suggestions or to ask for help. Our award-winning website also features inspirational travel stories, news and discussions.

Note: We may edit, reproduce and incorporate your comments in Lonely Planet products such as guidebooks, websites and digital products, so let us know if you don't want your comments reproduced or your name acknowledged. For a copy of our privacy policy visit lonelyplanet.com/privacy.

A – Z
Index

Symbols & Map Key

Look for these symbols to quickly identify listings:

- ◎ Sights
- ✪ Activities
- ⊖ Courses
- ◉ Tours
- ✪ Festivals & Events
- ✪ Eating
- ⊖ Drinking
- ✪ Entertainment
- ⊜ Shopping
- ⓘ Information & Transport

Find your best experiences with these Great For... icons.

 Budget

 Food & Drink

 Drinking

 Cycling

 Shopping

 Sport

Art & Culture

Events

Photo Op

Scenery

Family Travel

 Short Trip

 Detour

 Walking

 Local Life

 History

 Entertainment

Beaches

Winter Travel

Cafe/Coffee

Nature & Wildlife

These symbols and abbreviations give vital information for each listing:

🌱 Sustainable or green recommendation

FREE No payment required

- ☑ Telephone number
- ⊘ Opening hours
- Ⓟ Parking
- ⊝ Nonsmoking
- ❋ Air-conditioning
- @ Internet access
- 🛜 Wi-fi access
- ⊠ Swimming pool
- ⊞ Bus
- ⊞ Ferry
- ⊞ Tram
- ⊠ Train
- 🗎 English-language menu
- 🖊 Vegetarian selection
- 👪 Family-friendly

Sights

- Ⓑ Beach
- Ⓑ Bird Sanctuary
- Ⓐ Buddhist
- Ⓒ Castle/Palace
- Ⓒ Christian
- Ⓒ Confucian
- Ⓗ Hindu
- Ⓘ Islamic
- Ⓙ Jain
- Ⓙ Jewish
- Ⓜ Monument
- Ⓜ Museum/Gallery/ Historic Building
- Ⓡ Ruin
- Ⓢ Shinto
- Ⓢ Sikh
- Ⓣ Taoist
- Ⓦ Winery/Vineyard
- Ⓩ Zoo/Wildlife Sanctuary
- Ⓞ Other Sight

Points of Interest

- Ⓒ Bodysurfing
- Ⓒ Camping
- Ⓒ Cafe
- Ⓒ Canoeing/Kayaking
- • Course/Tour
- Ⓓ Diving
- Ⓓ Drinking & Nightlife
- Ⓔ Eating
- Ⓔ Entertainment
- Ⓢ Sento Hot Baths/ Onsen
- Ⓢ Shopping
- Ⓢ Skiing
- Ⓢ Sleeping
- Ⓢ Snorkelling
- Ⓢ Surfing
- Ⓢ Swimming/Pool
- Ⓦ Walking
- Ⓦ Windsurfing
- Ⓞ Other Activity

Information

- Ⓢ Bank
- Ⓔ Embassy/Consulate
- Ⓗ Hospital/Medical
- @ Internet
- Ⓟ Police
- Ⓟ Post Office
- ☑ Telephone
- Ⓣ Toilet
- ⓘ Tourist Information
- • Other Information

Geographic

- Ⓑ Beach
- ⋈ Gate
- Ⓗ Hut/Shelter
- Ⓛ Lighthouse
- Ⓛ Lookout
- ▲ Mountain/Volcano
- Ⓞ Oasis
- Ⓟ Park
-)(Pass
- Ⓟ Picnic Area
- Ⓦ Waterfall

Transport

- Ⓐ Airport
- Ⓑ BART station
- Ⓑ Border crossing
- Ⓣ Boston T station
- Ⓑ Bus
- ⊞ Cable car/Funicular
- Cycling
- Ⓕ Ferry
- Ⓜ Metro/MRT station
- Monorail
- Ⓟ Parking
- Ⓟ Petrol station
- Ⓢ Subway/S-Bahn/ Skytrain station
- Ⓣ Taxi
- Train station/Railway
- Tram
- Ⓣ Tube Station
- Ⓤ Underground/ U-Bahn station
- • Other Transport

Charles Rawlings-Way

English by birth, Australian by chance, All Blacks fan by choice: Charles's early understanding of Aotearoa was less than comprehensive (sheep, mountains, sheep on mountains...). Mt Taranaki's snowy summit, Napier's art deco deliverance and Whanganui's raffish charm have helped him realise that there's more to it, and he's now smitten with the country's phantasmal landscapes, disarming locals, and determination to sculpt its own political and indigenous destiny.

Contributing Writers

Professor James Belich wrote the History chapter. James is one of NZ's pre-eminent historians and the award-winning author of *The New Zealand Wars, Making Peoples* and *Paradise Reforged*.

John Huria (Ngai Tahu, Muaupoko) wrote the Māori Culture chapter. John has an editorial, research and writing background with a focus on Māori writing and culture. He was senior editor for Māori publishing company Huia and now runs an editorial and publishing services company, Ahi Text Solutions Ltd (www.ahitextsolutions.co.nz).

Gareth Shute wrote the Music section in the Arts & Music chapter. Gareth is the author of four books, including *Hip Hop Music in Aotearoa* and *NZ Rock 1987–2007*.

Vaughan Yarwood wrote the Environment chapter. Vaughan is an Auckland-based writer whose books include *The History Makers: Adventures in New Zealand Biography, The Best of New Zealand: A Collection of Essays on NZ Life and Culture by Prominent Kiwis,* which he edited, and the regional history *Between Coasts: From Kaipara to Kawau*.

Our Story

A beat-up old car, a few dollars in the pocket and a sense of adventure. In 1972 that's all Tony and Maureen Wheeler needed for the trip of a lifetime – across Europe and Asia overland to Australia. It took several months, and at the end – broke but inspired – they sat at their kitchen table writing and stapling together their first travel guide, *Across Asia on the Cheap*. Within a week they'd sold 1500 copies. Lonely Planet was born.

Today, Lonely Planet has offices in Dublin, Melbourne, Franklin, London, Oakland, Beijing, and Delhi, with more than 600 staff and writers. We share Tony's belief that 'a great guidebook should do three things: inform, educate and amuse'.

Our Writers

Brett Atkinson

Born in Rotorua, but now a proud resident of Auckland, Brett explored the top half of New Zealand's North Island for this book. Excursions to Northland, the Coromandel Peninsula and Tongariro National Park echoed family holidays from an earlier century, and rediscovering his home town also evoked great memories. Brett's contributed to Lonely Planet guidebooks spanning Europe, Asia and the Pacific, and covered around 50 countries as a food and travel writer. See www.brett-atkinson.net for his latest adventures.

Sarah Bennett & Lee Slater

Sarah and Lee specialise in NZ travel, with a particular focus on outdoor adventure including hiking, mountain biking and camping. In addition to five editions of the *New Zealand* guidebook, they are also co-authors of Lonely Planet's *Hiking & Tramping in New Zealand* and *New Zealand's Best Trips*. Read more at www.bennettandslater.co.nz.

Peter Dragicevich

After nearly a decade working for off-shore publishing companies, Peter's life has come full circle, returning to his home city of Auckland. As Managing Editor of *Express* newspaper he spent much of the '90s writing about the local arts, club and bar scene. He has contributed to many New Zealand guidebooks and, after dozens of Lonely Planet assignments, it remains his favourite gig.

◄————— More Writers ◄—————

STAY IN TOUCH LONELYPLANET.COM/CONTACT

EUROPE Unit E, Digital Court, The Digital Hub, Rainsford St, Dublin 8, Ireland

AUSTRALIA Levels 2 & 3 551 Swanston St, Carlton, Victoria 3053
☎ 03 8379 8000,
fax 03 8379 8111

USA 150 Linden Street, Oakland, CA 94607
☎ 510 250 6400,
toll free 800 275 8555,
fax 510 893 8572

UK 240 Blackfriars Road, London SE1 8NW
☎ 020 3771 5100,
fax 020 3771 5101

 twitter.com/lonelyplanet

 facebook.com/lonelyplanet

 instagram.com/lonelyplanet

 youtube.com/lonelyplanet

 lonelyplanet.com/newsletter